T0266454

'*The Buddha on Wall Street* is an orig
evaluation of our economic situation
social implications of Buddhist teach
– **David R. Loy**, author, *Money, Sex, War, Karma: Notes for a Buddhist*
Revolution

'Many Western Buddhists regard Buddhism as primarily a path to
personal insight and inner peace, thus as a virtual escape route from
the madness of the modern world. Yet deep within the Dharma are
the seeds for a new vision of human relatedness, a web of ideas about
how our social and economic systems can promote authentic well-being
rather than the oppression, violence, and exploitation so widespread
today. Vaddhaka Linn here boldly uses the lens of Buddhism to closely
examine the dominant structures of corporate capitalism. He lays bare
the pernicious consequences of these structures and draws forth from
the Dharma its suggestions for creating benign alternatives conducive to
true human flourishing. This book helps us to better see the Dharma as
a comprehensive message that has much to offer to the emergent global
community in its broadest dimensions. It should also help Buddhists to
understand more clearly the potential relevance of Buddhism to the crises
of our age.' – **Bhikkhu Bodhi**, editor, *In the Buddha's Words*

'Buddhism arose at a time of rising inequalities, partly as an answer as
to how to behave in, understand, and remedy such times. *The Buddha on
Wall Street* is an invaluable guide to how this time, faced again with crisis,
there are alternatives to believing there is no alternative.' – **Professor
Danny Dorling**, School of Geography and the Environment, University
of Oxford, and author, *Inequality and the 1%*

'Slavoj Zizek has written that Western Buddhism is the "perfect
ideological supplement" to capitalism. Zizek the provocateur thinks
Western Buddhism is complacent about the terrible harms of unbridled
neoliberal capitalism. Vaddhaka Linn's essay makes the argument for an
activist Buddhism that responds to Zizek's challenge.' – **Professor Owen
Flanagan**, Department of Philosophy, Duke University, and author, *The
Bodhisattva's Brain: Buddhism Naturalized*

'Do ever greater income levels lead to greater human fulfilment?
Vaddhaka Linn does an outstanding job exposing the false accounting of
social ills that make it into a list of goods as measured in GDP statistics.
More fundamentally, he questions any definition of well-being that does
not rest on a firm ethical foundation, developing a refreshing Buddhist
critique of the ends of economic activity.' – **Dominic Houlder**, Adjunct
Professor in Strategy and Entrepreneurship, London Business School

The Buddha on Wall Street

What's wrong with capitalism and what we can do about it

Vaḍḍhaka Linn

(𝑊)indhorse Publications

Published by

Windhorse Publications
169 Mill Road
Cambridge
CB1 3AN
UK

info@windhorsepublications.com
www.windhorsepublications.com

Cover design by Sagarapriya
Cover image © Navid Baraty
Typesetting and layout by Ruth Rudd
Printed by Bell & Bain Ltd, Glasgow

British Library Cataloguing in Publication Data
A catalogue record for this book is available from the British Library.

ISBN: 978 1 909314 44 3

Contents

Preface

Buddhism is not just about meditation. It's a whole-life practice involving ethics, meditation, and wisdom. Economics is not just for economists. Economics affects all aspects of life and requires everyone's attention, including Buddhists'. Buddhism is grounded in a set of values different from those of the economics of modern neoliberal capitalism. For anyone interested in economics, Buddhism offers a radically alternative perspective to the market fundamentalism that dominates the world today.

Acknowledgements

Thank you to Alokavira, who inspired the original idea for this book in a discussion in Birmingham, England in May 2012. Thanks also to my friends at Budakoda, the lovely Triratna Buddhist Centre in Tallinn, Estonia, who throughout 2013 patiently listened to a series of talks about economics. I would like to express my appreciation to those who took the time to read different drafts of the book and give thoughtful advice and encouragement, especially Bhikkhu Bodhi, David Loy, Vajragupta, Akuppa, Jukka Nuutilainen, Dhivan, Maitrisara, and Jinananda. Many thanks to Priyananda, Hannah, and Michelle at Windhorse Publications for seeing the book through to publication. Most of all, thank you to Sangharakshita, whose teachings opened my mind to a different perspective on the world and led me to Buddhism.

Publisher's acknowledgements

Windhorse Publications wishes to gratefully acknowledge a grant from the Triratna European Chairs' Assembly Fund towards the production of this book.

We also wish to acknowledge and thank the individual donors who gave to the book's production via our 'Sponsor-a-book' campaign.

Introduction

On the front of a British £20 note is an image of Queen Elizabeth II. On the back is an image of Adam Smith, the eighteenth-century Scottish philosopher who in 1776 produced *The Wealth of Nations*, a book that lays the foundations of modern economics and capitalism. On the £20 note, Adam Smith is looking across at a pin factory. A caption below the image of it reads: 'The division of labour in pin manufacturing and the great increase in the quantity of work that results'.

In the first chapter of *The Wealth of Nations*, Smith points out that the best way to increase productivity is to take complex work tasks and divide them into small segments. He describes how the manufacture of a single pin can be broken down into eighteen separate tasks. If one worker does all eighteen tasks by himself, it would take him the best part of a day to make at most twenty pins. If, however, ten workers are formed into a production line and each worker specializes in one or two of the tasks, together they can make 48,000 pins per day. Instead of a maximum of twenty pins per day, each worker is now in effect making 4,800 pins per day.[1]

That was in 1776, at the beginning of the rise of the economic system we call capitalism. Subsequent studies have shown that by 1832, factories were producing about 8,000 pins per worker per day. And by 1980, pin factories were producing 800,000 pins per worker per day.[2] Since Adam Smith's time, the principle of the division of labour, combined with developments such as scientific management, the assembly line, and advances in mechanization facilitated by the division of labour, has dramatically increased productive efficiency around the world. Before the eighteenth century, there was very little improvement in the standard of living for two thousand years. Since then, the increase in productive efficiency has been accompanied by unprecedented growth in the standard of living, by longer lives, by better healthcare, and by better education. But these immense increases in productivity and well-being come at a cost. What is being celebrated on the £20 note is also the beginning of a monotony of working methods that have condemned many people to mindlessly repeating the same small tasks.

Adam Smith himself recognized this drawback. Towards the end of *The Wealth of Nations*, he admits that the cost to workers of the division of labour was a 'torpor of the mind' and a 'loss of tender sentiment'. He wrote that 'the man whose life is spent in performing a few simple operations . . . has no occasion to exert his understanding, or to exercise his invention.'[3] He recognized that such production methods can deaden a person's creativity and their emotions. This is a side to Adam Smith that most modern economists tend to ignore.

The impact of the division of labour illustrates how capitalism has divergent effects. On the one hand, it can dramatically reduce suffering and improve the quality of life. The creative energy of capitalism has to be acknowledged. On the other hand, capitalism perpetuates suffering. Some may argue that the suffering inflicted by capitalism is a necessary price for progress. It's true that because of the progress made under capitalism over the past three hundred years, there is now a realistic possibility of providing everyone with decent shelter, clean water, and enough food to provide for a fulfilling life. But our current economic system also seems to be locking us into a world of increasing inequality, high levels of unemployment, especially for young people, worsening satisfaction with life, and the destruction of the environment, threatening the lives of many species, including our own.

The Buddha taught how to end suffering. His concern was with helping to bring about a fundamental transformation in the mind of individuals. He understood too that the existence of a society in which material and other forms of collective suffering were overcome would help to create the conditions in which individuals could transform themselves. To respond in our modern world to the Buddha, and to help in the process of reducing collective suffering, I believe that Buddhists need to engage in a serious questioning of our current economic order and our attitude towards it. Is there something in the nature of modern capitalism that prevents further progress towards an economic system that reduces suffering and allows individuals to fulfil their human potential while preserving and protecting the environment? Can Buddhism help us to conceive of something better than our current economic system? What can we do to help reduce suffering?

I have been pondering these questions ever since I heard a comment about Buddhism by Slavoj Zizek. Zizek is a controversial Slovenian philosopher and cultural critic who is becoming increasingly well known in the West, including by way of his occasional column for the *Guardian* newspaper in England. According to Zizek, what he calls 'Western Buddhism' is the 'perfect ideological supplement' to capitalism. He believes that the emphasis in 'Western Buddhism' on meditation encourages

Buddhists to create an inner distance from the 'mad dance' of modern capitalism, to give up any attempt to control what's going on, and to take comfort in the view that all the social and economic upheaval in the world today is 'just a non-substantial proliferation of semblances that do not really concern the innermost kernel of our being'.[4] Zizek's claim implies that when faced with injustice, pain, and suffering in the world today, Western Buddhists take cover in their meditation practice in order to avoid the full impact of this reality.

When I heard Zizek's statement, I have to admit that I reacted strongly against it. For the first twenty-five years of my adult life, I had worked in politics and trade unionism trying to build a better world and, as I saw it, to rid us of the suffering caused by capitalism. I was an idealist. I'm still an idealist. But although there are many good people involved as political activists and trade unionists and although independent and free trade unions continue to be essential in a democratic state, I became disillusioned after twenty five years – disillusioned not with the ideal of a better world but by the hatred I sometimes experienced around me, by the power games, and by the increasing sense that fundamental change was becoming ever more distant.

In the midst of that disillusionment, I came across a Buddhist meditation class in Sheffield in the north of England led by a member of the Triratna Buddhist Community. I was fortunate to find a path that offered a different way to fundamentally transform self and world together. It's a path that I have now followed for more than twenty years, thus my discomfort with Slavoj Zizek telling me, in effect, that I was wasting my time with Buddhism if I really wanted to reduce suffering in the world. Fortunately, I was mindful enough to realize that an instinctive emotional reaction wasn't good enough. I realized that this was an opportunity, an invitation to explore economics and capitalism and how Buddhism relates to them. I decided to examine the modern capitalist world from the perspectives of economics and Buddhism, and this book is the result.

What is capitalism? Dr Ha-Joon Chang of Cambridge University gives us a good starting definition.[5] Capitalism is an economy in which production is undertaken in order to produce a profit. This distinguishes it from a subsistence economy, in which food is produced for own consumption and not for profit, as well as from economies in which production is organized to fulfil political obligations, as in feudal societies or in planned socialist economies, in which the lords of the manor or central planners decide what is produced. Profit is simply the difference between what is earned by selling a product in the market and the costs that are incurred in producing that product, such as wages paid to the workforce, the costs of raw materials and costs of using and running machines and the factory. Capitalists are those who privately own the means of production, that is the factories and machines that are used to make a product sold in the market. The market is where goods and services are bought and sold.

Adam Smith believed that competition between sellers in the market would ensure that profit-seeking capitalists would produce at the lowest possible costs, thereby benefiting everyone. Since his time, capitalism has of course undergone many changes. For example, he would have made the assumption of small-scale firms operating in local markets where consumer tastes and technological know-how would be either essentially unchanging or very slow to change. But the competition for profit nowadays is much more among large multi-national companies that can change prices and reinvent technologies over short time periods and can also shape and fashion consumer tastes through advertising and brand identification. The ownership of capital has shifted away from individual owners to shareholders. The financial system has changed and become a much more important and complicated part of the economy. There are as well significant differences in the role of government as the regulator of markets, production, and financial systems and in the size of the public sector as employer and provider of welfare services outside the market. These changes have had an impact in different ways in different countries, to the extent that different types or labels of capitalism can now be applied such as 'welfare capitalism', as found in European and particularly Scandinavian countries, or 'state capitalism', as in China.

Notwithstanding these developments, the starting point for the book is that although there are different kinds of capitalism (and, indeed, different schools of economics – see the Note at the end of the book), the contemporary world of economics and of capitalism is in thrall to one particular brand of capitalism, 'neoliberal' capitalism or 'free market' economics, which has gained an increasingly influential global position over the past thirty years, ever since the rise to political power of Margaret Thatcher and Ronald Reagan in the early 1980s. 'Neoliberal' or 'free market economics' emphasizes policies such as reduction of public expenditure and the role of government, deregulation of finance and businesses, privatization, and globalization. I shall show how it promotes individualism and inequality, celebrates greed, encourages rampant consumerism, and has passionate faith in economic growth as a panacea for all world problems.[6] I shall argue that at the heart of neoliberal capitalism are values that are incompatible with Buddhist values (Chapter 1), epitomized by the promotion of greed and selfishness in neoliberal capitalism contrasted with generosity and altruism in Buddhism (Chapter 2).

I shall then explore particular areas of modern life from the different perspectives of free market economics and Buddhism, looking at the decline of community (Chapter 3), work (Chapter 4), nature and the environment (Chapter 5), the waste economy (Chapter 6), the attention economy (Chapter 7), the happiness industry (Chapter 8), and inequality (Chapter 9). I shall offer suggestions about what Buddhists might do in these areas in order to promote a Buddhist view and give alternatives to our current economic system. I shall take a special look at the corporation (Chapter 10) and present ideas for action from different Buddhist voices (Chapter 11).

In this way, I hope to persuade you of the conclusion towards which this book leads (Chapter 12). Capitalism has led us to a situation in the world today in which it is possible to conceive of a fulfilling life for all, but further progress is being suffocated by a neoliberal form of capitalism that threatens the environment and perpetuates suffering in the world. Primitive instincts for individual survival, such as greed and hatred, served us well in earlier evolutionary times. But as Charles Darwin argues, the human species has succeeded because of characteristics such as sharing and compassion.[7] Especially now, in our interconnected world where our actions richochet rapidly from place to place and can threaten our very survival, the progressive evolutionary impulses of sharing and compassion need to flourish. Instead of neoliberal capitalism with its emphasis on greed and selfishness, we need a different form of economic organization, one that combines thoughtful self-interest and the creative energy and dynamism in capitalism with the values of generosity and altruism. Buddhists can play a significant role in helping this to come about.

Throughout the book, the examples I give of Buddhist lifestyle, community, and livelihood draw mostly on my direct experience of living and working in the Triratna Buddhist Community. I give these examples because I am intimately familiar with them, not as a way of singling out the Triratna Buddhist Community as in some way unique. There are certainly other examples in the Buddhist world, and the wider world, of successful intentional communities, both national and international, of harmonious residential communities, of ecologically and socially orientated spiritual organizations, and of ethical business ventures. I do not have direct experience of them, and this is why I have not included them here. Similarly, in Chapter 11, in giving examples of distinctive Buddhist voices on economics, I draw from my own personal connection and inspiration, singling out some of the individuals who I believe have something unique to say. The list is not intended to be exhaustive. There are even more voices in the Buddhist world that are making important contributions to this vital debate on alternatives to the free market economy, as there are of course many voices beyond the Buddhist world.

1

An 'invisible hand'

Margin Call is a film that tells the story of a fictional Wall Street company.[1] When it realizes that the majority of its assets are basically worthless mortgage-backed securities, it launches a desperate attempt to save itself. A decision is made to sell the worthless securities to an unsuspecting set of clients, who buy them at grossly inflated prices compared to their real value. The more the company's sales team is successful at lying and offloading the securities, the greater are the bonuses they earn: more than a million dollars per person. The story might seem far-fetched. And yet, it emerged in 2011 that the US-based Citigroup, one of the largest financial services companies in the world, had to pay a $285 million fine to settle a legal case. In 2007, it had sold a package of worthless mortgage-backed securities to unsuspecting customers – securities that it knew were likely to go bust. In addition, Citigroup, unknown to the customers buying the securities, had engaged in another financial manoeuvre that was in essence a bet that the securities would indeed go bust and end up worthless, a bet that it won handsomely. The result was that those who invested in the deal lost hundreds of millions of dollars while Citigroup made $160 million in fees and trading profits. As a journalist for the *New York Times* commented, 'It doesn't get any more immoral than this.'[2]

Was this a random immoral act or was it an act based in a more deeply rooted set of values, of modern capitalism? To begin to understand the basic values of modern economics and capitalism, we must return to Adam Smith and *The Wealth of Nations*. In particular, we need to look at what he called 'an invisible hand'. Advocates of neoliberal capitalism and free market economics have seized upon the idea of the 'invisible hand' and placed it at the core of their beliefs, although Adam Smith only ever mentions it once in *The Wealth of Nations*. He writes:

'It is not from the benevolence of the butcher, the brewer, or the baker, that we expect our dinner, but from their regard to their own interest. We address ourselves, not to their humanity, but to their self-love, and never talk to them of our own necessities, but of their advantages.'

And he continues:

Every individual . . . necessarily labours to render the annual revenue of the society as great as he can. He generally, indeed, neither intends to promote the public interest, nor knows how much he is promoting it . . . *He intends only his own gain, and he is in this, as in many other cases, led by an invisible hand to promote an end which was no part of his intention.* Nor is it always worse for the society that it was no part of it. By pursuing his own interest he frequently promotes that of the society more effectually than when he really intends to promote it.[3] (my italics)

He is arguing that what motivates the butcher or the brewer or the baker – what drives them – is their own self-interest, their own profit. And this, he says, is a good thing because as long as every individual in society pursues their own gain or profit, chases after their own self-interest, then, through the working of the market, everyone in society benefits. All this comes about through the operation of an 'invisible hand'. Where did Adam Smith get the idea of the 'invisible hand' from? Most probably, he took it from a religious metaphor that was in use in his time. In other words, the working of the economy and the benefits of the pursuit of self-interest and profit are God-given. This is how God made the world.

Later the 'invisible hand' also came to be associated with the more secular idea of the 'survival of the fittest' from Darwinian theories of evolution. Just as the survival instinct drives the process of evolution, so it drives economic success. In this way, it is believed, economic progress depends on the 'survival of the fittest'. In fact, Darwin did not use the term until the fifth edition of his book *On the Origin of Species*. Before that, he used the term 'natural selection'.[4] He borrowed the phrase 'survival of the fittest' from Herbert Spencer. Because Spencer was associated with economic theories supporting unrestrained capitalism, Darwin inadvertently encouraged a narrow interpretation of his theory by economists and others. In reality, he had a broader view of evolution. In his book *The Descent of Man*, he argues that the human species has succeeded because of characteristics such as sharing and compassion. 'Those communities', he writes, 'which included the greatest number of the most sympathetic members would flourish best, and rear the greatest number of offspring.'[5] Nevertheless, the damage was done, and the link between economics and the 'survival of the fittest' was established.

But whether the 'invisible hand' is believed to come from God or from the theory of evolution, the implication drawn by neoliberal capitalists and free marketeers is the same. The pursuit of selfishness promotes the well-being of the whole of society. This mantra has become the core ethic of modern neoliberal capitalism. It is the ethical principle that supersedes other ethical considerations. As the Nobel prize-winning economist Joseph Stiglitz has said, 'To the morally uninspired, it's an appealing idea: *selfishness as the ultimate form of selflessness.*'[6] (my italics).

If you are a businessman or a banker, it doesn't matter how selfish your behaviour is. You can always justify your actions by saying that at the end of the day, you are selflessly giving of yourself to promote the interests of all.

At this point, the reader may have noticed that I have slipped from talking about *self-interest* to talking about *selfishness*. To act in one's self-interest means to act in pursuance of one's own interest. To act selfishly is to act not just in one's own interest but to deliberately act to the exclusion of the interests of others. To take Adam Smith's example of the baker, I can imagine someone setting up in business as a baker because they believe that they can provide tasty and nutritious food at a reasonable cost to customers and thereby make a living, make a profit, provide for themselves and their family, and put money aside for improvements in the machinery necessary for the manufacture of their products.

In Adam Smith's ideal world, competition in the market is the chief means for matching the ambition of the producer with the wishes of the consumer, and it then decides who will succeed and who will fail. In my view, there is nothing inherently wrong with this kind of self-interest and personal ambition. It's one of the main sources of the creative energy and dynamism of capitalism. Problems arise when the motivation shifts to a desire to put others out of business and to increase profits out of greed, when the concerns of others are ignored and when selfishness takes over. For neoliberal economists, selfishness has taken over.

But let's turn to the teachings of the Buddha and compare the basic values of Buddhism with the values of neoliberal capitalism.

Of course, the Buddha lived 2,500 years ago, far removed from modern capitalism. But he was an astute observer of the emerging economy of the Ganges plains, being very familiar with the working activities of farmers, merchant traders, and crafts people. He gave advice to business owners on how to run their businesses and to use their wealth and to rulers on their social and economic policies. Most of all, he had unrivalled insight into human nature and the causes of suffering. To illustrate this, I'm going to look at a teaching in the *Aggañña Sutta* from the *Dīgha Nikāya*, the Long Discourses of the Buddha.[7]

In the *Aggañña Sutta*, the Buddha tells a mythological story of the beginnings of our world and its socio-economic structure. Because it's a myth told by the Buddha, we don't have to believe the story literally. Some believe that this discourse is a parody by the Buddha of Brahmin creation texts. Nevertheless I think it contains important truths about human beings and the development of human society. In the story, the Buddha identifies *taṇhā*, thirst or craving, as an important part of the human condition. Once *taṇhā* has arisen, it causes humans to crave and exhaust one foodstuff after another. After they exhaust various foodstuffs, the crux of the story comes when humans are dependent on rice for food. The rice grows wild and replenishes itself overnight. But because the rice has to be collected every day, eventually some become tired of this. They begin to hoard, and accumulate increasing amounts of rice so that they don't have to go out and gather it every day.

As the rice is hoarded, problems arise with its supply. People start to divide the land and to establish boundaries and to grow their own supply of rice. This is the emergence of private property. Then, driven by *taṇhā*, some begin to steal others' crop of rice. Violence and the threat of violence appear.

Eventually the problem becomes so severe that people decide to appoint one of their number to oversee the division of the land and crops and to administer punishments to those who steal. In return, they give a share of their rice to the appointed ruler. Government and taxation appear. And later on, people divide themselves further, into Brahmins, traders, ascetics, and servants. 'Servants', the largest group, work for the other classes. The Buddha comments that 'servants' experience mean and cruel lives. The caste system appears.

What can we learn from this myth? Firstly, I think the Buddha is telling us that the socio-economic order of society is made by human beings; it's not god-given. Secondly, he is telling us that the restless search to quench *taṇhā*, to satisfy thirst and craving, is at the heart of the human condition and is a key driver of our individual and collective behaviour. The Buddha combines this fundamental insight into the nature of the human condition with what he could no doubt observe happening 2,500 years ago in the emerging socio-economic structure of the Ganges plains to tell the myth of the *Aggañña Sutta*. In it, he is showing us how suffering and the causes of suffering arise in dependence upon *taṇhā*.

Does this mean that the Buddha would agree with those who argue that selfishness and greed are a fixed characteristic of human nature, a dominant part of our evolutionary inheritance that cannot be transcended? No. In his teaching of the four noble truths, the Buddha tells us that the suffering described in the *Aggañña Sutta* is not inevitable and that there is a way to remove suffering. Suffering exists (first noble truth) and arises from *taṇhā*, the restless search for the satisfaction of our desire (second noble truth). We seek the satisfaction of our desire in craving and clinging to things that are impermanent and subject to change; and when they change, we experience *dukkha*, suffering or unsatisfactoriness. Things that are impermanent and change in dependence upon conditions are incapable of giving us lasting fulfilment. Because of our ignorance, we do not see this. This is the 'ignoble' search, the *anariyapariyesenā*, the restless and fruitless search to satisfy desire with conditioned and impermanent things.

But there is an alternative. It was the realization that seeking satisfaction and fulfilment in conditioned and impermanent things was bound to fail that led to the Buddha leaving home and starting out on the *ariyapariyesenā*, the 'noble' search. The Buddha channelled his *taṇhā* into a desire to find a deeper and lasting source of fulfilment. When he gained Enlightenment, he succeeded in this noble search. He overcame craving and showed that it is possible to end suffering and find a lasting source of peace and fulfilment (the third noble truth). The Buddha teaches us that the way to end suffering is through cultivating another, equally powerful side of human nature, that of caring and compassion. With generosity and loving-kindness and the practice of ethics, with meditation, and with reflection and the gaining of wisdom, a path opens up to the gaining of Enlightenment and the end of suffering (a path spelled out in the noble eightfold path, which is the fourth noble truth).

Those who start out on the Buddhist path may be motivated by self-interest, by a desire to overcome their own suffering, but they learn that to achieve their aim they must attend to the needs of others. But we are living in an economic society dominated by, and dependent on, the kind of *taṇhā* that manifests in the restless, ignoble search. Two present-day commentators illustrate this very well. The first, Charles Handy, is regarded as one of the most influential business gurus of the second half of the twentieth century and the second, Tim Jackson, is Professor of Sustainable Development at Surrey University and the author

15

of an important book *Prosperity Without Growth*. Charles Handy writes that 'Economic growth depends, ultimately, on more and more people, wanting more and more, of more and more things.'[8]

And Tim Jackson says, 'It's a story about us, people, being persuaded to spend money we don't have, on things we don't need, to create impressions that don't last, on people that we don't care about.'[9]

The treadmill of economic growth relies upon an ever-growing army of consumers who must desire more and more of more and more goods and services. To this end, potential consumers are bombarded with advertising that pushes them into spending beyond their present means on things they didn't even know they needed, to keep up appearances with the spending patterns of people with whom they have very little meaningful connection. We are deluded into wanting more and more in the belief that it will bring us happiness. The Buddha, however, is telling us that we have a choice. We can go down the path of selfishness and greed that perpetuates suffering or we can follow the path of generosity and kindness, the path of altruism, a path that leads to liberation and the ending of suffering.

In the next chapter I shall explore the economist's view of altruism.

2

The gift relationship

In 1970, a book called *The Gift Relationship* was published.[1] Written by Richard Titmuss, Professor of Social Administration at the London School of Economics, it compared the blood donation systems then existing in the US and the UK. Blood donation in the UK relied on people giving blood voluntarily, for no financial reward. Blood was given as a gift. Donations of blood were then used for strangers, who received the blood at no charge. The UK system existed outside the market rules of economics and relied upon altruism. Blood donation in the US at that time relied upon commercial blood banks that paid donors for their blood and then sold the blood on. The system there was market-based and relied upon monetary transactions. The contrast between these blood donation systems gives useful background to a discussion about the difference in values between free market economics and Buddhism.

I have shown how, according to the (one-sided) presentation of Adam Smith's ideas by modern free market economists, selfishness lies at the heart of a successful economy. Moreover, in *The Wealth of Nations*, Adam Smith appears to dismiss the economic possibilities of altruism: 'I have never known much good done by those who affected to trade for the public good. It is an affectation, indeed, not very common among merchants, and very few words need to be employed in dissuading them from it.'[2] He contends that business people who trade from altruistic motives, from an unselfish concern for the welfare of others, will not in practice do much to increase public welfare compared to those acting out of self-interest. With arguments such as this, he is presented as one of the fathers of neoliberal capitalism. But in fairness to him, it must again be pointed out that he did have another side. I mentioned in Chapter 1 how he paused in *The Wealth of Nations* to consider the detrimental effect of the division of labour on people's minds and emotions. Before I move on to explore more modern views of altruism, I think it's worth pausing to examine this other side of Adam Smith.

Seventeen years before *The Wealth of Nations* was published, Adam Smith had published another book, *The Theory of Moral Sentiments*. In it, he reveals a different view of human motivation, writing in its opening lines: 'How selfish soever man may be supposed, there are evidently some principles in his nature, which interest him in the fortune of others, and render their happiness necessary to him, though he derives nothing from it, except pleasure of seeing it.'[3] He expounds a theory of 'sympathy' (closer in meaning to the present-day usage of the word 'empathy'), in which he argues that 'our fellow feeling for the misery of others' is founded on our imaginative capacity for 'changing places in fancy with the sufferer'. He gives an example of how we put ourselves in the place of others without intending any benefit to ourselves:

> When I condole with you for the loss of your only son,
> in order to enter your grief, I do not consider what I, a
> person of such character and profession, should suffer, if
> I had a son, and if that son was unfortunately to die; but
> I consider what I should suffer if I was really you; and

I not only change circumstances with you, but I change persons and characters. My grief, therefore, is entirely upon your account, and not in the least upon my own. It is not, therefore, in the least selfish.[4]

A thousand years earlier, in the eighth century, Śāntideva, a great Indian Buddhist teacher, had spoken of meditating on, to begin with, the equality of oneself and others: 'At first one should meditate intently on the equality of oneself and others as follows: "All equally experience suffering and happiness. I should look after them as I do myself."' Then he advocated meditating on the exchange of self and other, substituting one's own identity with that of another person: 'Whoever longs to rescue quickly both himself and others should practise the supreme mystery: exchange of self and other.'[5] Something of Śāntideva's spirit is present in the other side of Adam Smith: a caring and compassionate side ignored by free market economists. Unlike him, they do not see a human being as an economic actor with both self-interested and altruistic tendencies. Unlike him, they display an alarming lack of imaginative identification with others, especially those suffering from the negative effects of their economic policies.

However, to give you a sense of how modern economists have appropriated Adam Smith's later words on self-interest and altruism, I want to look, first, at a relatively unknown but influential figure in modern global capitalism. Ayn Rand was a twentieth-century writer, now dead, of whom you may have never heard but her ideas continue to have a major effect on important figures in the world economy. Next, in the context established by *The Gift Relationship*, I shall examine the views of several powerful economists, including Lawrence Summers, a man who has influenced the economic policies of presidents

Bill Clinton and Barack Obama. Then I shall present a Buddhist perspective on altruism.

Although she died in 1982, Ayn Rand remains popular among some powerful people. For example, several hundred bankers, economists, political advisors, and business leaders gathered in the City of London in October 2013 at an event hosted by the Adam Smith Institute to hear a talk by the chief executive officer of a Danish investment bank. The speaker argued that 'the world is on the wrong track' and propose that 'Ayn Rand is the only answer.'[6] In the 1990s, a survey of book of the month members by the United States Library of Congress named one of Ayn Rand's books, *Atlas Shrugged*, as one of the most influential books in the US, second only to the Bible. Paul Ryan, the Republican vice-presidential candidate in the 2012 US presidential election and a prominent member of Congress who prepares the Republican Party's budget proposals, cites Ayn Rand as a major formative influence on his thinking. Alan Greenspan, who from the late 1980s was for twenty years the head of the US Federal Reserve Bank, one of the most important economic institutions in the world, was a friend and admirer of Ayn Rand.[7]

Who was Ayn Rand? She was a Russian émigré, born in 1905, who lived for most of her life in the United States and wrote several novels to promote her philosophical views. She saw altruism as a disease that was 'incompatible with freedom, with capitalism, and with individual rights'.[8] For her, altruism was a kind of primitive social instinct, left over from our earlier evolution as humans. She held the view that we may still be in evolution as a species and may be living side by side with some 'missing links'. These 'missing links' can be found, she thought, in those people who fail to utilize their rational selfishness to its full potential. She deeply believed that 'each man must live as an end in himself and follow his own rational self-interest.'[9] In *Atlas Shrugged*, the hero, John Galt, exclaims, 'I swear – by my life and my love of it – that I will never live for the sake of another man, nor ask another man to live for mine.'[10] Her conclusion was that 'if any civilization is to survive, it is the morality of altruism that men have to reject.'[11]

It's difficult to imagine a view more completely opposed to everything that Buddhism stands for. The Buddha exhorted his disciples to 'Go forth for the good of the many, for the happiness of the many, out of compassion for the world, for the welfare, the good and the happiness of gods and men.'[12]

How much do Ayn Rand's views represent the views of modern economists? To find out, let's take a closer look at *The Gift Relationship*. When comparing the UK and the US, Richard Titmuss finds that the quantity and quality of the blood donated in the UK is higher than that in the US. In particular, the quality of the blood in the US was poorer because in a market for blood, those who had the greatest incentive to supply it for money were those with the unhealthiest blood, especially drug and alcohol addicts, who also had the strongest incentive to lie about their medical condition. (In those days, the testing of blood donations was much less well developed than now.)

But Titmuss had a deeper objection to the commercialization of the blood donor system. He believed that commercialization of the blood donor system eroded the spirit of altruism and generally diminished the propensity of people to give to others. In this way the 'gift relationship' in society was undermined, something that he very much regretted. What Titmuss feared was the general erosion of *moral* values in society by the crowding-out effect of *market* values, through the process of commercialization. By eroding opportunities for people to be altruistic, the culture of giving would be diminished; others would have fewer examples of altruistic behaviour from which to learn.

Titmuss's thesis did not go unchallenged by economists. One of Titmuss's main critics was Kenneth Arrow, a distinguished American economist of the time. In his criticisms, Arrow relies upon two assumptions about human nature that economists tend to take for granted. The first of his assumptions is that commercialization doesn't change people's propensity to be altruistic. In the case of blood, he argues, commercialization means that those who wish to buy and sell it can do so. Those who wish to avoid the market and prefer to see blood as a priceless gift can continue to do so, and can give blood for nothing. In this way, everyone gains. Arrow argues:

> Economists typically take for granted that since the creation of a market increases the individual's area of choice it therefore leads to higher benefits. Thus, if to a voluntary blood donor system we add the possibility of selling blood, we have only expanded the individual's range of alternatives. If he derives satisfaction from giving, it is argued, he can still give, and nothing has been done to impair that right.[13]

Arrow contends that in the US, a person can choose to give blood as a gift or to sell their blood. The prospective donor had two options. Because in the UK the option to sell your blood is denied, Arrow argues that the freedom of the potential donor is restricted. And as two freedoms are better than one, the system that includes the market alternative, the possibility to sell your blood at a price, is superior to the one that denies that choice.

Peter Singer, a moral philosopher and professor at Princeton University points out, however, that there are in fact three freedoms at stake here: the freedom to donate blood for no financial reward, the freedom to sell blood, but also the freedom to give blood as a priceless gift whose value hinges solely on the need of the recipient, because it cannot be bought.[14] That freedom was not available in the US. It was available in the UK. It turns out that each country contains the same number of freedoms, two, and that in each you lose a freedom. So Singer concludes that there is a choice to be made. Do you dispense with the freedom to sell your blood or with the freedom to give a priceless gift? This is ultimately a decision about the kind of society we want to live in.

Michael Sandel also challenges Arrow's reasoning and shows how commercializing blood can change the meaning of donating. He asks us to consider:

> In a world where blood is routinely bought and sold, is donating a pint of blood . . . still an act of generosity? Or is it . . . [a] practice that deprives needy persons of gainful employment selling their blood? If you want to contribute to a blood drive, would it be better to donate blood yourself, or to donate $50 that can be used to buy an extra pint of blood from a homeless person who needs the income? A would-be altruist could be forgiven for being confused.[15]

The consequence can be that many people who would give blood if it had no price will not do so if it can be sold and bought.

But perhaps Arrow's second assumption tells us most about the mindset of modern economists and their discipline. Arrow argues that altruism and generosity are resources and that, like other resources, their supply is limited and therefore needs to be economized. According to him, markets, which rely on people acting purely out of self-interest, save us from having to use up a restricted supply of altruism. Accordingly, if the supply of blood depends on people's generosity, there will be less generosity left over for other situations. If, on the other hand, people are paid to supply blood, then their generosity and altruism will be preserved. This is what Arrow says: 'Like many economists, I do not want to rely too heavily on substituting ethics for self-interest. I think it best on the whole that the requirement of ethical behavior be confined to those circumstances where the price system breaks down. . . . We do not wish to use up recklessly the scarce resources of altruistic motivation.'[16]

Arrow was not the first, nor the last, economist to argue this point. In 1954, Sir Dennis Robertson, a Cambridge University economist, gave a lecture entitled 'What does an economist economize?'. Robertson acknowledged that economists promoted a system that relies upon 'the aggressive and acquisitive instincts' of human beings but argued that they nevertheless fulfil a moral purpose. The promotion of the higher virtues of altruism and generosity, he argued, are best left to the preacher, but the economist helps by reducing the preacher's task to manageable proportions. How does the economist help? By supporting free market policies that rely upon self-interest rather than altruism, he saves society from wasting its scarce supply of virtue. Robertson continued: 'If we economists do [our] business well, we can, I believe, contribute mightily to the economizing . . . of that scarce resource Love, which we know, just as well as anybody else, to be the most precious thing in the world.'[17] Well after Sir Dennis Robertson and Kenneth Arrow has come Lawrence Summers, a former Secretary of the Treasury under President Bill Clinton and later Director of the National Economic Council for President Barack Obama. Between working for Clinton and Obama, Summers was President of Harvard University from 2001 to 2006, and it was at Harvard that he spoke on 'what economics can contribute to thinking about moral questions'.

> One of the things that bothers many people of faith about market mechanisms is the idea that there is something wrong with a system where we are able to buy bread only because of the greed or profit motive of the people who make the bread. Here I would be very cautious. *We all only have so much altruism in us. Economists like me think of altruism as a valuable and rare good that needs conserving. Far better to conserve it by designing a system in which people's wants will be satisfied by individuals being selfish, and saving that altruism for our families, our friends, and the many social problems in this world that markets cannot solve.*[18] (my italics)

I conclude that unlike Ayn Rand, economists such as Arrow, Robertson, and Summers do see value in altruism and believe themselves to be preserving virtues for use where they are really needed. But to anyone not immersed in economics, their way of thinking about altruism, generosity, and love – as resources of limited supply, like a fossil fuel that is diminished with every use – is bizarre. I agree wholeheartedly with Michael Sandel when he argues that 'Altruism, generosity, solidarity, and civic spirit are not like commodities that are depleted with use. They are more like muscles that develop and grow stronger with exercise. One of the defects of a market-driven society is that it lets these virtues languish. To renew our public life we need to exercise them more strenuously.'[19]

For Stephen Marglin, a professor of economics at Harvard University, economists like Arrow, Robertson, and Summers fail to distinguish between 'private' goods such as bread and 'public' or 'collective' goods such as love, which he describes as a 'hyper' public good. Love increases in size by being used and may shrink to nothing if left unused for any length of time. Marglin summed this up in a little ditty:

> *Love is a very special commodity,*
> *An irregular economical oddity.*
> *Bread, when you take, there's less on the shelf.*
> *Love, when you make it, it grows of itself.*[20]

Although the impression might be given from this discussion that economists wish to preserve some kind of balance between contrasting values in the market and the non-market spheres of public life, the current reality is that market values are more and more crowding out non-market values; and in the process, they are undermining general moral standards. In his book *What Money Can't Buy* Michael Sandel gives us two examples of how market thinking works and how it is creeping more deeply into our lives. The first one concerns immigration and refugees and the second one has to do with life insurance.[21]

Gary Becker was a Nobel Prize-winning free market economist at the University of Chicago. Responding to the contentious debate over how many immigrants to admit into the United States, he recommended that the US should simply set a price and sell American citizenship for $50,000 or perhaps $100,000. Immigrants willing to pay a large sum of money, Becker argued, are likely to be young, skilled, ambitious, and hardworking, and, even better, they are unlikely to make use of welfare or unemployment benefits. Like me, I hope you would agree with Michael Sandel's view that asking a refugee fleeing persecution to hand over $50,000 to gain sanctuary is callous.

But for those of us unwilling to go as far as Gary Becker would like, there is another market-based proposal. This proposal to solve the refugee problem doesn't make the refugees themselves pay out of their own pocket. An American law professor has proposed that an international body should assign each country a yearly refugee quota based on national wealth. The wealthier the country, the higher the quota of refugees the country is assigned. However, states can buy and sell these quotas or obligations among themselves. For example, if Japan is allocated a quota of 20,000 refugees per year but doesn't want to take them, it could pay Poland or Uganda to take them in. According to standard free market logic, everyone benefits: Poland or Uganda gains a new source of national income; Japan meets its refugee obligations by outsourcing them; and more refugees are rescued than would otherwise find asylum. Sandel ironically asks, 'What could be better?' and answers:

> There is something distasteful about a market in
> refugees, even if it's for their own good, but what exactly
> is objectionable about it? It has something to do with
> the fact that a market in refugees changes our view of
> who refugees are and how they should be treated. It
> encourages the participants – the buyers, the sellers and
> also those whose asylum is being haggled over – to think
> of refugees as burdens to be unloaded or as revenue
> sources rather than as human beings in peril. What this
> worry shows is that markets are not mere mechanisms.
> They embody certain norms. They presuppose, and
> also promote, certain ways of valuing the goods being
> exchanged. *Economists often assume that markets are inert,*
> *that they do not touch or taint the goods they regulate. But this*
> *is a mistake. Markets leave their mark.*[22] (my italics)

This is the nub of Richard Titmuss's original worry about a market in buying and selling blood. He argues in *The Gift Relationship* that it's not just the blood that gets contaminated; people's minds and values are also contaminated. The place in our society of important qualities such as generosity and community is eroded, to be replaced with selfishness and greed. Human beings and human qualities become commodities, things to be traded just like other commodities.

Sandel also tells us about another developing market. 'Dead peasants insurance' refers to the increasingly widespread practice in the US of companies buying life insurance on the lives of their workers.[23] When Michael Rice, a 48-year-old assistant manager at a Walmart store, collapsed at work and later died from a heart attack, the insurance policy on his life paid out about $300,000. None of that money went to his family. Indeed neither Michael Rice nor his family knew anything at all about the existence of the policy taken out on him by Walmart. Walmart took the lot.

Walmart now holds life insurance policies on hundreds of thousands of its employees. Using the records kept by government social security agencies, Walmart is even able to track the lives and deaths of its former employees. Many US companies invest millions of dollars in such policies. By 2008, US banks alone held $122 billion in life insurance on their employees. As the *Wall Street Journal* commented, 'It adds up to a little-known story of how life insurance morphed from a safety net for the bereaved into a strategy of corporate finance.'[24] In this manner employees become less an essential part of a working community and more a source of potential profit, even in death.

This is one of the many ways in which the modern marketplace corrupts our values and attitudes. Another way in which the market diminishes a sense of moral responsibility is in its naked rejoicing in greed. Perhaps the most famous statements in support of selfishness and greed were made by Ivan Boesky, a real-life Wall Street trader, and Gordon Gekko, a fictional Wall Street trader played by Michael Douglas in the film *Wall Street*. In May 1986, Boesky, at the time a tremendously successful and famous trader, gave a speech at the University of California Berkeley School of Business commencement ceremony. He said, 'Greed is all right, by the way. I want you to know that. I think greed is healthy. You can be greedy and still feel good about yourself.' According to a newspaper report, people in the audience laughed and applauded.[25] Later that year, Boesky admitted that he had amassed some of his wealth through illegal trading and went to jail. But his words lived on in the 1987 film character Gordon Gekko:

'The point is, ladies and gentlemen, that greed, for lack of a better word, is good. Greed is right, greed works. Greed clarifies, cuts through, and captures the essence of the evolutionary spirit. Greed, in all of its forms, greed for life, for money, for love, knowledge has marked the upward surge of mankind.'[26]

And in late 2013, Boris Johnson, London's mayor and a leading British Conservative politician, declared that inequality is essential to fostering 'the spirit of envy'. He hailed greed as a 'valuable spur to economic activity', calling upon the 'Gordon Gekkos of London' to display their greed in order to promote economic growth.[27]

Behind this public glorification of greed, three recent experimental research studies suggest that the academic discipline of economics encourages a culture of greed.[28] The first study relied on a method known as the Dictator Game. In this game there are two players, one of whom receives a cash prize. The other player is passive. The player who has been given the cash prize is then told that they can keep it all for themselves, or they can share it with the other player. Results generally show that individuals often give money to the second player. It's a test of how selfish or how altruistic people are. In this first study, the experiment showed that students specializing in economics kept more money than others. Economics students were more greedy. In the second study, it was found that economics education was associated with more positive attitudes towards greed and towards one's own greedy behaviour. The third study found that reading a short statement on the societal benefits of self-interest led to more positive ratings of greed's moral acceptability, even for non-economics students. As the authors of the studies point out, these effects suggest that economics education may have serious consequences for students' attitudes towards greed.

A fourth study, written by a pair of researchers from universities in Montreal and Madrid, examined whether or not the study of economics made students more likely to lie for financial gain. They found that in the research experiment, many students from all disciplines lied. But students of business studies and economics were much less honest than students from other fields. Whereas 53 per cent of humanities students were honest, only 23 per cent of students from business studies and economics were honest. Such a result could occur either because studying economics and business make students more dishonest or because dishonest students are more likely to study business and economics. But, the researchers concluded, their analysis showed that 'Economists lie more in our study in part because they have learned to do so.'[29]

Buddhism offers an alternative ethical system and world view. Generosity, kindness, and love can be cultivated and developed, just like, as Sandel says, developing muscles with exercise. In the *Mettā Sutta*, a discourse on loving-kindness, the Buddha urges us as follows:

Even as a mother protects with her life
Her child, her only child,
So with a boundless heart
Should one cherish all living beings;
Radiating kindness over the entire world:
Spreading upwards to the skies,
And downwards to the depths;
Outwards and unbounded,
Freed from hatred and ill-will.
Whether standing or walking, seated or lying down
Free from drowsiness,
One should sustain this recollection.
This is said to be the sublime abiding.[30]

This is why Buddhists practise *mettā bhāvanā* meditation, the cultivation of loving-kindness: to grow and strengthen the virtues of kindness and love and to diminish the power of self-centredness. Loving-kindness is not a commodity in limited supply. It is a quality of mind that can be cultivated in meditation and that grows in strength with repeated application in everyday life.

The Buddha identified greed, hatred, and delusion as the root causes of the human predicament. *Mettā bhāvanā* meditation is an antidote to hatred, and also weakens the delusion that we exist separately from others and the world around us. The antidote to greed is generosity, the practice of giving. In stark contrast to the sayings of Ayn Rand, the Buddha once commented, 'Those who don't praise giving are fools.'[31] In the teaching of the Buddha, the practice of giving is the foundation and the seed of spiritual development. In the Pali suttas, the earliest recorded teachings of the Buddha, we read time and time again that 'talk on giving' was the first topic to be discussed by the Buddha whenever he was teaching. In the Pali canon, the practice of giving is the first of the ten *pāramitās* (perfections). In the later Buddhism of the Mahāyāna, the practice of giving is the first of the six perfections – the perfections are virtues to be cultivated by all who wish to gain Enlightenment. Sangharakshita, the founder of the present-day Triratna Buddhist Order, comments that it's as if the teaching is saying that 'You may not be morally scrupulous. You may not be able to meditate even for five minutes at a time. You may not dip into the scriptures from one year to the next. But if you aspire to lead any sort of higher life, then at the very least you will give.'[32]

This practice is not concerned just with giving something to another. It's more about cultivating a personal quality of generosity, an inward disposition to give, a disposition that is strengthened by outward acts of giving. Interestingly, studies of blood donors show that although the initial decision to give blood may be influenced by a variety of factors, such as the convenience of a nearby clinic or by an appeal for blood, the sense of an inner moral duty and the desire to help or to act on a feeling of responsibility to the community become more dominant over time. Furthermore, studies suggest, learning to give in one context may carry over into other contexts.[33] The cultivation of generosity directly debilitates greed and hate while facilitating that flexibility of mind that helps to destroy delusion.

I am not arguing that we should now completely shift our whole economy from one based on priced monetary transactions to one based simply on generosity. A modern economy based on generosity is an ideal that requires a fundamental shift in general attitudes. However, Buddhists can encourage this shift in attitudes in a small but important way. For Buddhists, '*dāna*' means giving. The basic principle of a '*dāna* economy' is give what you can, take what you need. At Buddhist centres practising a *dāna* economy, those who come to classes are encouraged to give what they can afford, to help enable the spread of the Dharma. In this way, the teachings of the Buddha are open to anyone regardless of their financial circumstances. The same principle of give what you can, take what you need applies when it comes to levels of financial support given to those who work full-time at Buddhist centres and businesses operating a *dāna* economy. The chairperson of a retreat centre or the managing director of a business is treated the same as everyone else. They are financially supported according to what they need. They give according to the best of their ability. In this way, the practice of generosity challenges selfishness, encourages a culture of sharing, and encourages a basic ethos at the heart of sangha, the Buddhist community.

As well as this example of the *dāna* economy, Taitetsu Unno tells a story that reminds us of the power of individual acts of giving. It's a story about three grapefruits.[34] In 1968, Unno and his family were visiting Japan. They received a gift of three grapefruits, at the time a very rare and expensive fruit in Japan. As Unno and his family were just about to return to California, where grapefruits were abundant and cheap, they decided to give the three grapefruits to the wife's teacher at a flower-arranging class. A few days later, the teacher sent them a letter. Taitetsu Unno describes its contents:

> She wrote that she shared the first grapefruit with her grandchildren, who were thrilled with the fragrance and taste of an exotic fruit that they had never seen before. The second grapefruit she peeled and ate together with an old friend whom she hadn't seen for over twenty years, making the reunion a very special event. The third grapefruit she took to a hospital, where her best friend

was dying of a terminal illness. She hadn't eaten for more than a week, but when she saw the grapefruit she wanted to try tasting just a little piece. When she finished the first morsel, she asked for one, then another one, until she ate half the grapefruit. The family members watching all this were in tears, happy that their loved one was enjoying something to eat. . . . The teacher thanked us profusely from the bottom of her heart for the three grapefruits.

Unno reflected that according to Huayan Buddhism (a Chinese Buddhist tradition based on a teaching known as the Flower Garland Sutra), a small act of giving has wider effects in an interdependent and interconnected world. He concluded that

'No one can measure the effects of a single act of giving, for its repercussions are beyond our limited imagination.'

3

The decline
of community

At the centre of Buddhism are the Three Jewels: the Buddha (the
ideal of Enlightenment), the Dharma (the path of the teachings
of the Buddha), and the sangha (the community of the followers
of the Buddha).[1] Community, both in the sense of the followers
of the Buddha and in its wider sense of the social ties that help
to bind people together, was a vital interest for the Buddha. But
it can be argued that community is lost with capitalist economic
development. This is the thesis put forward by Stephen Marglin,
Professor of Economics at Harvard University and author of
*The Dismal Science: How Thinking Like an Economist Undermines
Community*.[2] Marglin argues that the cause of loss of community
is greed and selfishness, the subject of our previous chapters.

For Marglin, community 'provides a kind of social glue,
binding people together in relationships that give form and flavor
to life.' Community relies upon 'constraints and obligations' that
go beyond simple self-interest.[3] Where might we find this 'social
glue', this sense of community? I believe it can be found in five
particular aspects of life: family and close friends, work, locality
or neighbourhood, the state or the nation, and shared interest
or commitment. From my own life, I can think of examples of
these types of community, in particular as a child brought up
in the 1950s in a shipyard town in the north of England. My

family, with aunts and uncles, grandmother and grandfather, lived either together or very close by each other, and everyone in the locality depended on the shipyard for work and income. The 'family' extended to include neighbours on the same street, whose doors were rarely locked, and people moved easily in and out of each other's houses. That was more than fifty years ago, and communities that combine family and friends, work, and neighbourhood are rarer today.

Nevertheless, I can draw on my own experience and think of two more recent examples of the persistence of community. In the mid-1990s, I did some research for the British Fire Brigades Union. This involved interviewing working fire fighters at all levels, from rank-and-file fire fighters up to Chief Fire Officers (the chief executive officers of regional fire brigades). The fierce loyalty and comradeship that the fire fighters felt for each other was remarkable. I remember one Chief Fire Officer speaking about the difficulties of changing the attitudes of middle-level officers towards the role of managing. Because middle-level officers started life in the fire service as rank-and-file fire fighters, they saw themselves firstly as fire fighters, secondly as union members, and only thirdly as managers. And later in the 1990s, I was fortunate to live for six years in a Buddhist community of eighteen men at a retreat centre. This was one of the most positive and formative experiences of my life: it was a shining example of an intentional community of shared interest and commitment.

What about community at the level of the state or nation? Citizens coming together and agreeing to pay taxation in return for a variety of collective provisions and services is a form of community. The nature and character of that community can of course be contested in democratic countries with elections. From my own life in Britain, I would like to highlight a particular example of the state as a caring and compassionate community. I was born in 1948, one month after the foundation of the National Health Service (NHS), a free medical service available to all in Britain. The vast majority of politicians and people in Britain in the 1940s favoured introducing the NHS. Its introduction came about in the immediate aftermath of an intense practical experience of community and an enthusiastic communal discussion of what was expected of the post-war state.

For example, faced with a long war and maybe with long periods when soldiers were stuck at base, the British army introduced the Army Bureau of Current Affairs, prompted by the belief that it was not only a soldier's right but also his duty 'to reason why'. Compulsory adult education and discussion in small groups for at least one hour per week, to be taken from training time, was introduced throughout the army. Just how far enthusiasm for communal discussion went is illustrated by the experience of one officer. Seeking shelter in a barn from German bombardment in north-western Europe after D-Day, he found a corporal and twelve men earnestly discussing 'What shall we do with the Germans after the war?'. This and many similar instances prompted the master of Balliol College at Oxford University to remark that 'there had not been an Army in England which discussed like this one since that famous Puritan Army which produced the Putney Debates and laid the foundations of modern democracy.'[4]

What was happening in the army reflected a wider spirit of the age, a concern to avoid returning to the unemployment of the 1920s and 1930s, and a wish to address the gaps in social provision left by an uncaring form of capitalism. A specific worry was the system of health insurance: some people were covered by a national government-run scheme, others were covered by private insurance, and some were not covered at all. The benefits provided by the schemes were inadequate to the extent that a prolonged illness could lead to real financial difficulty and poverty. When the Beveridge Report, by a committee set up by the wartime coalition government to consider these and other issues, was published in December 1942, some of the longest queues of the war appeared outside the shops of His Majesty's Stationery Office. More than 600,000 copies of the report and a shorter, summary version were sold; and within two weeks of its publication, a Gallup poll found that nineteen people out of twenty had heard of the report and that nine out of ten believed that its proposals should be implemented.

The report laid the foundations for what became known as the 'welfare state' in Britain, and led to the creation of a system of national insurance and the formation of the National Health Service. The objects of the NHS were spelled out in another government paper, published in 1944:

1. To ensure that everyone in the country – irrespective of means, age, sex, or occupation – shall have equal opportunity to benefit from the best and most up-to-date medical and allied services available.
2. To provide . . . for all who want it, a comprehensive service covering every branch of medical and allied activity.
3. To divorce the care of health from questions of personal means or other factors irrelevant to it; to provide the service free of charge . . . and to encourage a new attitude to health – the easier obtaining of advice early, the promotion of good health rather than only the treatment of bad.[5]

In this way the NHS was to be funded from taxation, and all hospital and other medical treatment was to be free. Some might argue that shifting the burden of care and compassion from family and friends in the community to institutions run by the state involves a loss of intimacy and reciprocity, important factors in the maintenance of community.

As we shall see shortly, this is, in an extreme form, the argument used by the Amish community in the United States. I prefer to think that the massive increase in the equality of treatment that came with an institution such as the NHS and the peace of mind afforded to all was founded upon the strength of community pressure. Of course, it's also the case that for some politicians, the decision to go along with the NHS was an instrumental one, made from fear that if a more benevolent form of capitalism weren't offered, then capitalism itself might be at risk. The alternative to capitalism in the form of communism and the Soviet Union was a very real fear and motivator for European democracies in the mid-twentieth century. Nevertheless, I believe that the formation of the NHS gives a good example to us today of how the state can act as the agent of a caring and compassionate national community. But I would add that without pressure from below, without an active sense of community at the local level, pressure may well rise to diminish the role of the state as a caring community and to weaken caring institutions such as the NHS.

Stephen Marglin elaborates his description of community with his distinction between communities of 'necessity' and 'affinity'. A classic example of a 'community of necessity' is the manor of mediaeval times, where men and women of radically different degrees of individual freedom were brought together in the common activity of agricultural production. People were not equal there but it was necessary that they worked together in order to survive. 'Communities of affinity' are held together not by adversity but by 'shared affections, common goals, a unity of vision and ideology, and mutual responsibilities'.[6] Religious communities, like the retreat centre community I lived in, and other intentional communities are examples of 'communities of affinity'. Necessity and affinity are not exclusive; they may together give a community cohesion. The community of mediaeval times was by no means ideal, with harsh and unequal relationships between the lord and serfs, but it also had the relationships of master and apprentice, of family, of religious beliefs, and of the village. These made up a network of ties that encompass four of the five different types of community I identified earlier and that gave mediaeval life a social cohesiveness.

But in Britain and Europe between the fifteenth and nineteenth centuries, traditional forms of mediaeval community were destroyed in a process that created the conditions for capitalism to emerge. In what is known as the 'enclosure movement', lands previously held in common were forcibly transformed into private property and the people who lived on the common land were evicted. Joyce Appleby, an economic historian, says that the process of enclosure dissolved what she describes as 'the moral economy', in which 'the weak, the irresponsible, and the unlucky were knit into the same village responsibilities with the able'.[7] The enclosure movement created a new order in which the individual landlord was free to pursue his own interests independent of the needs of others in the community. As Appleby says, 'Enclosure disentangled each person from this web of community obligations.[8] And the consequence was that 'The bond between the land, the people, and the divine had been broken and replaced by the emergence of land as an economic resource, what much later became known as "natural resource", and [by the emergence] of the people on the land as only "labor" or what, also much later, became known as "human resources"'.[9] In this way people were separated from the land, so that they no longer felt the same responsibility towards each other or towards the land itself. It was this change from the mediaeval to the more modern, capitalist structure of society that accompanied the emergence of the economist's emphasis on the purely self-orientated individual. And it was this change that created the large number of landless labourers that would become the workforce for the industrial revolution and the evolution of capitalism.

Was the enclosure movement a good or a bad thing? The conventional economic view of enclosure is that it represented the triumph of efficiency. Enclosure, it is argued, enabled a rapid growth in the economy from which all benefited, as outdated and inefficient methods of agricultural production were abandoned. In other words, the community had to be pushed aside because individuals, concerned with their own selfish needs, could do better, both for themselves and for the rest of society by acting on their own.

But not all economic historians accept this point of view. Some argue that the main impact of the enclosure movement was to redistribute income away from tenants to landlords. It was not the size of the economic pie but its distribution that motivated the enclosure movement. Traditional community organization stood in the way of landlords getting a bigger share of the economic pie. I am not making this point as an argument for a return to the mediaeval manor – far from it. I am simply indicating that the motivation behind this process of change can be seen as an example of the emerging prioritization of self over community.

Not all older forms of community organization have been lost. In the United States and in Ontario, Canada, there are around a quarter of a million members of the Amish community, in several hundred communities or settlements in which members live and worship. The Amish belong to the Anabaptist Christian community and combine 'affinity', their religious beliefs, with 'necessity', a set of rigorous rules that largely but not entirely preclude participation in modern technological and economic society. Basing their lives on their interpretation of the Bible, the Amish try to settle where they can separate themselves from the world and use the land for farming and other livelihoods. I remember watching the film *Witness*,[10] set among the Amish people, and being astonished by the barn raising scene. Barn raising is one of the defining examples of Amish economic and social life. The community comes together to help build a neighbour's barn and all the labour is given for free. More usually in modern society, if a farmer's barn is burnt down, the farmer will turn to the insurance company through a faceless transaction rather than to the community. The example of barn raising shows how the Amish combine both affinity and necessity by prohibiting insurance and encouraging mutual dependence.

Of course, not everyone would want to subscribe to the rules of necessity in Amish society. Marglin tells of the tragic consequences of the refusal of the Amish to accept money from the government. This led one Amish family to refuse medical aid for a young boy, who subsequently died. When asked why he would not accept government medical aid, the boy's father said, 'If we take money from the government, then we are not Amish.'[11] Some of the rules of necessity of the Amish are, in my view, too high a price to pay for the continued existence of community. On the other hand, recent trends concerning the elderly in modern American and European society may well be seen as the high price of the depletion of community.

A new financial product in the US is the 'life-settlements business'.[12] This is a growing marketplace in which people approaching the end of their lives sell their life insurance policies to a third party for a price, perhaps because they cannot afford necessary health care. Here is how it works. Once a person decides to sell their life insurance policy, the potential third party investor researches the seller's medical records, to see how long the person is likely to live. Then the investor and the seller agree on a price. For example, if the seller has an insurance policy that will pay $500,000 on their death and the best indications from medical research are that the seller will live for maybe another two or three years, the investor might offer to buy the policy, and to pay all remaining premiums, for a sum less than $500,000. In this way, the investor hopes to make a profit, which will be higher or lower depending on how much less than $500,000 they pay for the policy and on how long the seller lives. And the seller gets access to badly needed cash in order to help support them in their old age and in sickness.

In Europe, increasing numbers of elderly and sick Germans are being sent overseas for long-term care in retirement and rehabilitation centres because of rising costs and falling standards in Germany. According to the *Guardian* newspaper, this trend, which has seen thousands of retired Germans rehoused in homes in eastern Europe and Asia, has been severely criticized by social welfare organizations as 'inhumane deportation'.[13] But, the newspaper goes on, with increasing numbers of Germans unable to afford the growing costs of retirement homes and with an ageing population, the number expected to be sent abroad in the next few years is only likely to rise.

What do these stories from the US and Germany tell us about modern society? In my view, they point to a trend in which the ability to rely on community support is declining, whether it's the family as community, the local neighbourhood as community, a religious group as community, or the state as community and compassionate provider of free caring services. Marglin argues that this is an inevitable consequence of our free market economy:

> It is the importance of the ties of necessity that puts community at odds with the foundational assumptions of economics. Markets, based on voluntary, instrumental, opportunistic relationships, are diametrically opposed to the long-term commitments and obligations that characterize community. By promoting market relationships, economics undermines reciprocity, altruism, and mutual obligation, and therewith the necessity of community. The very foundations of economics, by justifying the expansion of markets, lead inexorably to the weakening of community.[14]

The increasing encroachment made by economic markets into more areas of people's lives leaves its mark on their mind, weakens traditional community values, and replaces community with economic transactions carried out at a price.

This is not to say that the notion of community is not without tensions. Perhaps the most fundamental tension is the potential conflict between building communities that provide a strong human connection and allowing enough room for the flourishing of individual diversity and creativity. Marglin recognizes that this is a problem but points out that in economics 'This much is sure: we will never find the answer to this question as long as we are blinded by an ideology, the ideology of the market, which makes community invisible.'[15] Free market economics simply ignores community.

But this tension between community and individual is not going to go away. Indeed, the recent social trend for people to live more on their own and not with others implies that its importance as an issue is growing. In 1950, four million people lived by themselves in the US. More recent figures suggest that thirty-one million now live alone. Single-person households are also increasing appreciably in most developed economies.[16] Many reasons for this trend have been put forward. Young people delaying marriage in order to achieve career goals; high levels of divorce and the breakdown of traditional family values and structures; the ageing of populations, with widows and widowers living alone; the women's liberation movement and feminism; urbanization and the rise of urban culture with its gyms and coffee shops; and online communications technologies such as Facebook that can dissolve the boundaries between isolation and social life – all these have been identified as possible causes for the trend. It may be explained also simply that as a result of growing wealth, individuals are enabled to live alone for the first time. But perhaps there is a more fundamental reason for this trend, a reason identified originally in the late nineteenth century by Emile Durkheim as 'the cult of the individual', arising then with the shift from rural communities to industrial cities, a shift that has been intensified by modern trends.[17]

I have sympathy in some ways with those caught up in this trend. The wish to have more control of one's life and to seek security in a place of one's own in an uncertain world are impulses I have experienced myself. But the growth of solitary living is a problem when it comes to community. In his book *Bowling Alone*, Robert Putnam notes that in the US between 1973 and 1994, the number of people who held leadership roles in a local organization fell by more than a half. He writes about a decline in civic participation and the networks of support and reciprocity that helped to join people together, that is a weakening of community. Writing in 2000, he finds that 'older strands of social connection were being abraded – or even destroyed – by technological and economic and social change.'[18] The pace of these changes has intensified since 2000. Although some may see developments of all the forms of social media via the Internet and of the digital connection as a counterweight to the loss of community, Putnam believes that they offer too weak a link to reverse the loss of community. His view that face-to-face social interactions are a precondition for meaningful life online has been supported more recently by those such as Sherry Turkle, who believe that real community, far from being enhanced by technology, has been displaced by 'the half-light of virtual community'.[19]

The Buddha lived 2,500 years ago in a society much more like Western mediaeval society than modern society. What can we learn from the Buddha about 'community'? The broader community of the Buddha's followers included monks and nuns and lay people, who co-existed in an interconnected relationship of affinity and necessity and gave support to each other. In the morning alms rounds, the monks and nuns, forbidden by rule to hoard and to cook food, went to towns and villages to receive food from the lay people. They in turn expected exemplary behaviour and to receive nourishing teachings from the monks and nuns.

The foundation of both parts of the community was good, or spiritual, friendship. In many texts, the Buddha extols the benefits of good friendship. Good friends, says the Buddha, are those who are there to help when one is in need, who stay loyal in bad times as well as in good times, and who offer advice about what is the best course of action and give sympathy. Helping a friend, for example, may mean looking after the friend's property when the friend has lost their way or is unable to look after the property themselves, or it can mean providing comfort in times of fear and distress. Staying loyal consists of being a trusted confidant. Opposite to the true friend is the false friend, who encourages wasting time, spending money foolishly, pursuing frivolous goals, and indulging in gossip and small talk. The false friend seeks to flatter rather than to offer constructive criticism and entices with temptation instead of giving sound advice. Ānanda, who was the Buddha's companion and attendant for more than twenty years, was once so struck by the importance of friendship that he went to the Buddha and exclaimed, 'Venerable sir, this is half of the holy life, that is, good friendship, good companionship, good comradeship.' To which the Buddha replied, 'Not so, Ānanda! Not so, Ānanda! This is the entire holy life, Ānanda, that is, good friendship, good companionship, good comradeship.'[20]

When he made this statement, the Buddha might have been thinking specifically of Anuruddha and his two companions Nandiya and Kimbila, monks who left home and came to live together in the wilderness. Once, on a visit to Anuruddha and his companions, the Buddha asked whether they were living in harmony. Anuruddha replied, 'Surely, Lord, we are living in concord, with mutual appreciation, without disputing, blending like milk and water, viewing each other with kindly eyes.' When the Buddha asked further how they managed to maintain such harmony, Anuruddha explained, 'I maintain acts and words and thoughts of loving-kindness towards these venerable ones both in public and in private. I think, 'Why should I not set aside what I am minded to do and do only what they are minded to do?' and I act accordingly. We are different in body, Lord, but only one in mind, I think.' The Buddha was very impressed by the example of Anuruddha and his companions and said that if all the world should remember the three young men with 'confident heart', that would lead to the welfare and happiness of the whole world for a long time.[21]

Looking after each other applied as well in lay life. One of the best-known Buddhist texts for householders or lay people is the *Sigālovāda Sutta*.[22] In it is described how a Brahmin youth named Sigālaka had promised his father that every day he would perform a ritual that required him to pay respects to each of the four directions of north, south, east, and west and also to the nadir and the zenith. One day, he was worshipping the different directions when the Buddha happened to see him and enquired what he was doing. When Sigālaka explains the promise he had made to his father, the Buddha says that Sigālaka can honour the six directions in an additional way. He can think of each of the directions as representing a particular kind of social relationship. The six basic social relationships that the Buddha relates to the six directions are parents and children, teacher and pupils, husband and wife, friend and friend, employer and workers, and lay follower and religious guides. The Buddha tells Sigālaka that his parents are the east, his teachers the south, his wife and children the west, his friends the north, his workers the nadir, and religious guides the zenith. The Buddha then gives to each member of each pair five obligations with respect to his or her counterpart; and when each member fulfils these obligations, the corresponding direction comes to be 'at peace and free from fear'.

As Bhikkhu Bodhi, the foremost translator of the Pali canon, comments, the Buddha thus reinterprets an ancient Indian ritual and infuses it with a new ethical meaning. He focuses on a society sustained by a network of interlocking relationships in which its members carry out their reciprocal duties and responsibilities in a spirit of kindness, sympathy, and goodwill. Bhikkhu Bodhi concludes that social stability and security depends upon each member of society carrying out the duties and responsibilities of their social position. In this way, 'Each person rises above the demands of narrow self-interest and develops a sincere, large-hearted concern for the welfare of others and the greater good of the whole.'[23] Buddhism also emphasizes the four 'means of unification' or 'ways of building a community' (saṃgrahavastu) by which a Bodhisattva draws to himself, and maintains, a following. The four means are generosity, kindly or affectionate speech, beneficial activity such as teaching the Dharma, and exemplification or acting in accordance with one's teachings. These four means are not just for a Bodhisattva to follow; they are desirable elements in the successful building of spiritual community.

But it would be a mistake to assume that all went well in the Buddha's spiritual community. Two examples in particular illustrate that problems did occur. They also throw interesting light on the roles of affinity and necessity in community.

The first example concerns monks and involves a case of dysentery.[24] The Buddha, accompanied by Ānanda, discovers a monk ill with dysentery lying on the ground in his hut and covered in excrement. Questioning the monk, the Buddha learns that no one is taking care of him. After first helping Ānanda to bathe and clean the monk and lifting him back into bed, the Buddha calls all the monks together and admonishes them, saying, 'Monks . . . you have no mother and no father to care for you. If you don't care for each other, then who will care for you? If you would care for me, then tend to the sick.' Despite the teachings of the Buddha, the monks fail to look after their fellow monk, who lies ill in his own excrement. The Buddha points out to them that as they have no father and mother, they must of necessity look after each other, especially when they are ill. And even though there is a clear spiritual hierarchy in the community of monks, everyone is expected to help by caring for another. The Buddha exemplifies this by himself cleaning and looking after the sick monk. The higher the spiritual rank, the more important it is that senior members are seen to uphold the values of the community.

The second example is a story about fractious monks. The story is called 'The Quarrel at Kosambī'.[25] A serious split developed among a group of monks staying at Kosambī. Originally caused by a trivial dispute – whether or not it was allowable to leave water in a container in the toilet area – it rapidly got out of control, with two deeply entrenched sides each refusing to give way. When the Buddha heard about the dispute, he attempted to resolve it but failed. Even he could not persuade the monks to end the dispute. The Buddha gave up and left. However, as we have noted before, monks have to go into villages and towns each morning to receive food. This was one of the rules of necessity in the community of monks and nuns. When the villagers, the lay people, heard about the dispute and that the monks had refused to listen to the Buddha, they refused to give them any food. Only when this happened did the monks decide to solve the problem. They all left Kosambī and went to see the Buddha, finally seeking his help in resolving the dispute. It's interesting to note the role of the lay people. Only their boycott forced the monks to do anything. In this case, at least they had more power than the Buddha in bringing the monks to their senses.

From the teachings of the Buddha, we've looked at the importance of good friendship. We've seen this at work among the monks. We've heard how the Buddha taught the importance of friendship and respect in all social relationships, in both lay and monastic life. We've looked at the qualities that help to maintain a community and we've discussed two examples of community life going wrong.

I wish to tell one more story relating to spiritual community, this time a myth or story originally told by the Buddha himself. It's called 'The Lion's Roar on the Wheel-Turning Monarch', from the *Cakkavatti Sīhanāda Sutta*, and it illustrates the important role a spiritual community can play at times of severe crisis.[26] (It also has relevance to the discussion on inequality and the effects of inequality in Chapter 9.)

A wheel-turning monarch is so called because, according to myth, a radiant 'wheel-gem' appears as a symbol of just rule. If the symbol disappears, it indicates that something is wrong with the method of rule. The wheel-gem cannot be passed down as an inheritance but must be earned by the just governance of each new king. In the discourse, the Buddha tells the story of a wheel-turning monarch and his successors. Concerned about the future of his kingdom, the monarch gets advice and is told that everything will be fine as long as he fulfils certain conditions: he must seek the counsel of wise people of high integrity; he himself must follow the teachings of the Buddha on morality and wisdom; and he must protect all his people, prevent crime, and meet the needs of the poor. In this way, his rule will be just and the symbol of the wheel-gem will remain visible. The king follows this advice; and for seven generations, his descendants follow his example, each of them by their policies and actions renewing the symbol of the wheel-gem.

Eventually, however, one of his descendants begins to neglect the poor. As a consequence of this neglect, poverty becomes increasingly widespread. As poverty spreads and the poor have no means of making a living, some of them began to steal from those who have enough for their needs. In order to forestall the increase in theft, the king introduces capital punishment for theft. Thieves then begin to arm themselves in order to protect themselves from the police. This leads to a general increase in weapons among the population, as people with property take up arms for protection against the thieves. As more and more people take up weapons, murder increases among the population. As crime increases, law enforcement becomes tougher and indiscriminate. People fearing arrest begin to lie. Meanwhile some see an opportunity to get their rivals into trouble with the law and begin making accusations against their neighbours. This eventually leads to a breakdown in people's trust of one another. As trust erodes, animosity increases. As animosity increases, people care less and less for each other. Eventually this leads to incessant strife among the population.

The Buddha tells the dismal story of the descent into chaos that eventually results from neglect of the poor. But then he continues the story and tells how the situation was eventually reversed. A few people grow tired of chaos. They simply decide to live differently. They go to a relatively secluded place and begin to live in harmony together. Essentially they live according to the Buddha's ethical guidelines. Eventually other people see that those who live in harmony are much happier and more prosperous than those who fight with one another. And so gradually all the conditions are reversed, and finally a government is established that that looks after the poor. Those first people who grew tired of incessant fighting are described as living lives remarkably like the life that the Buddha recommended for monks and householders. They lived as a sangha, a Buddhist spiritual community.

This is the key to what Buddhists can contribute to the preservation and development of community in the face of the historical and current trends towards the greater atomization of society. It is not an easy task to build and sustain a community with the right balance between the bonds of affinity of a shared spiritual goal, on the one hand, and rules of necessity, on the other hand, while allowing the flourishing of individual creativity and diversity. In my own Buddhist tradition of the Triratna Buddhist Community, there is a strong emphasis on community and the role of spiritual friendship, both in the form of friendships between more and less experienced practitioners and those between practitioners at the same level. This combines with an emphasis on exemplifying ethics and the four 'means of unification' (see above) at our urban and rural teaching centres and in our interactions with others, both Buddhist and non-Buddhist. For example, at the retreat centre where I used to live, we consciously reached out to the local community, holding the village fête on our grounds and one of us taking up a position on the board of governors of the local school.

In the Triratna Community generally, there is also much experience of establishing residential communities of Buddhists. These are sometimes formed from people working together in Buddhist businesses or at Buddhist centres, sometimes just by bringing Buddhists together under one roof. Occasionally there have been significant mistakes and problems in these endeavours, some of which have been described in *The Triratna Story*.[27] But a great deal of practical knowledge has been gained, not least that to build a spiritual community requires a balanced approach to Buddhism, one that includes meditation as an aspect of spiritual life and not as the only or necessarily the most important element.

4

Work

When I was at university in the 1960s studying economics, the number of unemployed in the UK averaged around half a million people. But after the 1960s, unemployment began to rise until in the 1980s more than three million were unemployed.[1] I particularly remember the anger and dismay when unemployment first went over one million in the 1970s. This was when I became actively involved in politics and trade unionism. Although I joined others in campaigning for the right to work, I did not think very much about the nature of work and its deeper role in people's lives until the late 1970s, when I came across a book written by the Hungarian writer Miklós Haraszti. In *A Worker In A Worker's State*, Haraszti, a dissident writer and poet, tells of life as a worker in the Red Star tractor factory.[2] Although Hungary was a communist state, management methods at the factory in practice closely resembled conditions in western factories: detailed supervision, very little autonomy for the workers, and individual pay tightly linked to the amount produced by each worker. In the absence of truly free and independent trade unions, the scope for resisting the system of production was very limited.

But Haraszti describes how the workers nevertheless found a way to rebel and assert their independence, by making what he calls 'homers'. When the factory supervisors were not watching, a worker surreptitiously looked around for junk pieces of metal, explored the available, unused machines near his work station, and decided what he would make. He didn't necessarily set out to make something useful, and he definitely didn't set out to make something to sell. Haraszti calls these two steps, producing something useless and renouncing payment, two steps towards the senseless and two steps in the direction of freedom. The worker, temporarily at least, won back power over the machinery, subordinating his skill to a sense of beauty. Haraszti comments that however insignificant the object was, its form of creation was artistic. The beauty of the 'homer' came first and foremost from the labour itself. He wrote:

> The tiny gaps which the factory allows us become natural islands where, like free men, we can mine hidden riches, gather fruits, and pick up treasures at our feet. We transform what we find with a disinterested pleasure free from the compulsion to make a living. It brings us intense joy, enough to let us forget the constant race: the joy of autonomous, uncontrolled activity, the joy of labour without rate-fixers, inspectors, and foremen.[3]

For writing the book, Haraszti was brought to trial by the communist authorities and given a suspended jail sentence. The manuscript was suppressed but was later published in the west. Haraszti's words inspired in me a vision of work as a central part of a fulfilling life. But although I personally have been very lucky in my life in finding emotionally rewarding jobs, work for the vast majority of people is a means to an end, a necessary affliction to earn money. A recent worldwide survey of 142 countries investigated how many employees were engaged with their work (psychologically committed to their job), were not engaged (lacking motivation), or were actively disengaged (unhappy and unproductive). The survey's results show that a quarter of all workers in the world today are actively disengaged, that two-thirds are not engaged, and that only one in eight workers is engaged with their work.[4]

On top of this, we live in a world where in 2013 over 200 million people were unemployed, 75 million of whom were young people between 15 and 24 years, and where in some countries almost a quarter of young people were neither employed nor in some form of education or training.[5]

Marie Yahoda was a well-known twentieth-century social psychologist and specialist on the effects of unemployment. Jewish, a socialist, brought up in Austria in the first half of the twentieth century, and like Haraszti in nearby Hungary later on, she suffered political persecution. She was imprisoned by the fascist government in Austria in the 1930s, as she had been one of the authors of a major study of the consequences of unemployment during the 1920s in Marienthal, a small industrial community. After fleeing to a new life in the UK and the US, she codified five categories that she said were vital to feelings of well-being. These were time structure, social contact, collective effort or purpose, social identity or status, and regular activity. She argued that the unemployed are deprived of all five and that this causes much of the reported mental ill health among unemployed people.[6]

Work, and the lack of work, are major sources of suffering in the world. How did we get to this situation and can we do anything to change it?

Historically the Judeo-Christian tradition has played an important role in attitudes to work. The Garden of Eden was a place of abundance where everything was provided for Adam and Eve; but because they chose to eat of the fruit of the Tree of Knowledge, God tells Adam:

> *Because you have listened to your wife*
> *and have eaten from the tree which I forbade you,*
> *accursed shall be the ground on your account.*
> *With labour you shall win your food from it*
> *all the days of your life. . ..*
> *You shall gain your bread by the sweat*
> *of your brow until you return to the ground.*[7]

It's true that for much of recorded history and for most of humankind, life has involved drudgery and hard physical work. Work was something unpleasant and had to be endured as an unquestioned part of the economic structure of society, at least in the Judeo-Christian west, as ordered by God. But with the Protestant Reformation of the sixteenth century came a changed perspective on work, which would eventually help to pave the way for the Industrial Revolution and the emergence of capitalism. As highlighted by the German economic sociologist Max Weber in his book *The Protestant Ethic and the Spirit of Capitalism*,[8] published early in the twentieth century, the Protestant work ethic involved diligence, punctuality, deferment of gratification, and the primacy of work.

But some elements of it did not fit well with the industrial age. One of the central aspects of the work ethic was that individuals could be the master of their own fate through hard work. Within the context of a world dominated by agricultural and craft-based production, this was to some extent true. But with the industrial age began a radical process of the deskilling of work, with the introduction of machine manufacture and the detailed division of labour. As I have already noted, people had been forced off the land by the enclosure movement. Home-based crafts were destroyed as production shifted from the countryside to factories in the towns and cities. In this way knowledge of the overall process of work was monopolized by the owner of the means of production.

Although the Industrial Revolution first took hold in England and western Europe, it was in the US that the potential of the division of labour and deskilling was most prominently realized upon the advent of mass production. A pivotal moment came at the end of the eighteenth century, when John Adams and Thomas Jefferson, the second and third presidents of the United States, met with the arms manufacturer Eli Whitney. Until that time, everything was made as a one-off, unique object. Whitney had brought ten muskets with him, and proceeded to take them apart and scramble the parts on a table. At random, he took a part from one musket and attached it to another until he had reassembled the ten muskets from the scattered parts. Jefferson immediately realized the potential of what he had seen. He had just witnessed a demonstration of the invention of interchangeable parts, and granted Whitney a contract to manufacture muskets.[9]

The shift to a new culture of work was accelerated in the nineteenth and early twentieth centuries by two further developments: first, the assembly line of mass production, where tasks are broken down into smaller and smaller parts in a more and more detailed division of labour and, second, scientific management, of which Frederick Winslow Taylor was the great proponent. Taylor brought time-study analysis into the picture, and the human being was harnessed to the assembly line to become part of the machine. Work became more and more of a 'mindless, stultifying, boring, and demeaning enterprise for a great many people caught in the factories, a phenomenon all too well known to us.'[10]

Deskilling and the spread of the division of labour continued apace throughout the twentieth century, spreading into more and more areas of work, with efficiency, productivity, and speed-up as the watchwords of production. For example, in English-speaking parts of the west, a telephone call to the bank now often involves speaking to someone who could be in a call centre anywhere in the world, who greets you and responds to you with predetermined, set phrases, whose knowledge and initiative is strictly limited by the employer, and whose productivity is measured by the number of transactions carried out in a fixed period of time. Calls are recorded and the efficiency of operators is assessed hour by hour. The methods of the factory are now reproduced in human conversations. And lest we believe that industrial factory conditions could not return to those of the nineteenth century, we should note the reports from mainland China of the terrible lives of the 500,000 (half a million!) workers at the Shenzhen and Chengdu factories. These are owned by Foxconn (a Taiwan-based company), which produces millions of Apple and other computer products each year. Conditions in them were so bad that after a spate of suicides in 2010, workers were asked to sign a statement promising not to kill themselves and pledging to 'treasure their lives'.[11]

Problems such as those at Shenzhen and Chengdu will not go away as long as we are stuck with the fundamental approach to work of modern economics. E.F. Schumacher in his groundbreaking essay 'Buddhist Economics' succinctly describes the modern economist's take on labour and work:

Now, the modern economist has been brought up to consider 'labor' or work as little more than a necessary evil. From the point of view of the employer, it is in any case simply an item of cost, to be reduced to a minimum if it cannot be eliminated altogether, say, by automation. From the point of view of the workman, it is a 'disutility'; to work is to make a sacrifice of one's leisure and comfort, and wages are a kind of compensation for the sacrifice. Hence the ideal from the point of view of the employer is to have output without employees, and the ideal from the point of view of the employee is to have income without employment.[12]

In this way, a vision of fulfilling work as an end in itself is lost, and the battle lines between employer and employee are drawn within a very limited perspective on the role of work. The outcome is that the employer is determined to cut his costs to the minimum in a competitive market and the employee is bent on securing more income for the least effort.

How does this compare with the Buddhist attitude to work? The Buddha lived in a predominantly agricultural society, but with many trade and craft specialisms. He was well aware of these crafts and often used similes drawn from different crafts in order to illustrate a point he wished to emphasize when giving a teaching. For example, in the *Satipaṭṭhāna Sutta*, when teaching how to follow the breath and to distinguish between a long and a short breath, the Buddha adds: 'Just as a skilled turner or his apprentice, when making a long turn, discerns, "I am making a long turn", or when making a short turn discerns, "I am making a short turn"; in the same way the monk, when breathing in long, discerns, "I am breathing in long"; or breathing out long, he discerns, "I am breathing out long" . . .'[13]

But the Buddha also gave some specific directions on work, and what he called 'right livelihood' is an important element of the noble eightfold path to Enlightenment ('right' means ethically positive). He mentions five specific work activities that harm other beings and that one should thus avoid: dealing in weapons and arms, dealing in living beings (including raising animals for slaughter as well as the slave trade and prostitution), working in meat production and butchery, selling intoxicants such as alcohol and drugs, and dealing in poisons. Any other occupation that would violate the principles of right speech and right action was to be avoided. (Right speech and right action are two other elements of the noble eightfold path.) So the Buddha encouraged his lay followers to make a living in a way that does not cause harm and is ethically positive. He advised his followers to avoid deceitfulness, hypocrisy, high-pressure salesmanship, trickery, and any dishonest way of acquiring means of support.[14]

The Buddha also gave more general advice to his followers on the sources of welfare and happiness in life, which relate to the purpose and activity of work. He often talked of 'wealth righteously gained', of the importance of persistent effort and balanced living, of associating with people of virtue, of being neither extravagant nor miserly, of being generous and not stingy, and of delighting in giving and sharing. All these would contribute to a balanced working life for those of the Buddha's followers who remained at home.[15] But for those who left home to become monks or nuns, manual labour was restricted to the construction of temporary huts or shelters. Monks or nuns did not engage in agricultural work.

This was not always well received, as a confrontation between the Buddha himself and a farmer illustrates. One morning, the Buddha went to the field where Kasibharadvaja, a Brahmin and farmer, had five hundred ploughs at work. He arrived when it was time for the Brahmin to distribute food to the workers. The Buddha waited there for his alms food; but when the Brahmin saw him, he sneered and said, 'I plough and sow, and having ploughed and sown, I eat. You also should plough and sow, and having ploughed and sown, you will eat.' 'Brahmin, I too plough and sow,' replied the Buddha. 'And having ploughed and sown, I eat.' When the puzzled Brahmin said, 'You claim that you plough and sow, but I do not see you ploughing,' the Buddha replied, 'I sow faith as the seeds. My discipline is the rain. My wisdom is my yoke and plough. My modesty is the plough-head. The mind is the rope. Mindfulness is the ploughshare and the goad. I am restrained in deeds, words, and food. I do my weeding with truthfulness. The bliss I get is my freedom from suffering. With perseverance I bear my yoke until I come to nirvana. Thus, I have done my ploughing. It brings the fruit of immortality. By ploughing like this, one escapes all suffering.'[16] Today in the Theravadin countries of Sri Lanka, Thailand, and Myanmar, monks still do not do agricultural work. But when Buddhism went to China, this was not possible, as Chinese people and culture expect monks to work. And so it became necessary for monks to work, to farm. As Buddhist communities took on a definite shape and structure within the Chan tradition, later to become Zen communities in Japan, work became an essential part of monastic life. Baizhang, who is credited with creating the first true monastic structure for Chan monks, was well known for his saying that 'A day without work is a day without eating.'[17]

In another well-known story, Dōgen Zenji, the founder of Sōtō Zen in Japan in the thirteenth century, travelled to China to study Buddhism. He met an old *tenzo* (head cook), who had walked twelve miles to buy some mushrooms brought over from Japan on

Dōgen's ship. Dōgen was puzzled by the distinguished monk and asked him, 'Venerable Tenzo, in your advanced years why don't you wholeheartedly engage the Way by doing zazen [meditation] or studying the sutras instead of troubling yourself by being Tenzo and *just working*? What is that good for?' The *tenzo* laughed loudly and said, 'Oh, good friend from a foreign country. It is clear you have no idea what it means to wholeheartedly engage in the Way'[18] (my italics). A present-day Buddhist teacher, my own teacher Sangharakshita, puts it this way: 'If your work is not your meditation, then your meditation is not your meditation.'[19]

E.F. Schumacher in his essay 'Buddhist Economics',[20] first published in 1966, lays out more fully what he thinks is the Buddhist attitude to work. He sees work as having three main purposes:

- to give a person the opportunity to make the most of their potential;
- to help them to overcome their ego-centredness by joining with other people in a common task;
- and to produce the goods and services needed for a becoming existence.

He continues:

> To organize work in such a manner that it becomes meaningless, boring, stultifying, or nerve-racking for the worker would be little short of criminal; it would indicate a greater concern with goods than with people, an evil lack of compassion and a soul-destroying degree of attachment to the most primitive side of this worldly existence. Equally, to strive for leisure as an alternative to work would be considered a complete misunderstanding

of one of the basic truths of human existence, namely
that work and leisure are complementary parts of the
same living process and cannot be separated without
destroying the joy of work and the bliss of leisure.[21]

Schumacher's essay is a wonderful refutation of the approach
to work of modern economics. I want to explore three particular
implications of his argument, relating to technology and mechanization, productivity, and employment and unemployment.

First, in relation to technology and mechanization, Schumacher
makes the point that two types of mechanization must be clearly
distinguished: one that adds to a worker's skill and power and
one that detracts from the worker's skill and power, turning
them into the slave of a machine. An example of a machine that
helps a craftsperson is the carpet loom, a tool that allows the
craftsperson to hold warp threads at a stretch for them to weave
the pile round them with their fingers. On the other hand, the
power loom is a machine that takes over the human part of the
work and is a destroyer of culture.[22] For Schumacher, there is a
fundamental conflict between Buddhist economics and capitalist
economics. Buddhism sees the essence of civilization not in the
multiplication of material wants but in the purification of human
character. And character, says Schumacher, 'is formed primarily
by a man's work'.[23]

As Arthur Zajonc, President of the Mind and Life Institute,
emphasizes, this is a very different and uplifting understanding
of the nature of work. By work, as well as by learning skills, we
educate ourselves morally.

What we do shapes who we are as well as produces the
goods and services needed for life. If we do something

that is demeaning, stultifying, soul-crushing, nerve-
racking, boring –then what we do gradually works
its way inside us and debilitates and demoralizes us,
diminishing our full capacity. If, on the other hand, we
can find a way of working by fashioning convivial tools
. . . with which to work, then work can be ennobling,
it can be nourishing, and the full capacity of our own
humanity can unfold through that nourishment.[24]

With the right technology, with the right tools, a productive connection between the inner and the outer can be forged. The Buddha sensed this when he used so many similes and metaphors from the world of work when teaching techniques for the inner life of meditation and contemplation.

Second, let's look at the obsession in modern economics with productivity. Growth of output as measured by Gross Domestic Product is everything. Increasing the amount of output delivered per person per hour – increasing productivity – is the holy grail of modern economic management. But ever-increasing productivity means that if our economies don't continue to expand, we risk putting people out of work. If more is possible each passing year with each working hour, then either output has to increase or there is less work to go around. Like it or not, it appears that we are hooked on growth if we are to avoid less work being available. But what if we decide that the relentless pursuit of economic growth is destroying our planet and that we must seek a different economic strategy that limits growth? Is growing unemployment inevitable?

Not necessarily. As the economist Tim Jackson points out, one solution would be to accept increases in productivity, shorten the workweek, and share the available work. These proposals have been around since the 1930s and are now enjoying something of a revival in the face of continuing economic difficulties. Jackson tells us that the New Economics Foundation, a British think tank, proposes a 21-hour workweek. If you are a workaholic, this may not sound so attractive but, as he says, it's certainly a strategy worth thinking about.[25]

Jackson puts forward another strategy for keeping people in work when economic growth is either not available or not desirable. It fits Schumacher's idea of what a Buddhist approach to work involves, as listed in the three purposes highlighted above. What is the strategy? It is to let go of the relentless pursuit of productivity. It is to deliberately seek to increase employment in sectors of the economy and in jobs that are traditionally seen as low-productivity sectors, such as the caring professions of medicine, social work, education, and crafts and culture.

At first, as Jackson recognizes, this may sound crazy because we've become so conditioned by the language of efficiency. But there are sectors of the economy in which chasing growth in productivity doesn't make any sense at all. Certain jobs and tasks rely on people giving their time and attention and care. Professions such as medicine, social work, and education are good examples. Expanding jobs in these sectors, and giving people more time to do their job, directly improves the quality of our lives and of their working lives. Making these professions more and more efficient is not desirable. For example, because of the drive for 'efficiency' and its associated form filling, teachers in the UK spend only sixteen hours in an average forty-eight-hour working week actually teaching and learning with pupils.[26] What sense does this make?

He is surely right to argue that instead of imposing meaningless productivity targets, we should be looking to improve the quality of care and the experience of the caregiver. 'The care and concern of one human being for another is a peculiar "commodity". It can't be stockpiled. It becomes degraded through trade. It isn't delivered by machines. Its quality rests entirely on the attention paid by one person to another. Even to speak of reducing the time involved is to misunderstand its value.'[27]

Support for Jackson's argument comes from an unlikely source: research into the placebo effect. Medical researchers have known for some time that placebo treatments – interventions with no active drug ingredients – can stimulate real physiological responses, from changes in heart rate and blood pressure to chemical activity in the brain. But exactly how the placebo effect works is a puzzle. Recent medical research carried out at several hospitals affiliated to Harvard University has focused on trying to isolate the ways in which the placebo effect works, using patients suffering from irritable bowel syndrome. To the researchers, the results were not surprising. The patients who experienced the greatest relief were those who received the most care. The longer the doctor spent with the patient, the more empathetic and thoughtful the doctor was, the better the results for the patient. As a report on the research commented, in an age of rushed doctor's visits and packed waiting rooms, this was the first study to show that the more care people get – even if it was fake, even if it was a placebo – the better they tended to fare.[28]

The journalist Jackie Ashley describes an excellent example of a care initiative in the UK that is not caught up in the modern preoccupation with productivity indicators. Instead, the initiative simply gets on without fuss with providing care and advice to patients with neurological conditions such as Parkinson's disease, multiple sclerosis, and stroke, conditions that affect movement, memory, balance, and communication. Founded as a charity in

1999, Integrated Neurological Services (INS) tries in a small but important way to fill a gap left by the National Health Service. In 2014, it is helping 600 people a year with various physical therapies and mutual support systems. Compared to the 300,000 people a year in the UK who are now affected by neurological conditions and who often live for another fifteen or twenty years, the number helped by the charity might seem insignificant (although not to those helped!). But nurtured by the local community and volunteers, it is a shining example of caring and compassion. I agree that it is important in an enterprise as large as the NHS that best practices are shared and disseminated around the organization, but the current management preoccupation with productivity measures and privatization means that the values of care and compassion can be forgotten and sidelined, leaving it to organizations such as the INS to keep them alive.[29]

Jackson argues that care is not the only low-productivity profession that might serve as a source of economic employment. He points also to crafts and culture. With crafts, it is the accuracy and detail inherent in crafted goods that gives them lasting value. The time and attention paid by the carpenter or the seamstress or the tailor is what makes this detail possible. The same is true of the cultural sector. It is the time spent in practising and rehearsing that gives performances their enduring appeal. Jackson rhetorically asks, 'What – aside from meaningless noise – would be gained by asking the New York Philharmonic to play Beethoven's Ninth Symphony faster and faster each year?'[30]

He believes that the modern tendency to view low productivity as a disease 'highlights the lunacy at the heart of the growth-obsessed, resource-intensive consumer economy'. We end up, he says, in a ridiculous situation in which 'a whole set of activities that could provide meaningful work and contribute valuable services to the community are denigrated because they involve employing people to work with devotion, patience and attention.'[31] He concludes that avoiding the 'scourge of unemployment' may have less to do with chasing after growth and productivity and more to do with building an economy of care, craft, and culture. In this way, he hopes we can restore the value of decent work to its rightful place at the heart of society.

But, and this relates to the third implication of Schumacher's argument, the tendency persists among modern economists to use mathematically sophisticated calculations to check whether full employment 'pays' or whether it might be more 'economic' to run an economy at less than full employment so as to ensure lower price inflation, all in pursuit of the greater output of goods and services. Writing in the 1960s, Schumacher reminds us that from a Buddhist point of view, this is standing the truth on its head by considering goods as more important than people and consumption as more important than creative activity. In his words, it's a 'surrender to the forces of evil'.[32]

Earlier in life, I was fascinated by stories about the International Workers of the World (IWW), a union that organized among vagrants and itinerant workers in the US in the early part of the twentieth century. IWW members would have approved of the vision of a perfect world described in the folk song 'Big Rock Candy Mountain':

There ain't no short-handled shovels,
No axes, saws nor picks,
I'm bound to stay
Where you sleep all day,
Where they hung the jerk
That invented work
In the Big Rock Candy Mountain.[33]

Later in life, when I became a Buddhist, I came across a vision of a different kind of utopia in the Pure Land texts of Mahāyāna Buddhism. The perfect world (the Pure Land) is Sukhavatī, the 'land of bliss', where there is perfect peace with no pain or suffering, no old age or death. Food and clothing appear miraculously when needed, the land is flat, the weather is perfect, and no one ever has to work. To be honest, although the Pure Land texts are obviously of higher ethical and spiritual value and are on a different plane to the vagrant's dream, I don't like flat land and much prefer the challenge of mountains. But most of all, and this applies to both the vagrant's dream and the 'land of bliss', I find the thought of an existence without work is distinctly unappealing.

In Voltaire's *Candide*, the story is told of a series of unfortunate sufferings that happen to Candide and his companions, until they escape suffering and live quietly in a community. But they become bored, finding contentment only when they each take up meaningful work that contributes to the community's welfare.[34] This inspires me. I am inspired by the Buddha's use of agricultural and craft metaphors to describe meditation. I am also inspired by Miklós Haraszti's description of 'homers', by Marie Yahoda's account of how work contributes to well-being, by E.F. Schumacher's vision of a Buddhist economics, and by Tim Jackson's promotion of an economy of care, crafts, and culture.

But the challenge of finding work that is satisfying both individually and socially and that gives an adequate income is difficult in our current economic system, particularly for those with family responsibilities. What can we do to help change attitudes to work? Many, Buddhists among them, do not have the good fortune to work at a job that is a vocation. Sangharakshita suggests that for the individual Buddhist, in the context of an ethical approach, two aspects of the pursuit of right livelihood need attention.[35]

First, he distinguishes between four types of job. The first are those, like working in a slaughterhouse or in the manufacture of armaments, that cannot be right for a Buddhist under any circumstances. The second type concerns jobs that involve deliberately increasing people's greed, such as might be found in advertising or sales promotion. These need to be avoided by Buddhists. The third type involves jobs that, on the face of it, might seem neutral as regards right livelihood but, with conscientious application and an ethical approach, can be made into right livelihood. This is as much to do with the attitude that one brings to work as with the type of work itself. The fourth type is those occupations that involve significant mental strain and tension, to the extent that meditation becomes difficult. If possible, these too should be avoided. Second, Sangharakshita urges those people whose job is simply a means to earn a living to restrict their working hours to the minimum required to earn enough to live from, so as to free up time for Buddhist practice and the spreading of the Dharma.

In considering Sangharakshita's suggestions, we need to remember that he outlined this approach in a series of lectures given in Britain in 1968. Unemployment at that time was very low by current standards. Consequently a relaxed attitude to being in or out of work, especially among young people, was much more possible than today. Moreover, in the late 1960s an increasing standard of living seemed assured for the foreseeable future. In present-day circumstances, there is much higher unemployment and greater insecurity among those in work. With longer working hours for many and the decreasing real value of wages and salaries, the pressures to conform and take any job offered are much greater than in the 1960s. Because of this, it can be more difficult to decide whether or not to take jobs or roles that might conflict ethically with Buddhist values, especially when others depend on the income from the job. Careful and compassionate judgement needs to be applied in such situations. Nevertheless, I do believe that Buddhists have a particular responsibility to try to exemplify the values of right livelihood in their working lives. At the very least, such issues need to be discussed among friends in Buddhist communities. But Buddhists can also respond collectively.

Tim Jackson writes about the three 'c's of care, craft, and culture. Earlier in the history of the Triratna Buddhist Community, in the 1970s and 1980s, there was lots of talk about the three 'c's of 'centre', 'community', and 'cooperative'. Later, the term 'cooperative' changed into the rather more awkwardly expressed 'team-based right livelihood'. The idea behind 'team-based right livelihood' was to provide a context in which Buddhists could work together in teams in businesses that exemplified right livelihood. During the history of the Triratna Community, there have been at various times wholefood shops, vegetarian cafes, printing shops, building firms, estate agents, and second-hand clothes shops, all employing Buddhists in team-based businesses. Keeping these businesses going over the long term has been difficult, but some still exist; and the principles of this approach apply also to the teams that run retreat centres and the bigger urban Buddhist centres.

The longest survivor and best known of the 'team-based right livelihood' businesses is Windhorse:evolution, ethically trading in giftware. It started as a market stall in London in the 1980s and is now one of the leading suppliers of giftware in the UK with a small chain of shops and a central warehouse in Cambridge.[36]

The business was originally inspired by a vision of generating funds to be given to projects in the Triratna Buddhist Community in a conscious practice of generosity (*dāna*). In time, there was a growing awareness of the potential for work to be a place of individual and team-based spiritual practice. Today, not all the workforce is part of the Triratna Community, but hundreds of men and women from all backgrounds and many countries happily work and contribute within the business. The warehouse, with its huge aisles and Buddhist stupa at its centre, is seen as a sacred, ritual space. Team meetings explore spiritual practice or study Buddhist texts. Sometimes work in the warehouse is carried out against the background of silent mornings focusing on mindfulness. In a modest but important way, such collective examples of Buddhist activity offer an alternative approach to work.

5

Nature and the environment

'Anyone who believes in indefinite growth of anything physical on a physically finite planet is either mad or is an economist.'[1] These words were spoken in 1962 by Kenneth Boulding, then environmental advisor to President John F. Kennedy. They were true then, and are much more true now, more than 50 years later. The physicist Geoffrey West has calculated how much power a modern person needs, using a watt as the measurement. On average, doing nothing, resting, a person runs on 90 watts of power. A hunter-gatherer in the Amazon uses about 250 watts. Now take someone living in the US. Add up all the calories he or she consumes, all the power necessary to run their computer(s), all the other electronic devices of a modern household, and the car. The total power required for this person is around 11,000 watts. To put the figure into perspective, this person in the US demands more energy than a blue whale, the largest mammal that has ever existed. Imagine a world with seven billion blue whales and the scale of the problem we are creating becomes very clear.[2] And yet, despite the manifest evidence of declining biodiversity, ecological damage, and global warming, we seem incapable of taking decisive action to counter the dangerous effects of our demand for more growth. As the scientist Neil deGrasse Tyson said in 2014 on the television series *Cosmos*:

We just can't seem to stop burning up all those buried trees from way back in the carboniferous age, in the form of coal, and the remains of ancient plankton, in the form of oil and gas. If we could, we'd be home free climate wise. Instead, we're dumping carbon dioxide into the atmosphere at a rate the Earth hasn't seen since the great climate catastrophes of the past, the ones that led to mass extinctions. We just can't seem to break our addiction to the kinds of fuel that will bring back a climate last seen by the dinosaurs, a climate that will drown our coastal cities and wreak havoc on the environment and our ability to feed ourselves. All the while, the glorious sun pours immaculate free energy down upon us, more than we will ever need. Why can't we summon the ingenuity and courage of the generations that came before us? The dinosaurs never saw that asteroid coming. What's our excuse?[3]

Why is it that we seem incapable of action? In this chapter, I shall look at the problem from the perspective of economics and business and then from the perspective of Buddhism and our relationship with nature.

In the 1970s, I dimly remember owning and reading a couple of books by E.J. Mishan, a professor at the London School of Economics. Mishan wrote a book called *Welfare Economics* and in 1967 published *The Costs of Economic Growth*, in which he perceptively writes that the precondition of sustained growth is sustained discontent and warns developing countries of the 'wasteland of Subtopia' that comes with industrialization.[4] Unfortunately, these and other books on the problems of economic growth remained on the periphery of my reading, squeezed out of my mind by a revolutionary fervour for more economic growth as a solution to the world's ills. And as I mention in the Note (see p.219), the neoliberal approach has since the 1970s come to dominate the neoclassical approach in universities and in other economic institutions such as the International Monetary Fund and the World Bank, limiting the space allowed to alternative points of view.

David Orrell comments in his recent book *Economyths* that one of the things missing from present-day teaching of neoclassical economics is 'the rest of the planet'. According to Orrell, modern economics neglects the fact that the human economy is embedded in the biosphere.[5] In the mid-1970s, the Nobel prize-winning economist Robert Solow even said, 'The world can, in effect, get along without natural resources because human ingenuity and technology can always provide a substitute.'[6] Orrell concludes that what passes today as mainstream economics has become so disembodied and detached from reality, it's as if it thinks it can do without the physical world.[7]

The environment and the natural world are insufficiently taken into account in mainstream economics, and in business the same ignorance can lead to hasty decisions in the pursuit of profit, without proper consideration of potential hazardous effects. This tendency has been highlighted by two recent trends.

The first trend involves vultures in India. Vultures provide a vital ecological function. Farms in India have vast herds of cattle and, in the way of things, individual cattle are always dying, their corpses left to rot in the sun, but not for long. Vultures can devour a carcass in minutes, leaving only bones. In the mid-1990s, farmers in India began to use a new, anti-inflammatory drug on their cattle. Traces of the drug left in dead cattle proved to be lethal to vultures. It's estimated that up to 40 million vultures died, almost 99 per cent of all vultures. The 'free' cleaning service provided by them, which would normally remove around 12 million tonnes of dead livestock a year, failed. Dead cows and buffalo were left rotting in the fields; and as result, India's wild dog population burgeoned, accompanied by a massive increase in the transmission of rabies. It has been estimated that 48,000 people lost their life to rabies as a result of the death of vultures. The total cost to India's economy has been calculated at \$34 billion.[8]

The second trend concerns bees. Bees play a vital role in the world economy. Without them, one-third of worldwide agricultural production would be lost. Bees pollinate crops, including alfalfa (used for cattle feed), apples, pears, almonds, oranges and lemons, broccoli, carrots, onions, melons, and many other crops of fruit and vegetables. But in autumn 2006 in America, and soon after in Canada, the UK, mainland Europe, South and Central America, and Asia, bee hives began to collapse and the bee population was decimated. Entire industries, such as California almond farming, have come under threat. The phenomenon has been given a name, colony collapse disorder, CCD for short.

The cause of the phenomenon is still being vigorously debated. Possible causes include parasites, fungal infections, and environmental stress. Many bee colonies affected by CCD belong to commercial operations that regularly transport the bee hives around the countryside to pollinate crops. But increasingly it is thought that pesticides play a major role in CCD by exposing bees to deadly toxic chemicals; and in 2013, the European Union imposed bans on the use of various pesticides thought to be contributing to the collapse of the bee population. The ban is vigorously opposed by firms producing the pesticides. Commenting on the situation with bees, the world-famous insect biologist E.O. Wilson has said, 'We are flying blind in many aspects of preserving the environment, and that's why we are so surprised when a species like the honeybee starts to crash.' For Wilson, the honeybee is nature's 'workhorse'. 'We took it for granted. We've hung our own future on a thread.'[9]

Problems such as these come about because our modern economy is enslaved to what has been called the 'growth fetish'.[10] As Charles Handy has pointed out, faith in the 'growth fetish' requires more and more people, wanting more and more, of more and more goods and services, and E.J. Mishan's observation above also bears repeating – the precondition of sustained growth is sustained discontent. The high priests of the growth fetish are the leaders of companies and the owners of capital, who desire to be bigger and bigger and to outdo their rivals. As the nineteenth-century philosopher Karl Marx wrote, 'Accumulate, accumulate! This is Moses and the Prophets!'[11] To break the faith in unlimited economic growth requires people to reconsider their relationship to material goods and their idea of what makes them happy. I shall return to this issue later in the chapter and in Chapter 9, when I consider well-being and happiness. Although there are honourable exceptions among economists such as Tim Jackson, as expressed in his book *Prosperity Without Growth*,[12] it seems now that if left to their own devices, modern economists and business are not going to do much to help deal with the problem of global warming and environmental damage.

But what about Buddhism and nature? Is there anything we can learn from the time of the Buddha that can point towards a better relationship with nature and the environment? In his day, nature in the form of the wilderness or jungle was a source of fear and terror. But as my friend Vishvapani, a writer on the life of the Buddha explains in his article 'How the Buddha

Discovered Nature', a potential new relationship with nature did emerge from the Buddha's experiences as he pursued his path to Enlightenment.[13]

The Indian jungle then was for most people an unknown place of dread rather than a place for quiet meditation. Four great forests dominated northern India, with few safe settlements. Travellers had to face the dangers of poisonous snakes, tigers and wild boar, and bandits. Some reported frightening encounters with ghosts, spirits, and demons. Instead of living in harmony with nature, the Buddha's contemporaries felt that they were intruders in another world that belonged to the animals and spirits.

In the *Bhayabherava Sutta* (the Discourse on Fear and Dread),[14] the Buddha talks of certain spots in dark woodland or around sacred trees as possessing an unnerving atmosphere. But despite the terror that these places evoked, the Buddha deliberately visited them at the times during the moon's phases when they were at their worst. As he later recalled, 'There in the darkness or the moon-cast shadows I would hear an animal approaching, or a peacock would break off a twig, or the wind would rustle the fallen leaves, and I thought, "Is this it coming now, the fear and dread?"'[15] The Buddha was directly engaging with the powers associated with these places and with the forces in his mind that caused him to fear them. And when the fear and terror flooded his mind, he refused to be deflected. If he were meditating, he continued to meditate; if he were walking, he continued to walk. In this way, he directly faced the fear in his mind until it vanished. The Buddha's actions resembled in part a shaman's encounter with the spirit world, but he differed from a shaman in his focus on his state of mind. Using mindful awareness, the Buddha focused on his own fearful response to the spirits rather than on the spirits themselves. In facing the demons and conquering his mind, he eliminated the fear of nature that pervaded his culture.

The Buddha thereby formed a new relationship with nature, one that allowed him to become intimate with it. As Vishvapani says, the Buddha's lesson to us is this: 'to heal our relationship with the natural world, we must first heal ourselves.'[16] The full flowering of the Buddha's lesson is reflected in a wonderful set of nature poems, said to be uttered by followers of the Buddha after their Enlightenment. Here is an excerpt from a poem by Mahā Kassapa Thera:

At Home in the Mountains

Strung with garlands of flowering vines,
This patch of earth delights the mind;
The lovely calls of elephants sound —
These rocky crags do please me so!

The shimmering hue of darkening clouds,
Cool waters in pure streams flowing;
Enveloped by Indra's ladybugs —
These rocky crags do please me so!

Like the lofty peaks of looming clouds,
Like the most refined of palaces;
The lovely calls of tuskers sound —
These rocky crags do please me so!

The lovely ground is rained upon,
The hills are full of holy seers;
Resounding with the cry of peacocks —
These rocky crags do please me so!

Being clothed in flaxen flowers,
As the sky is covered in clouds;
Strewn with flocks of various birds —
These rocky crags do please me so!

Not occupied by village folk,
But visited by herds of deer;
Strewn with flocks of various birds —
These rocky crags do please me so!

With clear waters and broad boulders,
Holding troops of monkey and deer;
Covered with moist carpets of moss —
These rocky crags do please me so!

[But] there is not so much contentment
For me in the fivefold music,
As in truly seeing Dhamma
With a well-concentrated mind.[17]

The message that in order to heal the world we must heal ourselves is emphasized in the *Cakkavatti Sīhanāda Sutta*, to which I have already referred in Chapter 3. As we have seen in this discourse, the degeneration of human morals led to the disappearance of many foodstuffs and to a collapse of society. Only when a small group decided to start living in a morally better way did the situation reverse itself. The Buddha is telling us that there is a close link between human morals, the environment, and the natural resources available to humans. Humanity, the environment, and nature are woven into an interdependent relationship. If immorality takes hold of humanity, all deteriorate. If morality takes hold, then all improve. One modern commentator, Lily de Silva, expresses the Buddha's teaching this way: 'Thus greed, hatred, and delusion produce pollution within and without. Generosity, compassion, and wisdom produce purity within and without.'[18]

It is well known that the Buddha prescribed the practice of *mettā*, loving-kindness, towards human beings. But actually he prescribed the practice of *mettā* towards *all living creatures found in nature*. In the *Karaṇīyamettā Sutta*, he enjoined his followers to cultivate the following intention:

Whatsoever living beings exist,
Without exception, whether weak or strong,
Whether tall and large, middle-sized, or short,
Whether very subtle or very gross,
Whether visible or invisible,
Dwelling far away or not far away,
Whether born already or not yet born,
May all beings be happy in themselves.[19]

As well as enjoining us to practise *mettā* towards all living creatures, the Buddha asks us to direct our *mettā* towards those 'not yet born', towards future generations of humans, and towards other species. We are being asked to act with kindness towards our descendants and the descendants of other species. The Buddha advocated a gentle, non-aggressive attitude towards all nature. In the *Sigālovāda Sutta*, he says a householder should accumulate wealth as a bee collects honey from a flower.[20] When a bee collects pollen from a flower, it doesn't pollute its beauty, nor does it deplete its fragrance.

The Buddha had an affinity for trees. It's said that having been born under a tree, he gained Enlightenment while sitting under the bodhi tree, and he died between two trees at Kushinagar. When I visited the Mahabodhi Temple at Bodh Gaya and walked around the temple's grounds among thousands of pilgrims, one spot affected me more than any other. It was marked with a plaque stating that this was where, after his Enlightenment, the Buddha sat for a week gazing in gratitude at the Bodhi Tree. The rational part of me questioned how anyone could know that this was the true spot and how they could be certain that this had really happened. But at another level entirely, the story of the event moved me deeply. I know that for meditation, the Buddha instructed his followers to sit down in the forest or at the foot of a tree, but I think the story moved me because of the Buddha's gratitude and because it symbolized just how much we depend upon trees.

In June 2002, a bug called the emerald ash borer arrived in the US from abroad. Within four years of becoming infested with it, an ash tree dies. More than 100 million ash trees have died in the US since 2002. Outwardly the signs of the plague are seen in the urban parks and neighbourhoods, once tree-lined, that are now bare. Less apparent, but evident enough in statistics, is the effect of the plague on human mortality. When the US Forest Service looked at mortality rates in counties affected by the emerald ash borer, it found higher mortality rates than usual, with more people dying from cardiovascular and lower respiratory tract illnesses.[21] As the ash trees died, more humans died. It's not certain why this might be so. We know that trees produce oxygen and that without trees we cannot survive. (And when we breathe out, we give back the carbon dioxide necessary for trees' survival.) We also know that trees act as a natural filter, cleaning the air of pollutants, especially contaminants such as nitrogen dioxide, which contributes to the formation of photochemical smog. It's been estimated that in Washington DC, trees remove nitrogen dioxide to an extent equivalent to taking 274,000 cars off the highways. The US Forest Service puts a $3.8 billion value on the air pollution annually removed by urban trees.[22]

But perhaps the true value of our relationship with trees is reflected better in a short poem by the American Bill Yake:

Inside Out

Trees are our lungs turned inside out
and inhale our visible chilled breath.

Our lungs are trees turned inside out
and inhale their clear exhalations.[23]

However, not all the Buddha's followers were successful in forming a new relationship with nature, especially trees. I have already referred to the *Karaṇīyamettā Sutta* (see above, pp.31 and 83), in which the Buddha extols the practice of loving-kindness. After the Buddha's death, a story was created that told of the circumstances surrounding the teaching of this discourse. Here are the key features of the story. At the start of the monsoon period, when monks in the Buddha's Sangha found a place to spend the rainy season, one group of monks discovered and settled in a lovely spot in woodland in the foothills of the Himalayas. But the monks did not attempt to engage with the tree spirits, who were upset at the disturbance to their surroundings caused by the arrival of the monks. The tree spirits succeeded in driving away the monks by inducing fear and dread in them. The monks left and sought advice from the Buddha, who taught them the *Karaṇīyamettā Sutta* and then told them to return to the woodland chanting it. This they did, and, the story tells us, they were well received and accepted by the tree spirits.[24]

In explanations of the story's message, emphasis is usually put on overcoming fear through the practice of *mettā*. But there is another way to read it. When they first arrived at the woodland, something was missing in the attitude of the monks. They did not take sufficient care of their surroundings; they thought only of themselves. They did not seek a relationship of respect with the trees. But when they returned with the Buddha's teaching of *mettā*, which helped them to overcome their fears, they also brought with them a different attitude, sensitivity to their environment. This is represented in the story by the recital of the *Karaṇīyamettā Sutta* within the hearing of the tree spirits. A new relationship was forged.

In modern times, we tend to dismiss the idea of nature spirits and of rituals that might be used to strengthen the connection between humans and their natural surroundings. But it has not always been so. The anthropologist Frederique Apffel-Marglin reminds us of this, and illustrates how even today there are native societies that maintain and benefit from ritual connections with nature. While reading her book *Subversive Spiritualities: How Rituals Enact the World*, an image of the Buddha sitting expressing gratitude to the bodhi tree expanded in my mind to include all of nature, animate and inanimate. Apffel-Marglin describes how it used to be:

> Before the triumph of modernity . . . people lived in constant interaction with a host of beings, powers and spirits who tricked us, protected us, quarreled with us, guided us, taught us, punished us, and conversed with us. We were wealthy in our human and other-than-human communities. There was an abundance of beings to accompany us in our earthly journey. The multifarious

beings of this world taught us to share the bounty
of this world with them; they taught us the gestures
of reciprocity; they taught us to fear greediness and
accumulation. They taught us that the wealth of the plant
beings, the tree beings, the water beings, the soil beings,
the mineral beings, was not only ours, was not there for
the sole purpose of satisfying our needs. They had their
own reason for existing, their own requirements, and their
own agency. We needed to ask permission, to share, to
give back, and to give thanks. These very gestures made
us aware that we were only one strand in an immense
tapestry that wove the pattern of life on this earth.[25]

But now, she argues, owing to the age of enlightenment and
the scientific revolution (and also to economic processes such
as the enclosure movement), a process of alienation has led to
the objectification of the 'other-than-human' as natural resources,
things for us to own and use and throw away in the pursuit of
economic and technological salvation. But some of the world's
population still live in places that, although not completely
isolated from our modern technological world, retain the
connection to the spirits and voices of the 'other-than-human'
world. One such place, described by Apffel-Marglin, is the High
Andes of Peru in South America. Don Santos Wilca is a farmer
and shaman living on the shores of Lake Titicaca in the Peruvian
Altiplano (High Plain). Speaking for his people, he says that 'all
those who live in this pacha (world) are persons: the stone, the
soil, the plants, the water, the hail, the wind, the diseases, the
sun, the moon, the stars, we are all one family. To live together
we help each other mutually; we are constantly in a continuous
conversation and in harmony.'[26]

Ritual is the method for communicating with the 'other-than-humans'. Through ritual they are given a voice, and they remind the humans that this world is not just there to satisfy their unlimited desires. In the rituals, the humans practice *ayni*, a form of ritualized gift exchange with the 'other-than-humans'. One such festival is Yarqa Aspiy,[27] a festival celebrating the spirit of water, which takes place at the start of spring and focuses on the irrigation channels that funnel water down the mountainsides. The whole community is involved with the festivities, putting flowers gathered from the high mountains in their hats, making offerings to the water, running up and down the irrigation channels, cleaning the channels, dancing, eating and drinking, and performing other ritual elements.

The attitudes underlying the ritual are those of communal solidarity and reciprocity with the 'other-than-human' collectivity. They are very different from the attitudes found among economic development specialists, as instanced in a story told by Apffel-Marglin.[28] Traditionally the irrigation channels in Quispillacta are earthen channels dug carefully and with love. But the economic development specialists once tried to replace the earthen channels with cement-lined channels. The result? The water in the cement-lined channels reached only half as far down the mountainsides as did the earthen channels. According to the villagers, the engineers who designed the channels did not know how to 'nurture the water'. They did not respect the water by asking permission of it and by making offerings to it. But the villagers did not tell this to the engineers because they thought it would have been a waste of time; they would not have taken it seriously. The villagers told the specialists instead that because of the drastic reduction in vegetation that can grow on the border of cement-lined channels, the water surface is far more exposed to the sun, causing a much greater degree of evaporation than in the shaded and unlined earthen channels. The two explanations are not incompatible. Indeed, it is owing to the different attitude and ritualized way of being of the villagers that vital knowledge is learned and retained. Apffel-Marglin puts it this way:

> Respecting and nurturing the water means that its ways of travelling are intimately known. At the place where the water is diverted to enter the irrigation channels, the stream is surrounded by lush vegetation; in fact, the whole stream is thus surrounded. These plants are the water's companions, its familiars. The water and the plants have an affinity for each other, and the ancient earthen channels are made lovingly, respectfully, so that the water will not feel abandoned by its companion plants and will travel happily. The villagers' actions are ever mindful of the respect due to the beings of the pacha. The earth, the water, the sun, the seeds, and all that is needed to provide the sustenance for life is respected.[29]

Reading this account of the relationship between the villagers and the 'other-than-human' world, I was reminded of a very different kind of relationship between humans and nature, one with tragic consequences. You may remember Hurricane Katrina, which hit New Orleans in 2005. It killed 1,600 people, destroyed tens of thousands of homes, and caused total damage estimated at $81 billion. You probably won't remember that three weeks later, another hurricane, Hurricane Rita, hit the American coast west of New Orleans. This time, seven people died and there was comparatively little damage. The difference in the loss of human life and the general damage is partly explained by mangrove forest, which grows along the shorelines. Where

Hurricane Rita landed, the mangrove forest was relatively intact, forming a natural barrier against the huge waves generated by the hurricane. But around New Orleans, mangrove forests had been destroyed and shipping channels had been cut through them, creating pathways along which the floodwaters raced and inflicted their damage. Nature was therefore less able to protect the human population.[30]

At this time of increasing pressure to secularize the world and downplay myth and ritual, a pressure from which Buddhism is not immune, there is much that all of us can learn from those native traditions around the world that retain a living, ritualized connection with nature and the 'other-than-human' world. Twenty years ago, before I became interested in Buddhism, and perhaps for some years afterwards, I would not have written such a sentence. Until my mid-forties, I was a rationalist, steeped in economics and statistics and a materialist approach to life. But now I am very impressed by the attitude of Peter Whitely, a teacher of anthropology and the curator of North American ethnology at the American Museum of Natural History. Whitely has spent a great deal of time with Native communities in the US and Canada observing their persistent attachment to age-old ritual practices, especially those connected with the land. As someone brought up to approach problems rationally, I believe his conclusion, drawn from actual experience, warrants careful consideration:

> As an anthropologist, I am a scientist, and profess the standard commitment to search for objective truth via observation and reason; I cheerfully accept established scientific laws. Yet this commitment has often been challenged by my experiences with Native communities

in the natural world, which I am unable to explain
by scientific reason. I have come to believe that such
experiences point towards a different, genuinely
sustainable relationship with nature. But taking account
of them means listening much more carefully to other
people's world views than we have done to date.[31]

There is, however, another, central aspect of Buddhism that is
more in tune with modern scientific thinking, particularly the
study of systems, and that has much relevance for the relationship
between humans, the environment, and nature. Dependent
origination, or conditionality, is one of the core teachings of the
Buddha. Its basic principle is expressed by these words: 'When this
exists, that comes to be; with the arising of this, that arises. When
this does not exist, that does not come to be: with the cessation
of this, that ceases.'[32] The teaching of dependent origination tells
us that everything in our experience arises in dependence upon
conditions. Nothing exists in a fixed, separate way; things exist
instead as part of an interconnected flow of changing processes.
Our globalized world, ourselves as human beings, other living
beings, our economies, nature and the environment coexist in
such a manner that changes in one place can quickly lead to
changes elsewhere. A recent example illustrates this great degree
of interconnectedness.

Early in 2008, oil prices increased threefold in a few months.
The increase in oil prices pushed up the cost of fertilizer and
transportation, adding to the cost of food production. As oil prices
were rising and producers were looking for alternative supplies,
farmers saw that they could now make more money from biofuels.
They shifted land use from wheat for food to biofuels for energy.
Poor harvests further reduced the supply of wheat, at the same

time as demand for wheat increased in India and China. All these factors, together with the activity of speculators, resulted in what some have described as the worst food price inflation in history. Between 2007 and 2008, the price of wheat on the world market more than doubled. The price of bread, pasta, and tortillas all went through the roof. The people most affected by the price inflation were those living in developing countries, where up to 75 per cent of income is spent on food. Food riots erupted in Mexico, Egypt, Pakistan, Cameroon, and other countries around the world. The World Bank warned that 100 million people were threatened with starvation.

But not everyone was badly affected. One trader working for Citigroup, the America-based multinational financial services company, correctly forecast the price fluctuations in the oil market, and for his efforts he was awarded a bonus of $100 million. An American government spokesperson characterized the bonus as 'out of whack', to which David Orrell added, 'The 100 million threatened with starvation might have agreed.'[33]

This is not the first time that we have faced a complex set of dangers from an increasingly interconnected world. A recent book by the archaeologist and George Washington University professor Eric H. Cline entitled *1177 B.C.: The Year Civilization Collapsed* tells how a closely interconnected set of advanced civilizations in the Near and Middle East collapsed and disappeared.[34] The scientist and blogger Adam Frank reports on his exchanges with Eric Cline about similarities between what happened 3,000 years ago and now. When Frank asked Cline about parallels between then and now, he responded:

> The world of the Late Bronze Age and ours today have more similarities than one might expect, particularly

in terms of relationships, both at the personal level and at the state level. Thus, they had marriages and divorces, embassies and embargoes, and so on. They also had problems with climate change and security at the international level. These are not necessarily unique to just them and us, but the combination of similar problems (climate change and drought, earthquakes, war, economic problems) at the very same time just might be unique to both.[35]

With a complex trade network in copper and tin (to make bronze) as well as in grain and manufactured goods, the Egyptians, Hittites, Canaanites, Cypriots, Minoans, Mycenaeans, Assyrians, and Babylonians built what could be seen as the first version of a 'global' culture. What brought them down begins with climate change, in this case the onset of cooling sea surface temperatures leading to drought, famine, and war. But although climate change may have been the catalyst for the destruction that came so quickly, the deepest reason for the collapse may have come from within the structure of the society itself, from the very complexity of its interdependent existence. Cline points out: the similarities of our world to that of the Late Bronze Age include, 'as the British archaeologist Susan Sherratt has put it, an "increasingly homogeneous yet uncontrollable global economy and culture" in which "political uncertainties on one side of the world can drastically affect the economies of regions thousands of miles away".'[36] In an email to Adam Frank, he concludes that 'We should be aware that no society is invulnerable and that every society in the history of the world has ultimately collapsed. We should also be thankful that we are advanced enough to understand what is happening.'[37] But, as Adam Frank asks, are we advanced enough to do anything with our understanding?

Before considering some proposals for what might actually be done to help reduce our preoccupation with growth and to construct a better relationship with nature and the environment, I would like to summarize the argument so far in this chapter. We are in the grip of a growth fetish that is causing serious damage to the environment and to nature, with little hope of help on the required fundamental changes from mainstream economics or business. Buddhism offers the basis of an alternative approach with a dual emphasis on eradicating pollution within and without by tackling the root poisons of greed, hatred, and delusion. The core principle in Buddhism of conditionality or dependent origination can help us to understand our problems in this interconnected world. But modern Buddhism can also learn from native societies and their ritual relationship with the 'other-than-human' world.

What, then, can Buddhists and non-Buddhists do? Here are some ideas.

1. Work together to help promote a closer relationship with nature.

Many Buddhist organizations already consciously work together, and there are two with which I am directly familiar. The first is Buddhafield in the UK.[38] It is part of the Triratna Buddhist Community, and its vision is of nature as the primary context for life and practice. Attracted by the beauty of the natural world, by ancient sacred sites and landscapes, and by the living experience of interconnectedness these give, the Buddhafield community aims to live simply and to live lightly on the land using appropriate technology and exemplifying best practice in all that they do. Buddhafield offers outdoors retreats and camps such as a four-week meditation retreat, a Green Earth Awakening camp, and a family-friendly retreat. The other Triratna organization promoting greater environmental awareness is the Eco Dharma Centre in the Catalan Pyrenees in Spain. It offers courses and retreats combining the Buddha's teachings with ecological consciousness.[39]

2. Simplify your life.

Buddhism puts much emphasis on simplifying life. As E.F. Schumacher points out in *Buddhist Economics*, modern western economists consider consumption to be the sole end and purpose of all economic activity, but the Buddhist view is that its aim should be to obtain the maximum of well-being with the minimum of consumption.[40] In the Triratna Buddhist Community, the third ethical precept, in its positive form, is 'With stillness, simplicity, and contentment, I purify my body.' The process of simplification can bring a greater degree of fulfilment.

This chimes well with the Australian professor Clive Hamilton's contention that to achieve a radically different political approach requires a shift in consciousness. But, he argues, this will not necessarily come about by confronting people with more desperate facts about environmental decline.[41] Hamilton proposes instead that we ask people to reflect on whether a life of chasing after more consumer goods actually makes them happy. He argues that many are open to a conversation about happiness and the role of materialism, citing in support evidence that nine out of ten Americans believe that their society is too materialistic and puts too much emphasis on shopping.

In practical terms, the phenomenon of 'downshifting', that is reducing income and consumption in order to realize a better, more sustainable work-life balance, is one way to achieve greater simplification and happiness. According to Hamilton, around one-fifth of adults in the US, Britain, and Australia, from a variety of ages and classes, have a positive experience of voluntarily changing their lives to earn less money and choosing greater fulfilment over more consumption.

I can personally attest to the increased satisfaction and greater sense of meaning in life that comes with downshifting. In the mid-1990s, I gave up a well-paid but stressful career and a house of my own to live in a Buddhist community of eighteen men on a drastically lower income. Community living also markedly reduces environmental pressures, certainly as compared to the trend now for people to live more often in single-person households. Recent trends in the UK, the US, Scandinavia, and Japan show that more and more people are now living on their own. In the UK, 34 per cent of households have one person living in them; in the US it's 27 per cent. Why might this be a problem? Because, according to a recent study, single-person households consume 38 per cent more produce, 42 per cent more packaging, and 55 per cent more electricity per person than four-person households.[42]

3. Become vegetarian or vegan.

Another way in which environmental pressures can be reduced is by encouraging a shift to a vegetarian or vegan diet. Like many Buddhist groups, the Triratna Buddhist Community in which I am involved encourages people to become vegetarians. We do this out of empathy for other living beings. The Buddha's first ethical precept asks us to avoid killing or harming other living beings and instead to act towards them with loving-kindness. Some of our community go further and urge us to take on a vegan diet in view of the immense suffering caused to animals not only in meat production but also in the dairy and egg industries, where many animals spend their whole lives packed together in sheds in terrible conditions.

To be a vegetarian or a vegan, to act out of kindness and empathy for other living beings is to enlarge our 'compassion footprint'. But there is another argument in favour of veganism. As the United Nations reported in 2010, a global shift towards a vegan diet is vital if we are to save the world from hunger and from the impact of climate change.[43] As the world population heads towards an estimated 9 billion in 2050, the United Nations says that the western preference for a diet rich in meat and dairy products is simply unsustainable. It is already the case that the world's cattle consume enough food to sustain 9 billion people, because of the enormous amount of grain and other agricultural products fed to them in order to produce meat. A staggering 97 per cent of the world's soya beans are fed to animals. It takes 20 pounds of grain to make one pound of beef, 7.3 pounds of grain to produce one pound of pork, and 4.5 pounds of grain to make one pound of chicken meat.[44] Furthermore, meat and dairy production add significantly to greenhouse gas effects. According to a research report from Lancaster University, if everyone in the United Kingdom were to swap their current eating habits for a vegetarian or vegan diet, the greenhouse gas emissions savings would be equivalent to a 50 per cent reduction in exhaust pipe emissions from the entire UK passenger car fleet.[45] The same report points out that fresh meat has the highest greenhouse gas emissions of all food products.

Earlier I used the term 'compassion footprint'. The term *'carbon footprint'* is shorthand for describing the best estimate that we can get of the full climate change impact of something. For example, at the supermarket checkout in the UK, fresh meat has a carbon footprint of 17 kilograms of carbon dioxide equivalent per kilogram of meat. Cheese has a carbon footprint of 15 kilograms per kilogram of cheese. It's true that exotic vegetables have a carbon footprint of 9 kilograms, largely because of transportation by air and because of glasshouse heating costs, but fruit and vegetables grown without artificial heating and/or shipped to the UK by sea have low emissions. Potatoes, apples, milk, bread, and cereals have a carbon footprint of under 2 kilograms per kilogram of produce. Fresh meat has a carbon footprint eight times higher than potatoes, apples, bread, and cereals.[46] It is difficult not to agree with one commentator who writes, 'With hundreds of millions of hungry people worldwide, it is criminally wasteful to feed perfectly edible food to farmed animals in order to produce meat, rather than feeding it directly to people.'[47]

4. Act collectively.

In 2011, the Quaker movement in Britain made a commitment to become a low carbon sustainable community. Partly inspired by the Quaker example, the UK-based Network of Buddhist Organisations launched the Buddhist Action Month in June 2014 around the theme of care of the environment. Among the suggested activities were switching the local Buddhist centre to green electricity, making the Buddhist centre or retreat centre a Fair Trade centre and vegan (and not just vegetarian), making individual pledges not to fly for a specified period of time, and getting involved in Transition Towns. The Transition movement seeks to create local community networks for addressing climate change; its key words are 'resilience' and 'reskilling'. For it, local communities are more effective because they are intermediate in size between individuals (too small on their own to be effective) and government (too remote to influence).

5. Campaign to change the behaviour of industry and government.

But are the above actions enough? Annie Leonard, who created the animated film *Stuff* and who in 2014 became Executive Director of Greenpeace, USA, offers a cautionary story.[48] She tells how in 1971, in one of the most iconic advertisements of the twentieth century, a Native American is seen canoeing through a river full of trash. He leaves his canoe; and as he walks beside the river, a passenger in a passing car throws a bag of litter out of the window. A tear rolls down his cheek and the narrator says, 'People start pollution. People can stop it.' The advertisement had a tremendous impact on people's individual actions, just as its makers hoped. But its makers were the companies that produced much of what becomes rubbish when used up. Since the early 1950s, the Keep America Beautiful campaign has worked hard to ensure that rubbish was seen to be a problem only of individual responsibility and not the responsibility of the companies producing the disposable bottles, cans, and plastic bags that might otherwise be subjected to greater and stricter regulation.

Leonard emphasizes that individual actions do matter and that bringing our everyday small deeds into alignment with our values is essential, thereby creating moments of 'mindful living'. These small actions, she contends, are a good start but they are a terrible place to stop. The simple fact is obscured that rubbish from households accounts for less than three per cent of the total waste produced in the US. The bulk of waste comes from industries and businesses. By shifting the focus solely on to individual actions, they present environmental damage as the result of an epidemic of bad individual choices rather than as the responsibility mainly of an overarching economic, regulatory, and physical infrastructure that encourages environmentally damaging activities over beneficial ones.

She argues that calls for changes in individual behaviour need to be seen as first steps and tactical elements within much broader political campaigns. These campaigns need to engage people as citizens working together using a variety of methods, including protesting, lobbying, legal action, economic sanctions, creating alternatives, and peaceful civil disobedience.

6

The waste economy

Chindogu is a term used by the twentieth-century management guru Charles Handy.[1] It comes from a Japanese word meaning clutter and excess. Examples of *chindogu* include washing machines with 30 programmes when you might only ever use three or four and (Handy's favourite) spectacles with windscreen wipers. But it also includes the shoes or ties or other items of clothing bought but never used and books bought on impulse from Amazon that are never read. *Chindogu* products are especially prevalent at Christmastime: for example, a Darth Vader talking piggy bank, an individual beer can chiller, or bacon-flavoured toothpaste – all products that after a few days are thrown away. George Monbiot, an environmentalist and a columnist for the *Guardian* newspaper, calls them examples of pathological consumption: the unfortunate using up of rare materials, complex electronics, and much-needed sources of energy and transport. As he puts it, 'We are screwing the planet to make solar-powered bath thermometers and desktop crazy golfers.'[2]

Why are we creating so much waste? I discussed capitalism's growth fetish in Chapter 5. And as noted in earlier chapters, Handy writes, 'Economic growth depends, ultimately, on more and more people, wanting more and more, of more and more things'[3] while E.J. Mishan warns that 'the precondition of sustained growth is sustained discontent.'[4] But what happens if consumers move beyond their needs and can't be persuaded to want more than they have? How can discontent be rekindled? Handy comments that this was the problem faced in Japan in the 1990s, when the Japanese government even considered giving people vouchers to tempt them into the shops.[5]

To promote discontent requires new products and product upgrades to titillate consumer appetites and keep demand buoyant. Boosting the desire to have what we see others having, or to have what they don't have, through advertising and creating new fashions Handy recognizes to be an important stimulus to demand, as is envy. I remember Tim Jackson's words: 'It's a story about us, people, being persuaded to spend money we don't have, on things we don't need, to create impressions that don't last, on people that we don't care about.'[6] In other words, *chindogu* is one of capitalism's ways of stoking discontent and promoting economic growth. Considering all this, Handy writes:

> I was enough of an economist to recognize that chindogu has its uses in providing employment and more money for people to spend, but a part of me worried about the waste involved in all those unnecessary things, the waste of people's time as much as the waste of materials. It can't be much fun standing in those shopping malls all day and increasingly all night promoting chindogu, even if it is upmarket stuff, nor can it be satisfying to be one of those who produce it, in a factory or, nowadays, to be sitting in a call centre backing up yet another unneeded website. Not the best use of a life, I reflected, even if it does provide the bread to sustain that life.[7]

As well as *chindogu*, there are other ways in which our modern economy promotes waste in the pursuit of economic growth, and I shall look at some of them later in this chapter. But before that, I shall discuss the attitude to waste found in accounts from the life of the Buddha and his followers, using three examples.

First, in the Vinaya, the compendium of regulations governing the life of the Buddha's monks and nuns, there's a story about a king who is wondering whether to make a gift of cloth for robes to the Buddha's monastic followers, wondering whether the gift will be appropriately used. He investigates and discovers that once their robes become worn, monks use the cloth as mattress coverings or foot wipers and that the shreds left over after these uses are mixed with mud and used to build huts. This convinces the king that the monks and nuns do indeed make proper use of a gift of cloth. Nothing is wasted in the Buddha's Sangha.[8]

Second, in relation to his lay followers, the Buddha identified four worthy ways in which wealth might be spent: properly maintaining oneself, family, workers, friends, and colleagues in happiness; making provision against potential losses; making offerings to relatives, guests, ancestors, the king, and the gods; and giving alms to ascetics and other praiseworthy spiritual figures. The Buddha concluded: 'For anyone whose wealth is expended on other things apart from these four worthy deeds, that wealth is said to have gone to waste, to have been squandered and used frivolously. But for anyone whose wealth is expended on these four worthy deeds, that wealth is said to have gone to good use, to have been fruitfully employed and used for a worthy cause.'[9]

Third, as regards food, the Buddha laid down very specific guidelines to be followed by monks and nuns.[10] They were allowed to eat only what they had been given. They were not allowed to provide themselves with food. They were able to obtain food by collecting it from house to house or they could be invited to a meal by their lay followers. To collect food, monks would stand in silence with their bowl at a householder's front door. They had to accept whatever they were given regardless of its quality. If they were not given anything, the Buddha advised them not to feel displeasure or frustration. The monks and nuns were not allowed to prompt their benefactors; and unless they were ill, they were not allowed to express any requests or to make known their favourite kinds of food. In the stories of the Buddha's life, there are many instances of discussions and debates between the Buddha and lay followers ending with a request: 'Blessed One, may you accept to come and eat in my house with your disciples tomorrow.' Generally monks were not to store or to cook food themselves, although limited exceptions of particular kinds of food were made for sick monks. When during famine lay followers brought food to the more settled abodes of monks and nuns, the Buddha allowed food to be stored and cooked by monks. And when monks were to set out across a desert or through a large forest where food would not be available for some time, they were allowed to bring along a lay attendant to carry provisions for the journey.

Monks and nuns were allowed to eat only between dawn and noon. The reasons for this rule were explained by the Buddha: 'Monks, I do not eat in the evening. Because I avoid eating in the evening, I am in good health, light, energetic and live comfortably. You too, monks, avoid eating in the evening, and you will have good health.'[11] The rule on eating only between dawn and noon was also intended so that monks would not waste time that could be spent concentrating on their religious practice. It was also to prevent monks standing alone outside a house at night and possibly frightening householders.

Although the Buddha was always concerned that his disciples had enough nourishing food to keep them in good physical health, he was very critical of overeating or gluttony. Gluttony, like any other kind of desire, was an obstacle to inner progress. The Buddha said: '. . . as soon as a monk is able to control his senses, the Tathāgata [Buddha] leads him further still: now, monk, be moderate in your eating. Concentrate and be attentive when you eat: do not eat for pleasure or enjoyment, nor in order to be handsome and attractive; eat only for the benefit of the religious life.'[12] Because overeating causes heavy sleep, it was seen as an obstacle on the spiritual path of renunciation: it prevented the practice of meditation and mindfulness. Monks and nuns, who had entered the path of renunciation, had to restrict their eating in order to practise contemplation, to meditate for long periods of time without feeling sleepy, and to stay in good physical health.

To summarize, although applied in different ways to his lay followers and to his monks and nuns, the Buddha's advice was essentially to lead a life of stillness, simplicity, and contentment. Wealth was not to be used frivolously and food was to be consumed in moderation. Waste was to be avoided. However, modern society is deliberately structured to promote waste and to induce overeating. It faces an individual with many obstacles to a life of simplicity, stillness, and contentment.

For example, just how difficult has it become to get something repaired? The author Shannon Hayes tells the story of how her family tried to get its favourite stereo system repaired.[13] First, they contacted the manufacturer, to be told that 'Those systems can't be repaired any longer.' Then they approached Mr Kleinburger, who for many years had run a local electronics store. He didn't hold out much hope, explaining, 'Factories don't authorize repair people anymore. It used to be that we'd get trained by the manufacturers to repair and maintain their equipment. Nobody does that anymore. They wanna sell you the new thing.' Although he was pretty sure that the repair would cost just a few dollars, he could not find a way to open up the casing without breaking it. The people he contacted at the company refused to tell him how to do that because they were under strict orders not to release the information. But finally the persistent Mr Kleinburger did find someone at the company who shared his passion for the way things are made and told him how to open the casing. The repair was easily done and the stereo again worked perfectly. Mr Kleinburger's final words were 'That's your stereo. It's a beautiful piece of machinery, that thing is. Every single part is a standard American part, made here and easily replaced.'

But present-day manufacturers don't want it to be that way. Perhaps we could learn from the sixteenth-century Japanese tea master Sen no Rikyū. On one occasion, Sen no Rikyū steadfastly ignored a Song dynasty Chinese tea jar of which his host was inordinately proud, until the owner smashed it in despair at his indifference. After it had been painstakingly put together by the owner's friends, Rikyū declared, 'Now, the piece is magnificent.' When ceramics were broken in old Japan, it was an opportunity to make a new one from the pieces, and often a repaired bowl or container would be valued more highly than the original. The writer Philip Ball comments, 'The mended object is special precisely because it was worth mending. The repair, like that of an old teddy bear, is a testament to the affection in which the object is held.'[14]

A similar approach applied to the *boro* clothes of the Japanese peasant and artisan classes: they were stitched together from scraps of cloth. In the spirit of the Buddha, nothing went to waste. Both *boro* and the mending of ceramics had a strong aesthetic side that drew upon the Japanese tradition of *wabi-sabi*, a view of the world that emphasizes transience and imperfection. Unfortunately, we live in a society dominated by a consumerism that is prejudiced, even organized, against repair. It wasn't always this way. In Britain, mending clothes was a routine part of life for all classes, including the aristocracy. Mending in countries such as Britain and the US used to be a skilled manual trade, of which Mr Kleinburger is a reminder. But now, just as Shannon Hayes' stereo unit was sealed, more and more electronic items are sealed against repair; and if you start to tinker with them, you lose any guarantee. And, Ball comments, 'Add that to a climate in which you pay for the service or accessories rather than for the item – inks are pricier than printers, mobile phones are free when you subscribe to a network – and repair lacks feasibility, infrastructure or economic motivation.'[15]

Jacques Peretti, in the first episode of his 2014 BBC television series *The Men Who Made Us Spend*,[16] reveals how the idea of planned obsolescence goes back to the 1920s. A cartel of light bulb manufacturers agreed then to deliberately and artificially limit the lifespan of a light bulb to 1,000 hours when it could easily be manufactured to last for 2,500 hours. The result was a doubling of sales of light bulbs. This was the start of the cycle of endless spending and throwing away. As Peretti demonstrates in the programme, now we have printer cartridges made so that customers can't take a look inside them and see a counter there that tells them that it is finished and stops the cartridge working after a certain number of pages have been printed. In fact, Peretti says, the counter can be reset and used three times over. Or perhaps you have had the same experience as I have when your printer tells you that the ink cartridge has run out and needs to be replaced, only to discover that if you persist and continue to use it, many more pages can be printed before it actually does finish.

Apple and other manufacturers deliberately make electronic devices such as iPods or phones with batteries that run out after a fixed time. Sometimes they design their products in a way that makes it very difficult to replace the battery, even to the extent of creating an entirely new screw that needs an entirely new screwdriver to get into a phone! The choice for the customer is either to pay an exorbitant sum of money to the manufacturer to install a new battery or, better still (from the company's point of view), simply to buy a newer model.

Peretti also demonstrates other elements in promoting the cycle of endless spending and throwing way. In the 1950s, Alfred P. Sloan, the head of General Motors Corporation, initiated a psychological reprogramming of the consumer, creating the desire to buy a new car every year by continually modifying the style of new models. Alongside planned obsolescence being 'done to an object', planned obsolescence would now be 'done in the head'. General Motors called it 'the organized creation of dissatisfaction', a phrase echoed in the 1960s by E.J. Mishan's observation that economic growth requires 'sustained discontent'. When consumer demand abated in the 1970s, the response in the 1980s was to massively expand credit so as to make it easier to shop and aspire to a richer lifestyle. With the introduction of computer-aided design, it became much easier to make products with myriad design features and rapid turnover. For example, instead of watches being for life, they were now manufactured to be bought several times a year according to seasonal fashions. IKEA introduced the idea of household furniture as throw-away items just like other consumer products, and their advertisements mocked people for their attachment to old furniture and furnishings. Football supporters and their children need to buy expensive new shirts every year in the summer as football clubs change their club strips.

Another area of deliberately induced waste is the production and consumption of food, as two recent reports reveal. In 2012, the largest-ever study of the state of the world's health revealed that for the first time, the number of years of healthy living lost as a result of people eating too much surpassed the number lost by people having too little to eat. Dr Majid Ezzati, Chair in Global Environmental Health at Imperial College London and one of the lead authors of the report, said, 'We have gone from a world 20 years ago where people weren't getting enough to eat to a world now where too much food and unhealthy food – even in developing countries – is making us sick.'[17]

This not to say that problems of malnutrition have disappeared – far from it. Although great gains have been made in the past twenty years, not having enough to eat is still the eighth most important cause of disease.[18] But according to a second report issued in 2013, while people are still starving, as much as half of all the food produced in the world ends up as waste every year. The report, produced by the UK's Institution of Mechanical Engineers (IME), blames this appalling fact on a variety of factors, including unnecessarily strict sell-by dates, buy-one-get-one free sales campaigns, consumers conditioned to demand cosmetically perfect food, and also poor engineering and agricultural practices, inadequate infrastructure, and inefficient storage facilities.[19] In the UK, for example, as much as 30 per cent of vegetable crops are not harvested because they do not meet retailers' standards of physical appearance. And in Europe and the United States, up to half the food that is bought by consumers is thrown away. Tim Fox, the head of energy and the environment at the IME, says, 'The amount of food wasted and lost around the world is staggering. This is food that could be used to feed the world's growing population – as well as those in hunger today. It is also an unnecessary waste of the land, water and energy resources that were used in the production, processing and distribution of this food.'[20] Such is the cost of our throw-away culture. But perhaps the problem of obesity tells us the most about the consequences of promoting discontent and fuelling demand and growth.

One April evening in 1999, a meeting was held in Minneapolis in the US. Assembled there were the men who controlled America's largest food and drinks companies, among them Nestlé, Kraft, Nabisco, General Mills, Proctor and Gamble, Coca-Cola, Mars, and Pillsbury (taken over two years later by General Mills). The *New York Times* reporter Michael Moss tells the story of the meeting.[21] There was one item on the agenda, the growing worry about the obesity epidemic. The men gathered at the meeting were business rivals, used to fighting each other for what they called 'stomach share': the amount of digestive space that any one company's brand can grab from the competition. Some present were uneasy about childhood obesity and were aware of the parallels that could be drawn between the negative health effects of cigarettes and the damage done by certain kinds of food. Would this meeting of the most powerful men in American food manufacturing come to an agreement to help tackle obesity?

Any thoughts of that were scotched, according to Moss, when Stephen Sanger, then the head of General Mills, said, 'Don't talk to me about nutrition, talk to me about taste, and if this stuff tastes better, don't run around trying to sell stuff that doesn't taste good.' Sanger went on to say that consumers were fickle, sometimes worrying about sugar, sometimes about fat. He argued that because General Mills offered consumers a choice of products, including those designed to satisfy dieters and others with low sugar and added whole grains, he was not prepared to change anything. It was up to the consumer to decide. This was his argument despite knowing that sugary, salty, fatty foods cause obesity, type 2 diabetes, and high blood pressure. What mattered for Sanger was the drive for greater market share and profits for shareholders.

Moss discovered in his investigation that the food companies are pouring huge sums of money into research and development of new product lines designed to get people hooked on foods that are cheap and convenient. The aim is to find the 'bliss point', the design for a product that creates the greatest amount of craving. According to the food scientist Steve Witherly, one of the most successful food products in terms of creating craving is Cheetos potato chips. Witherly sees Cheetos as one of the most marvellously constructed foods on the planet in terms of pure pleasure. Cheetos has many attributes that make the consumer want more, but the one he admires most is the puff's uncanny ability to melt in the mouth. 'It's called vanishing caloric density,' he says. 'If something melts down quickly, your brain thinks that there's no calories in it . . . you can just keep eating it forever.'[22]

Moss tells us too how some of the largest companies are now using brain scans to study how we react neurologically to certain foods, especially sugar. Apparently companies have discovered that the brain lights up for sugar in the same way it does for cocaine. This knowledge is useful in formulating the right food ingredients, and it's also useful in promoting food products. For example, the world's largest ice cream maker, Unilever, used its brain research in a marketing campaign that promotes eating ice cream as a 'scientifically proven' way to make us happy.[23]

Despite this, many authorities still publicly endorse the view that the primary cause of the obesity epidemic is a lack of individual willpower. In the same way as the manufacturers of throw-away containers and other sources of rubbish seek to push responsibility on to the individual and away from themselves, food companies seek to push responsibility for obesity on to individual consumer choices.

It isn't too extreme to draw a comparison between this attitude and the attitude of the British in the opium wars of the nineteenth century. The import of opium was forced on the Chinese people against the wishes of their government, and the British argued that the sale of opium was not immoral because the Chinese people were only too willing to receive it. Moreover, just as one food company might argue that if it didn't provide unhealthy food for its customers, then others would, so the British argued that if they did not provide the opium, then other countries' merchants would.[24] To help us to deal with our own lack of willpower, a new industry, and a new source of profit, has appeared. Weight-loss food and drinks, medicines, services, surgeries, and new technologies, all designed to help us lose weight, are now big business. Apparently a Hong Kong company named Hapilabs offers an electronic fork that tracks how many bites you take per minute in order to prevent hasty eating: shovel food in too fast and it vibrates to alert you[25] – a modern-day reminder to eat mindfully? A May 2012 report by the consulting firm McKinsey & Co. predicted that 'health and wellness' would soon become a trillion-dollar global industry. Commenting that obesity is expensive in terms of healthcare costs, the report added, encouragingly, that 'dealing with it is also a big, fat market'.[26]

But many specialists do not believe that personal gluttony and laziness are the entire explanation for the obesity epidemic.

Richard L Atkinson, Emeritus Professor of Medicine and Nutritional Sciences at the University of Wisconsin and editor of the *International Journal of Obesity*, put it this way in 2005: 'The previous belief of many lay people and health professionals that obesity is simply the result of a lack of willpower and an inability to discipline eating habits is no longer defensible.'[27] We have already seen the deliberate attempt by food companies to encourage more consumption of food products. But additional research indicates that the problems caused by the food industry go deeper still.

The usual belief is that particular categories of people become fat because they simply consume more calories than others do. So one version of why poorer people become fat might go like this. Because being poor is stressful, stress makes you eat more, and the cheapest foodstuff available is the stuff with lots of 'empty' calories such as Cheeto chips, poorer people are more likely to become obese than the better-off. They simply consume more calories. However, a number of researchers have come to believe that all calories are not equal. As the science writer David Berreby points out, 'The problem with diets that are heavy in meat, fat or sugar is not solely that they pack a lot of calories into food; it is that they alter the biochemistry of fat storage and fat expenditure, tilting the body's system in favour of fat storage.'[28]

Sugar, trans-fats, and alcohol have all been linked to changes in 'insulin signalling', which affects how the body processes carbohydrates. This might sound like a merely technical distinction but it's a fundamental shift of understanding. If the problem is not the number of calories but the biochemical influences on the body's fat-making and fat-storage processes, then the sheer quantity of food or drink is not the all-controlling determinant of weight gain. Berreby observes, 'If candy's chemistry tilts you toward fat, then the fact that you eat it at all may be as important as the amount of it you consume.'[29] Worse still, things that can alter the body's fat-making and fat-storage processes, that can alter the body's fat metabolism potentially include much wider categories than just food. Sleeplessness (maybe associated with shift work), stress, industrial chemicals, electric light, heating, and air conditioning are all potential factors that can alter the activities of body cells, change the body's fat metabolism, and contribute to the obesity epidemic.

Moreover, there is some evidence that such changes may persist over longer timescales, even from one generation to the next. Berreby explains it this way. A developing foetus is very sensitive to the environment into which it will be born, and a crucial source of information about that environment is the nutrition it gets via the umbilical cord. Where mothers have gone hungry during pregnancy, their child is at much greater risk of obesity. Life in the womb attunes the baby's metabolism for a life outside the womb of scarcity, preparing the child's body to store fat whenever it can in order to get them through periods with little food. If, however, the bouts of scarcity don't materialize, the child's tendency to fat storage ceases to be an advantage and can become a problem. This is why the 40,000 babies gestated during Holland's 'Hunger Winter' of 1944–5 grew up to be more obese, to be more prone to diabetes and heart trouble than their fellow citizens who developed at a different time.[30]

Using a similar line of thought, Jonathan Wells, Professor of Child Nutrition at University College London, even proposes that the root cause of the modern epidemic of obesity in developing nations can be linked to the history of capitalism.[31] He asks us to imagine a poor farmer growing food crops in a poor country in Africa or Asia several hundred years ago. When Europeans take control of the economy in the late eighteenth or early nineteenth century, their new system pushes the farmer and his neighbours to stop growing their own food and instead to start cultivating a more marketable export commodity, such as coffee. As they are no longer growing their own food, the farmers must buy it. But the Europeans are aiming to maximize profit. Thus they pay as little as possible for the coffee crop, and so the farmers go hungry. Later, when the farmer's children go to work in factories, they also are paid as little as possible for their work and go hungry.

Eighty years on, some of the farmer's descendants rise out of the ranks of the poor and join the world's twenty-first-century middle class consumers. These descendants are now primed to live what Wells calls the 'obesogenic' life, a life full of factors such as stress and lifts instead of stairs in which they buy the kinds of food and beverages that are 'metabolic disturbers'. And because the human body's response to its nutrition can last a lifetime and even be passed on to the next generation, the descendants are more likely to become obese in a food-rich environment because their parents were undernourished. And if they do become obese, they pass on changes in metabolism that predispose their children to obesity too. Just as with the children of underfed people, the children of the overfed have their metabolism set in ways that tend to promote obesity.

Wells concludes that a past of *under*nutrition, combined with a present of *over*nutrition, is an obesity trap. He calls this double bind the 'metabolic ghetto', whose causes come from a history of profit-led manipulations of the global supply and quality of food. He concludes that the obesity trap is inextricably linked to the 'unifying logic of capitalism'. Capitalism requires that food companies seek immediate profits and long-term success, and its best strategy for that involves persuading people to choose foods that are the most profitable. This the companies do, both at the behavioural level through advertising, price manipulation, and restriction of choice and at the physiological level through the enhancement of the addictive properties of foods. Obesity is the result.

What can Buddhists do in response to the waste inherent in our modern economic system? Whether we live alone, in a family, or in a residential community such as a Buddhist centre, the obvious starting step is to review and improve ways for minimizing and recycling waste of all kinds. Following a life of simplicity without waste is important.

Another step involves becoming more knowledgeable about (and to help promote awareness within the Buddhist community of) local or national initiatives designed to encourage the repair and reuse of consumer products and to safely dispose of waste. One such initiative at the national level in the US is the Electronics TakeBack Coalition. This brings together a coalition of many diverse organizations, including the Communication Workers of America, Friends of the Earth, and Physicians for Social Responsibility and it aims to promote green design and responsible recycling in the electronics industry.[32] iFixit is a global community of people helping each other to repair things. Their slogan is 'Let's fix the world, one device at a time.' They point out that repairing can create local jobs, helping to shelter localities from the vicissitudes of globalization.[33]

Another local project, designed to reduce food waste is Original Unverpackt in Berlin.[34] Original Unverpackt, born as a social business with partners coming from backgrounds in Fairtrade, vegan supermarkets, and economics, will be the first supermarket in Germany without any disposable packaging. It sources its food mostly from local suppliers and simply offers everything in bulk, allowing customers to take as little or as much of the produce in any container they like.

A further, old-fashioned but nonetheless significant possibility is to open a second-hand clothes shop, like Lama's Pyjamas at the London Buddhist Centre.[35]

But as I concluded at the end of the previous chapter, securing fundamental change on issues such as the environment and waste requires going beyond the steps I have just described. The initiatives above are a platform to build on by connecting with much broader political campaigns that aim to change the behaviour of food companies and other manufacturers. With their emphasis on clarity of awareness and on simplicity and contentment as fundamental values, Buddhists have much to offer such campaigns.

7

The attention economy

In 1993, the Buddhist teacher Sangharakshita gave fifteen points of advice to members of the Western Buddhist Order.[1] The first one was to 'reduce input'. He commented, 'I do not know anything about computers, so this point is not intended to have anything to do with them.' Like many others, Sangharakshita was not aware of what was about to happen in the wider world, particularly apropos of information technology (IT) and its impact on all forms of communication media. He focused instead on disturbance from a variety of sources, including television, radio, and newspapers. He warned that we do not understand the great detrimental effect that they can have upon our mind.

1993 was a different world. The IT revolution was just starting. Mobile phones were a recent phenomenon and email and the worldwide Web were still in their infancy. There were no smart phones, netbooks, ipads, tablets, e-books, Facebook, or Twitter. The first text message (SMS) was sent from one mobile phone to another in Finland in 1993. In his talk Sangharakshita warned, with greater prescience than he realized, that 'We are a sort of receiving station all the time, but we do not have to allow these different factors and influences to play on us constantly without any sort of control or restriction.'

Others had different ideas. Later in the 1990s, Dr Eric Schmidt, who became Chief Executive Officer of Google, forecast that the twenty-first century would be synonymous with what he called the 'attention economy' and that the most successful global companies would be those that maximized the number of 'eyeballs' they could consistently connect with and control.[2] Companies such as Google and Facebook are now part of a generalized effort to mine individuals for information that can be used to predict, and even modify, their behaviour and thereby better target the selling of consumer products. With smart phones, ipads, and other tablet computers, there is now virtually no part of everyday life that is beyond the reach of the attention economy. As we shall see, even the world of sleep is under threat as the last bastion of resistance to the twenty-four hour, seven-days-a-week economy.

But to begin this discussion about time and attention, I shall consider what we might learn from the world of the Buddha 2,500 years ago. The daily life of the Buddha and his followers was much simpler than ours. The Buddha himself followed a daily routine in which he rose early, meditated, and then walked into the nearest village or town to receive food. After returning from his alms round and eating, he meditated again. In the hot season, he took an afternoon nap and received lay visitors and gave teachings in the evening. Then he received visits from monks. He would spend time pacing mindfully up and down practising walking meditation, and he would spend much of the night in the open air meditating with the monks before sleeping. Both the Buddha and his monks and nuns would walk mindfully from place to place giving teachings, collecting their daily food, and often meditating at the foot of a tree.

The Buddha and his community of disciples had no books or writings to help them with their practice. The Buddha's teachings were all verbal. His followers were called sāvakas, which means listeners. Listening was the only method of learning from others, and was the first level of a monk's path to wisdom. This path had three levels: listening, reflecting, and contemplating or meditating. Having listened to the Buddha or one of his senior disciples, the monk would memorize the teaching and then reflect upon it and examine its meaning.

Ratnaguna, in his book *The Art of Reflection*, describes the process of reflection as it might apply to a modern Buddhist:

> You see implications that you may not have noticed on first hearing. You may also encounter problems, things that you don't fully understand or that seem to contradict other teachings, and you have to work out the solutions for yourself. Or you may question something – 'Is this really true?' Or you may think about how the teaching might apply to you, and in this way you 'translate' what may be a general and theoretical teaching into something more specific and practical. As a result of reflecting in this way you come to a deeper understanding of the teachings than you did when you first heard them, and this deeper understanding the Buddha called a 'reflective acceptance'. You now accept the teachings, not out of faith – not because they have come from the Buddha and therefore they *must* be true or because you think that you *should* believe them – but because after careful examination you can see that they make sense.[3]

With reflection, you become intellectually convinced. But this does not equate to having direct insight. The third level, wisdom through contemplation, involves meditating on a teaching. It's different from reflecting because when you contemplate, you don't think about a teaching; you simply hold it in your mind and allow it to penetrate into the whole of your being. It's a deep and direct experience, unmediated by concepts, of the way things are. This is the experience of insight or vipassanā. In this way, the Buddha's followers made time for listening, reflecting, and contemplating upon a teaching.

But in order to singlemindedly focus on a teaching, the Buddha's followers needed to be able to resist the temptation for the mind to wander off to other things. Even in the Buddha's day, there were many opportunities for distraction. The Buddha himself reflected upon this problem in a teaching known as the *Dvedhāvitakka Sutta*, the teaching on two kinds of thought.[4]

The Buddha recalls in it the time in his life before he became Enlightened. He tells of how he became aware of how the mind could be turned in different directions. The Buddha-to-be decided to examine his own mind, and divided his thoughts into two broad classes: first, craving (desire), ill will (hatred), and cruelty and, second, renunciation (commitment and inspiration), non-hatred (loving-kindness), and non-cruelty (compassion). When a thought of desire arose in his mind, he applied his awareness, his mindfulness to consider the consequences of such thoughts. When he did this, he saw that thoughts of desire led to his affliction and to the affliction of others, causing difficulties and blocking the path to wisdom. Considering this and applying his mindfulness to the situation led to thoughts of desire subsiding and fading away. He applied the same method to thoughts of ill will and cruelty, removing them from his mind. The conclusion that the Buddha-to-be came to was that whatever a person frequently thinks about and ponders upon will become the inclination of their mind. The more a mind dwells upon something, the tendency for the mind to move in that direction is strengthened and the more the mind becomes bent in that mode of being.

W.H. Auden, a twentieth-century poet and writer, summed it up this way: 'Choice of attention – to pay attention to this and ignore that – is to the inner life what choice of action is to the outer. In both cases man is responsible for his choices and must accept the consequences. As Ortega y Gasset said: "Tell me to what you pay attention, and I will tell you who you are."'[5]

Andrew Olendzki, a Pali canon expert, reminds us the Buddha also warned that 'I know of no single thing more conducive to great harm than an unrestrained mind.'[6] A mind whose energy is dispersed in several directions loses its strength and purpose. An image in the Pali canon compares the flow of consciousness to a mountain stream flowing swiftly downhill. If there are several outlets through which the water is dispersed, it will be little more than a trickle when it reaches the plain. Auden, again, echoes this:

Or else we make a scarecrow of the day,
Loose ends and jumble of our common world.[7]

What can we learn from the Buddha? It is that we need to take seriously the importance of careful listening, which in the modern world extends to reading. This means also making time for reflection and contemplation, being careful and mindful about what we pay attention to, and focusing our mind and not allowing it to be distracted and dispersed. We can also bear in mind Sangharakshita's simple but important advice: reduce input.

However, this does not fit easily with the modern information-saturated world in which the average person now checks their mobile phone almost 150 times per day.[8] And it's important to remember the purpose of advertising. Leo Burnett, an advertising pioneer named by *Time* magazine as one of the one hundred most influential people of the twentieth century, put it this way: 'Good advertising does not just circulate information. It penetrates the public mind with desire and belief.'[9]

With the advent of the Internet, advertising is now infiltrating much more effectively every corner of our consciousness than it ever did in Burnett's lifetime (he died in 1971). Moreover, it is in the interest of the commercial Internet to have us shifting our minds rapidly from one thing to another, to absorb, however briefly, more and more input. Nicholas Carr, a writer and former executive editor of the *Harvard Business Review*, comments:

> The idea that our minds should operate as high-speed data-processing machines is not only built into the workings of the Internet, it is the network's reigning business model as well. The faster we surf across the Web – the more links we click and pages we view – the more opportunities Google and other companies gain to collect information about us and to feed us advertisements. Most of the proprietors of the commercial internet have a financial stake in collecting the crumbs of data we leave behind as we flit from link to link – the more crumbs, the better. *The last thing these companies want is to encourage leisurely reading or slow, concentrated thought. It's in their economic interest to drive us to distraction.*[10] (my italics)

The IT revolution drives the mind towards greater desire and away from reflection and contemplation, away from focus and towards a scattering of our consciousness.

One of the factors driving an increasing dependence on online networks and communication systems is called 'fear of missing out' (FoMO). FoMO is the feeling that we are missing out on something important going on somewhere else (something to which I myself am not immune!) or a fear of being forgotten by others. It is feeling uneasy that others just might be having a more enjoyable experience than you and that you are not part of it. In this way, our mind is prone to fragmentation.

In a Chinese Buddhist text, the Buddha says: 'Of all longings and desires, there is none as strong as sex. Sexual desire has no equal. Fortunately, it is one of a kind. If there were something else like it, no one in the entire world would be able to cultivate the Way.'[11] However, a recent study by a University of Chicago social psychologist seems to suggest that sex might indeed have a rival in the power to tempt people away from the Buddhist path to Enlightenment. The psychologist Wilhelm Hofmann's research found that in strength of desire, the most potent desires were for sleep, sex, and social contact. Hofmann also studied the use of willpower to resist temptation and discovered that participants in the study found it easier to abstain from food and sex through willpower alone than to stay away from media desires such as for television, checking emails, or surfing Facebook and the Web.[12] Hofmann speculated that these desires are influenced by the pervasive availability and ease of access to social media in modern lives. Perhaps if sex were as available as social media, the results might be different!

Another way in which the IT revolution is adversely affecting our minds is in our ability to reflect and to create. By being given access to hand-held computer devices at an early age, children are spending more time typing on a keyboard and less time learning handwriting. But children not only learn to read more quickly when they first learn to write by hand but also are able to better retain information and to create ideas. This is because the act of handwriting stimulates a part of the brain that is not stimulated by typing on a keyboard. Handwriting allows more of a process of reformulation and reflection that leads to better understanding and creativity.[13]

Earlier in this book, in Chapter 3 on the decline of community, I drew attention to the enclosure movement in Britain and Europe between the fifteenth and eighteenth centuries. This movement involved closing off common land and bringing its ownership under the control of a minority of landlords. Some people think we are now witnessing the 'ultimate enclosure – the enclosure of the cognitive commons, the ambient mental atmosphere of daily life' and the commodification of 'cognitive space'.[14] But, you might think, there are some areas of our lives that the enclosure of the cognitive commons cannot encroach upon, such as sleep and walking. If you do think this, you might be in for a rude awakening.

Among the migratory birds of North America is a species known as the white-crowned sparrow. Over the past five years, the US Defence Department has been pouring massive amounts of money into research on this bird. Why? The white-crowned sparrow has the unusual ability to stay awake for as long as seven days when migrating. The objective of the research is the creation of the sleepless soldier. Other researchers are investigating different techniques for inducing sleeplessness, including neurochemicals, gene therapy, and transcranial magnetic stimulation.[15] As we know from history, military innovations are often integrated into society, where the ultimate aim might be the sleepless worker or (better still?) the sleepless consumer. As Jonathon Crary puts it in his book *24/7: Late capitalism and the Ends of Sleep*, 'The huge portion of our lives that we spend asleep, freed from the morass of simulated needs, [remains] one of the great human affronts to the voraciousness of contemporary capitalism.'[16]

Sleep is under pressure everywhere. In Britain, one in three workers is chronically sleep-deprived.[17] The average North

American adult now sleeps approximately six-and-a-half hours a night, down from eight hours a generation ago and ten hours in the early twentieth century.[18] I personally prefer Shakespeare's enjoyment of 'the honey-heavy dew of slumber' but the modern capitalist view of sleep is now much closer to that of Thomas Edison, the inventor of the first commercially practicable electric light bulb. Four hundred years after Shakespeare, Edison said, 'Sleep is a criminal waste of time and a heritage from our cave days.'[19] For Russell Foster, the head of the Nuffield Research Laboratory on sleep at Oxford University, Edison's view is disastrously wrong. One of the most important and exciting functions of sleep is its ability to come up with novel solutions to complex problems. Sleeping at night, he tells us, enhances our creativity.[20] Just as children's creativity is being diminished by the use of the keyboard, adult creativity is lessened by lack of sleep, and both these trends are being stimulated by ubiquitous social media.

In addition, loss of sleep may contribute to the rise in obesity. Sleep loss gives rise to the release of the hormone ghrelin, the hunger hormone. When ghrelin is released, it goes to the brain, causing it to think 'I need carbohydrates', and the brain then prompts the body to seek out carbohydrates, particularly sugars. Disruption of normal sleep patterns also leads to stress; and among shift workers, studies show reduced immunity to infection and higher rates of cancer.[21] And for those of us fortunate enough not to be shift workers, many are taking smart phones and ipads into the bedroom, ready to respond to the latest nudge from the 24/7 attention economy.

If you are like me, one of the best ways besides sleep and meditation to refresh the mind, relieve stress, and step out of the pervasive pressure of the attention economy and reflect is to walk.

As a lover of mountain walking, I associate very strongly with John Muir, the Scotland-born naturalist and founder of the Sierra Club in the United States, who saw walking as an opportunity for deep reflection. He wrote, 'I only went out for a walk, and finally concluded to stay out till sundown, for going out, I found, was really going in.'[22]

Henry David Thoreau, another American, also saw the link between walking and reflection. 'Methinks that the moment my legs begin to move, my thoughts begin to flow.' Yet even Thoreau sometimes found it difficult to let go of daily concerns. He wrote, 'But it sometimes happens that I cannot easily shake off the village. The thought of some work will run in my head and I am not where my body is – I am out of my senses. . . . What business have I in the woods, if I am thinking of something out of the woods?'[23]

Since the time of Muir and Thoreau, the 'village' has grown exponentially and become much more intrusive. With the advent of the smart phone, it's much harder to walk away from 'the village'. More of us are surrendering to a life of distractions, with the result that we are living much of our lives out of our senses.[24] In the city this surrender is evident in those transfixed by their smart phones – 'the digital dead, shuffling slowly, their eyes fixed to a small screen in their hands'.[25]

In a study that focused on a single intersection in Seattle, it was found that one in three pedestrians were distracted, by either typing or talking on a phone or by using earphones.[26] For those who were distracted, it took almost twenty per cent longer to cross the street. Worse, if we can resist the lure of distraction, the public spaces we need to walk in relatively undisturbed in our cities and towns are at risk from commercial developers. In the UK, developers are being given more freedom to configure where we walk, what we visit, and who has access, because in this way they can maximize sales per square foot of shopping. For developers of shopping malls, public space simply means lost revenue.[27] And after going through security, entering the departures area of an airport requires being forced to navigate through expensive shopping arcades.

Earlier in this book, I had occasion to refer to the impact on work of Frederick Winslow Taylor's method of time and motion study and scientific management. Nicholas Carr, in his much quoted article 'Is Google making us stupid?', reminds us how Taylor's methods revolutionized industrial manufacturing. His aim was a restructuring not just of industry but also of society, to create a 'utopia of perfect efficiency'. Carr argues that Taylor's system is still very much with us. He says it remains the 'ethic of industrial manufacturing', and goes on: 'And now, thanks to the growing power that computer engineers and software coders wield over our intellectual lives, Taylor's ethic is beginning to govern the realm of the mind as well.'[28] Google's headquarters in California is described by Carr as the Internet's 'high church', where the religion of Taylorism is practised. 'What Taylor did for the work of the hand, Google is doing for the work of the mind.' Carr believes that Google sees information as a kind of commodity, a resource that can be mined and processed with industrial efficiency. The faster we can extract the gist of more and more pieces of information, the more productive we become as thinkers.

I believe that this fast and 'productive' thinking bespeaks a radically impoverished view of the creative capability of the human mind. What is lost in Google's drive for 'efficiency' is the ability to reflect, even the ability to read. The 'efficient' and 'immediate' style of reading promoted by Google and the

Internet may be weakening our capacity for the kind of deep reading that emerged with the earlier technology of the printing press. When we read online, we become 'mere decoders of information' while our ability to interpret text and to 'make the rich mental connections that form when we read deeply and without distraction remains largely disengaged'.[29] Deep reading is valuable for acquiring new knowledge and also for the intellectual reverberations set off in our mind. 'In the quiet spaces opened up by the sustained, undistracted reading of a book, or by any other act of contemplation . . . we make our own associations, draw our own inferences and analogies, foster our own ideas. Deep reading . . . is indistinguishable from deep thinking.'[30]

Losing those quiet spaces, or rushing to fill them with more data from the Internet, risks turning us into what the playwright Richard Foreman has called 'pancake people' – spread wide and thin but with no depth.[31] Besides diminishing our ability to reflect deeply, another outcome of this 'spreading thin' is that we become less patient. This is because our sense of time is conditioned by context. If that context is conditioned by increasingly pervasive information and communication technologies whose speed is becoming faster and faster, then we are being trained to become used to near-instantaneous interactions. As Nicholas Carr warns us in another article, 'The Patience Deficit', we become more and more likely to get frustrated and annoyed at even brief delays.[32] The risks are not just personal; they are also cultural. We shall be less willing to experience anything that requires us to wait, preferring instead instant gratification. But the greatest human creations take time and depth, both to be created and to be appreciated.

One of the main methods used by Buddhists to counter the pressures of the attention economy is mindfulness meditation. Recently the mindfulness techniques and skills learnt by

Buddhists have become much more widely available on a secular basis. Many thousands of people have benefited from the help of mindfulness trainers in dealing with pain and stress, with depression and addiction in more and more countries around the world. The care and compassion of these teachers is admirable. It is a welcome and wonderful development.

But now businesses are beginning to apply the techniques of mindfulness to the modern workplace. It's claimed that mindfulness helps with many things, from better teamwork and relationships to improved business creativity and reduced stress and anxiety. In several articles in 2012 and 2013, the *Financial Times*, one of the world's leading business newspapers, tells us that mindfulness is now used in organizations as varied as Google, Apple, General Mills, the London Underground, Marks and Spencer, and finance companies such as the world's largest hedge fund, Bridgewater.[33] Inevitably, much emphasis is put on the purely economic and organizational benefits of mindfulness. The following quotation is from the Search Inside Yourself Leadership Institute website: 'Developed at Google and based on the latest in neuroscience research, our programs offer attention and mindfulness training that build the core emotional intelligence skills needed for peak performance and effective leadership. We help professionals at all levels adapt, management teams evolve, and leaders optimize their impact and influence.'[34]

In another example, research into a mindfulness course at General Mills, led by Janice Marturano's Institute for Mindful Leadership, found that:

After one of Marturano's seven-week courses, 83 per cent of participants said they were 'taking time each day to optimise my personal productivity' – up from 23 per

cent before the course. Eighty-two per cent said they now
make time to eliminate tasks with limited productivity
value – up from 32 per cent before the course. And
among senior executives who took the course, 80 per cent
reported a positive change in their ability to make better
decisions, while 89 per cent said they became better
listeners.[35]

Reading these reports on mindfulness in business, I am concerned
that deeply meaningful Buddhist concepts such as 'equanimity'
are diminished in the jargon of business mindfulness. Ray Dalio,
the founder of Bridgewater and a strong supporter of mindfulness,
has commented that 'Meditation, more than anything else, is
responsible for whatever success I have had. . . . When I meditate,
I acquire an equanimity that allows me to see things from a higher-
level perspective and that allows me to make sensible decisions.'[36]
I agree that equanimity does offer a higher perspective, a looking
down from above. But this 'higher' perspective is very different
for a Buddhist than for a businessman. Dharmachari Manjusura,
writing in the Buddhist magazine *Tricycle*, captures this very well
in a lovely description of equanimity:

> When I visualize Avalokiteśvara, the Bodhisattva of
> Compassion, he's usually up above the world, suspended
> in a bright sky. His name tells us as much – *īśvara* means
> 'lord', and *Avalokita* is usually translated as 'the one who
> looks down', so Avalokiteśvara is the Lord of the Dharma
> who looks down. . . . Why is Avalokiteśvara so high up?
> Because that gives him a more comprehensive view of
> the lives of beings in the world, making it easier for him
> to see and respond to suffering. . . . When we cultivate a

view from above, we gain a proper perspective – we see our lives within the 'harmony of opposites', the endless transformations of birth, growth, joy, illness, prosperity, sadness, and death. And we see the countless others with whom we share our lives, to whom we are related by the very fact of having a body, with all the sufferings and joys that flesh is heir to.[37]

The Buddhist purpose of equanimity is to gain a perspective from which it is possible to better help alleviate the suffering of others. Without this, there is a danger that the notion of equanimity becomes like the perspective of Harry Lime in the film *The Third Man*. He looks down on the masses from the top of a big wheel and asks, 'Look down there. Tell me. Would you really feel any pity if one of those dots stopped moving forever?'[38]

The Buddhists I know who are teaching mindfulness to people in companies, government, and business schools are consciously attempting to increase ethical awareness. They seek kindness as an outcome to the sensitive teaching of mindfulness. There is for them an awareness that employers and organizations might use mindfulness as a means to make diffcult conditions tolerable rather than to tackle the root causes of the bad conditions. Perhaps the idea of a mindful and ethical organization can be stimulated in this way. But in some way there needs to be an understanding that, properly applied, mindfulness implies tackling the fundamental conditions that have led to suffering. Maybe the slogan could be 'Mindfulness is political' or even, as my teacher Sangharakshita has said, 'Awareness is revolutionary.'[39]

I hope I am wrong. But notwithstanding the sincerity of mindfulness teachers, the evidence of an ethical shift in business behaviour owing to the embracing of mindfulness is, as far as I can see, not encouraging. To the contrary, the evidence suggests a 'disconnect' between the practice of mindfulness and reality on the ground. A recent example from the US illustrates this disconnect. One of the most successful of the modern meditation and mindfulness movements is Wisdom 2.0. It promotes conferences bringing together business leaders from Silicon Valley companies such as Google, PayPal, eBay, and Apple as well as other western industries. Having held a succession of very impressive conferences in San Francisco, Wisdom 2.0 is expanding to New York and to Dublin for its first European conference. However, the proceedings of its most recent conference in San Franciso were disrupted by a demonstration led by someone who is a dedicated Buddhist meditator and a union and community organizer.

Amanda Ream helped to organize the demonstration and tells the story behind it.[40] According to her, the tech industry's great economic boom is creating a housing crisis in San Francisco. This is because state law allows what are called 'no-fault' evictions. These have increased by 175 per cent in the past year. The city doesn't keep track of how many people have been affected but independent estimates suggest that up to 3,580 residents were no-fault evicted in 2013. Ream, like generations of people before her, came to San Francisco because she wanted to find the freedom to live out her ideals. She wanted to practise Buddhism, and no other city has so many Buddhist teachers and centres. She describes how the tech industry, Google, Facebook, and their peers have adopted the culture of San Francisco. From her perspective, just as new, wealthier people displace others who have lived there longer, Buddhism is undergoing a process of 'gentrification' in San Francisco today. What is being lost, she argues, is 'the bigger picture of the teachings that asks us to consider our interdependence, and to move beyond self-help and addressing only our own suffering'.

While members of Eviction Free San Francisco held a banner across the stage and chanted 'San Francisco Not for Sale', Ream handed out leaflets to the more than 500 attendees that read 'Thank you for your practice. We invite you to consider the truth behind Google and the tech industry's impact on San Francisco.' She wanted conference participants to consider the campaign to keep families in their homes, to save the diversity of the city, and to repeal the state law that allows for no-fault evictions. But as protestors were marched out of the hall by conference staff, a Google presentation on corporate mindfulness carried on, asking the audience to 'check in with their body' about the conflict. Ream reports that no one addressed the issues she and other protestors were raising, not then or later on at the conference. This is a telling example of the 'disconnect' that can occur between the practice of mindfulness and the reality of people's everyday lives.

Even the *Financial Times* is not altogether comfortable with business mindfulness. Commenting on the spread of mindfulness into the world of high finance, the journalist John Paul Rathbone writes, 'Meditation may be one way to "go deeper". Certainly, it seems to have increased the willingness of some to explore their interiority. Whether that will make a difference to the ethics of the financial world is an open question.'[41] Others too have their doubts about the business mindfulness movement. Writing about Wisdom 2.0, Noah Shachtman comments:

> One of the reasons that Wisdom 2.0 – and the broader
> movement it represents – has become so big, so quickly,
> is that it stripped away the dogma and religious
> trappings. But it's hard not to consider what gets lost in
> this whittling process. Siddhārtha [the Buddha's original

name] famously abandoned the trappings of royalty to
sit under the Bodhi Tree and preach about the illusion of
the ego. Seeing the megarich take the stage to trumpet his
practices is a bit jarring. It also raises the uncomfortable
possibility that these ancient teachings are being used to
reinforce some of modern society's uglier inequalities.[42]

As you have been reading my critique of the attention economy,
you may have noticed a distinct irony. The irony is, of course,
that much of this chapter and this book could not have been
written without the help of the very technology that is at the
heart of what I have been criticizing. In today's world, the Internet
is virtually an indispensable tool for researching and analyzing
a topic. It's like a gigantic collective memory that is almost
instantly available. For this, I am thankful. I am thankful also
for the commons-based peer productions such as Wikipedia that
challenge the usual profit-driven model of business. So I'm not
going to say that I believe we should turn our backs completely
on the Internet, mobile phones, Skype, or any other features of
modern technology. Indeed, as a friend commented to me, there
is a sort of 'messy democracy' about social media that allows for
more freedom of expression compared to pre-Internet days when
governments and corporate media had more monolithic control.

One of the key battles against pressure for the enclosure of the
cognitive commons is precisely in this area, and we need to be
watchful. But I do believe very strongly that we should pay heed
to Sangharakshita's simple but powerful advice, given in 1993 but
still very relevant: to reduce input, maybe dramatically to reduce
input. As I can testify, this is not always easy, but simple steps
such as restricting the times of day when you access the Internet
are possible. Furthermore, we should value and unashamedly

promote meditation and mindfulness for their original purpose: to reduce suffering, to promote well-being, and to encourage a desire to help others.

And perhaps we can do something really radical: allow ourselves periods of idleness. As Tim Kreider, an American essayist and cartoonist, writes:

> Idleness is not just a vacation, an indulgence or a vice; it is as indispensable to the brain as vitamin D is to the body, and deprived of it we suffer a mental affliction as disfiguring as rickets. The space and quiet that idleness provides is a necessary condition for standing back from life and seeing it whole, for making unexpected connections and waiting for the wild summer lightning strikes of inspiration.[43]

Or we could follow Sangharakshita's advice and regard boredom as a positive opportunity:

> When you are really bored, the best thing you can do is sit down and let yourself experience the boredom more fully. It may not be a deep or satisfying state, but at least you are not indulging in the things with which you usually cover up this kind of experience. Your real state of mind is more nakedly exposed, because for the time being there are no distractions. If you can stay with the experience of boredom, you can try to feel your way through into something deeper, truer, and more spontaneous within yourself.
>
> This is likely to be more helpful than trying to force a more positive state into being or rushing to alleviate the boredom with a distraction. After a while you should find that the boredom passes. You will start to feel more

positive simply by virtue of experiencing yourself more truly. And feeling more positive, you will probably want to get on with actually doing something positive. But if the minute you start feeling bored you turn on the radio or pick up the newspaper or ring somebody up [or turn on the computer, access the internet, play with your smartphone etc], then you've lost the opportunity that the boredom has presented you.[44]

These are difficult practices but the alternative is, in T.S. Eliot's words, to end up 'Distracted from distraction by distraction'.[45]

8

The happiness industry

Aldous Huxley's 1932 novel *Brave New World* describes a society in which people are selectively bred in incubators to become alphas, betas, gammas, deltas, or epsilons and, once born, are trained to be content with their situation. (Alphas are the highest caste with the best jobs, epsilons are the lowest with the worst jobs.) If they become discontent, they are given soma, a drug designed to make them happy again. In his foreword to the second edition of the book, published in 1947, Huxley warned: 'The most important [projects] of the future will be vast government-sponsored enquiries into what the politicians and the participating scientists will call the problem of "happiness" – in other words, the problem of making people love their servitude.'[1] At present governments and social scientists around the world, including in Britain, France, Canada and the United States, are following the lead of the Buddhist state Bhutan and investigating the potential for implementing national measures of happiness. They are now part of what one respected financial commentator has described as the 'happiness industry'.[2] Should we be worried or should we welcome this as a much-needed alternative to the relentless emphasis on Gross Domestic Product (GDP) and economic growth in the modern capitalist world?

To try to answer this and other questions about happiness, I shall examine what the Buddha said about happiness. This will help to give us a perspective on modern economic discussions about happiness. The Buddha distinguished between different types of happiness. The first important difference is between what he called 'worldly' happiness and 'unworldly' happiness. Worldly happiness arises in dependence upon sensual pleasure. Unworldly states of happiness arise during deep states of absorption or concentration that can occur in meditation. There is the happiness we can find in external things and people and there is the happiness we can find internally, in our own mind and body, independent of any yearning for something outside us. The happiness that depends upon sensual pleasure is no match for the happiness found within. In one story, the Buddha compares the pleasure he experiences with that of a king. The king can't sit still and be silent in experiencing pleasure for even one day and night; the Buddha can do so for seven days and nights.[3]

The second important difference identified by the Buddha is that between happiness that comes with attachment and happiness that comes without attachment. For example, when we read the accounts and poems about Enlightenment given by disciples of the Buddha, we find many poems about the pleasure and happiness they experienced in nature. Cūḷaka, one such disciple, writes:

> *The peacocks – with lovely feathers, lovely wings,*
> *Lovely blue necks and lovely faces,*
> *Call out – a lovely song with a lovely sound.*
> *This great earth has lovely waters and grasses;*
> *There are lovely clouds in the sky.[4]*

Clearly Cūḷaka enjoys the pleasure and happiness of nature, but with a difference. As an Enlightened being, he enjoys nature while knowing that the cause of his pleasure will not last and is subject to change. He is not attached to the particular pleasure. In fact, his appreciation of nature and the happiness he derives from it is heightened by a clear understanding of its fleeting nature. By contrast, pleasure for me as an unenlightened being is often tied up with grasping and attachment and with a lack of appreciation of the impermanence of things.

If I look at the modern world and reflect upon the Buddha's distinction between worldly and unworldly happiness and between happiness with attachment and without attachment, I come to a clear conclusion: our modern economy depends upon people being persuaded to continually seek out worldly forms of pleasure, in a way that works against exploring and appreciating the happiness that can come from within. At the same time, a trick is repeatedly played upon us. We are promised that this or that product offers lasting pleasure; and when it doesn't, another product is offered in an endlessly replenishing flow of new goods and services. We thereby become attached to the idea that consuming more and more goods and services is the way to happiness. Moreover, chasing after sensually derived forms of happiness results in the strengthening of desires. The more we indulge in sensual pleasure, the more we shall be caught up in sensual desire, 'a vicious circle turning into a bottomless vortex of ever greater desires clamouring for satisfaction'.[5]

The Buddha's view is different. For the Buddha, the path to happiness requires a long-term perspective, a realization that what gives immediate happiness may lead to future happiness or unhappiness *depending upon its ethical quality.* When considering a lay person who, through their own ethically rooted efforts to earn a living, gains financial rewards, the Buddha points to four consequent elements of happiness that can be expected: the happiness of acquiring wealth by their own effort; the happiness of using this wealth to give pleasure to themselves, their family, and friends and to do meritorious deeds; the happiness of being free from debt; and the happiness of blamelessness, to be able to live a faultless and pure life. So although the Buddha acknowledges the economic and material happiness gained by the layperson, it is the fourth type, blamelessness, that brings the greatest benefit: 'Of these [types of happiness] the wise know that the happiness of blamelessness is by far the greatest householder happiness. Economic and material happiness is not worth one-sixteenth part of the spiritual happiness arising out of a good and faultless life.'[6]

This is not to say that economic and material things are completely irrelevant to a person's happiness. Unless a person is provided with at least a minimum standard of living that supplies the basic requirements of food and shelter with some degree of time available for leisure and reflection, it is pointless to talk about a spiritual path to Enlightenment. Given a minimum standard of living, the main wellspring of happiness lies in an ethical life, a life founded on the training of the mind. This, according to the Buddha, is the true source of happiness.

The Buddha tells us that as a source of happiness, nothing surpasses a mind that is well trained and developed. The famous twin verses at the beginning of the Dhammapada state:

Experiences are preceded by mind, led by mind, and produced by mind. If one speaks or acts with an impure mind, suffering follows even as the cartwheel follows the hoof of the ox drawing the cart.

Experiences are preceded by mind, led by mind, and produced by mind. If one speaks or acts with a pure mind, happiness follows like a shadow that never departs.[7]

If we speak and act with a pure mind, the Buddha tells us, it's possible to embark upon a path of progressively refined forms of happiness.[8]

The first stage of this ascending series is happiness owing to 'blamelessness', a happiness that results from maintaining moral conduct. It will grow once a frugal lifestyle and contentment become additional contributing factors. The next stage of happiness comes from leaving sensual distractions behind by practising sense-restraint. This type of happiness is 'unimpaired happiness', as the bondage of sensuality has temporarily been left behind. The path continues from the stage of unimpaired happiness owing to freedom from sensual distraction to the different types of happiness experienced with the deepening levels of meditative absorption and concentration. The path culminates in the happiness that comes with liberation or Enlightenment.

The path of transformation described here is a gradual one. The Buddha is telling us that we cannot shift from being dependent upon sensual pleasures overnight. We need to patiently work on our ethics and on the purification of our mind in order to create the conditions for the shift to take place so that we are happier in the long run. The process of working on our ethics and purifying the mind requires us to engage in turning both outwards to others and inwards to our own mind. This process of outward and inward movement is summarized in the five basic positive ethical guidelines laid down by the Buddha: practising loving-kindness; generosity; skilful speech towards others; cultivating stillness, simplicity, and contentment within; and practising mindfulness in all our daily activities.

Before I look at the issues around happiness and its measurement from this Buddhist perspective, I want to touch on a concern that is always raised about happiness. Once a person has attained the minimum standard of living required for decent housing and sufficient food and leisure time, the question arises: 'Does more money make you happier?' This is a controversial issue in economics. Until recently, it was generally claimed that once basic needs have been met, higher levels of income do not provide higher levels of happiness or well-being. More recent research appears to challenge this view. However, a careful reading of all the research reveals the following picture.[9] As an individual gets richer and richer, income matters less and less in terms of improving well-being; and although more income might 'buy' a little more happiness, other things such as having more friends would 'buy' much more.

Two important consequences flow from these findings. First, once basic needs are met, there are often better ways to spend our time to increase happiness than chasing after more money. Taking more time off and spending it with family and children or with friends will add more to a person's well-being. Second, as marginal increases in well-being from increases in income are smaller for the richest people and greater for the poorest people, a redistribution of income from the richest to the poorest would lead to an increase in the level of well-being in a country. For example, a loss of £1,000 in income for a rich person reduces their well-being by a small amount but an increase of £1,000 in income for a poor person increases their well-being by a much greater amount.

But now I shall turn to broader questions about happiness and well-being. In earlier chapters, I have emphasized the obsession in capitalism with consumption and economic growth. The obsession can be seen as stock exchanges, politicians, and the media anxiously wait for the announcement of the latest figures on GDP or gross national product (GNP). Invented in the 1930s,

GDP tries to measure the total amount of goods and services produced in a country. GNP measures the total value of goods and services produced by all nationals of a country, whether within or outside the country. GDP is used throughout the world to gauge economic progress. Growth in GDP is greeted as good news; reduction in GDP is bad news. The limitations of GDP as a single indicator have been well known for a long time.

The inventor of GDP, Simon Kuznets, wanted to include only activities he believed contributed to the well-being of a society. He didn't want to include spending on armaments because war clearly detracted from human welfare. He thought advertising was useless and shouldn't be included in GDP, and financial and speculative activities were dangerous and should be excluded from calculations. Contrary to Kuznets' desires, and somewhat paradoxically, all these economic activities are now included in calculations of GDP. Kuznets would have been appalled that recorded GDP in the UK has recently grown by £10 billion because of the addition of heroin sales and prostitution into the calculations.[10] The country Macau has registered very high rates of growth in GDP because of a boom in gambling. Countries with high rates of crime will show higher rates of growth in GDP because of spending on security guards. The list goes on. GDP is amoral.[11]

These problems and others have been known and discussed for a long time. In March 1968, Robert F. Kennedy (brother of President John F. Kennedy) criticized the indicator, pointing out that its calculation included 'jails, cigarette advertising, nuclear warheads and armored police cars'. But GDP 'does not allow for the health of our children, the quality of their education, or the joy of their play. It does not include the beauty of our poetry or the strength of our marriages . . . it measures everything in short, except that which makes life worthwhile.'[12] Other anomalies abound in the measurement of GDP. We add to GDP if we eat out in a restaurant, and add nothing to it if we cook and eat at home. Caring for a family member at home does not count, but being paid to work as a carer in someone else's home does count. Cleaning up the 2010 oil spill in the Gulf of Mexico was worth more economically, in GDP terms, than the carbon absorption provided by the Amazon rain forest. As a measure of national wealth and well-being, GDP is at best partial and at worst misleading.

It is thus understandable that recently, especially since the onset of the global economic crisis in 2008, there has been a burgeoning interest in constructing differently based indicators of well-being or happiness. This field in economics is evolving very rapidly. Psychologists, behavioural economists, leading opinion poll companies, governments, and international economic organizations such as the OECD and others are working to produce indicators to supplement or to replace GDP.

To try to simplify all this, I shall look at arguments for a single indicator of happiness, such as one measuring 'life satisfaction'. Next I shall examine those indicators that try to measure a more complex concept, well-being or 'flourishing'. Then I shall examine the specific case of the Buddhist state Bhutan and its use of 'Gross National Happiness' as an alternative to Gross National Product. I shall look at these critically from a perspective informed by the Buddha's teachings on happiness and also bear in mind other criticisms made by modern commentators.

First, single indicators of happiness. Richard Layard is Director of the Wellbeing Programme at the London School of Economics and is an advisor to various national and international bodies on happiness indicators, including the UK government. He is a strong advocate of the single-indicator approach. His view is that over the past fifty years, 'the grip of GDP as the talisman of national performance [has become] ever stronger. We shall only displace the use of GDP by providing a single, convincing alternative.'[13] For him, that alternative is the quality of life as people subjectively experience it; and of all the measures of subjective well-being, life satisfaction, he says, has been the most intensively studied.

An example of life satisfaction indicators is provided by Gallup, probably the leading private company in the collection and analysis of global data and measurements. Gallup measures life satisfaction by asking respondents to rate their present and future lives on a 'ladder' scale: steps are numbered from 0 to 10, where '0' indicates the worst possible life and '10' the best possible life.[14] Individuals who rate their current lives '7' or higher and their future life '8' or higher are considered to be 'thriving'. Individuals are 'suffering' if they report their current *and* future lives as '4' or lower. All other individuals are considered to be 'struggling'.

Gallup supplements these measures with what it calls a 'daily well-being average' (0-10 scoring), based on responses to ten items measuring daily experiences (feeling well rested, being treated with respect, smiling/laughter, learning/interest, enjoyment, physical pain, worry, sadness, stress, and anger). Higher scores represent better days, i.e. more positive and less negative daily experiences. For those interested in results, here are the top and bottom nations from the 2010 survey of the forty countries included in Gallup's European group. Denmark is top, with 82 per cent of people thriving, 17 per cent struggling, and only 1 per cent suffering. Their daily experience indicator stands at 7.9. Bulgaria is bottom, with only 6 per cent thriving, 58 per cent struggling, and 36 per cent suffering. Their daily experience indicator stands at 6.5.

Martin Seligman, the inventor of the Positive Psychology movement, criticizes the single indicator approach because, he claims, 70 per cent of the score a person gives themself on a scale of 0 to 10 is determined by their mood at the time of asking. In other words, it measures mostly how good a person is feeling at that moment. And, he continues, you do not achieve the highest human good simply by feeling good.[15] Another critic, Jules Evans, the author of *Philosophy for Life and Other Dangerous Situations*, calls the single-indicator approach the 'Hedonic' approach, arguing that it does not allow for the possibility that some forms of happiness are higher and better than others. The Buddha's distinction between worldly and unworldly happiness comes to mind here. And single indicators, Evans points out further, ignore that nature gives us a range of emotional experience for a reason, so that sometimes it is appropriate to be sad or angry or disappointed or restless. Putting all the emphasis on happiness reduces 'the rich complexity of life'.[16] The goal of life and of society is not for everyone to experience 'pleasant feelings'. If it were, the government should simply give everyone a dose of Aldous Huxley's soma or, in modern times, a dose of Prozac.

The start of the Buddha's path to Enlightenment came with the realization of suffering and the determination to solve the problem of suffering and find meaning in life. This was the shift from the ignoble search for happiness to the noble search for happiness, a search that involved mistakes and more suffering as well as joy and happiness. The Buddha would agree with Jules Evans when he says, 'We don't want just to feel good. We want lives of genuinely rich activity, engagement, striving, achievement and fulfilment. Feeling good is the bonus to those experiences – it shouldn't be the goal itself. In fact, an important part of the striving life is moments of dissatisfaction and restlessness. Those emotions have their place in human experience.'[17]

But what about those approaches to measuring well-being that go beyond the single-indicator approach? Martin Seligman, mentioned above as a critic of the single-indicator approach, is a proponent of scientifically measuring the more complex notion of 'flourishing'. The components of his measurements can be summed up by the acronym PERMA, in which:

P   stands for positive emotion (for example, the experience of peace, gratitude, satisfaction, pleasure, inspiration, hope, curiosity, and love);

E   stands for engagement (for instance, when we're truly engaged in a situation, task, or project, we experience a state of flow; time seems to stop, we lose our sense of self, and we concentrate intensely on the present);

R   stands for meaningful and positive relationships with others;

M   stands for meaning that comes from serving a cause larger than ourselves; and

A   stands for accomplishment (for example, mastering a skill or achieving a goal).

It is suggested that Seligman's approach and the other approaches that try to go beyond simple measures of 'feeling good' seek to align themselves with Aristotle's theory of eudaemonia. (Eudaemonia means a contented state of being happy and healthy and prosperous.) If this is so, then, as Evans points out, something fundamental to Aristotle's theory is missing: ethics or virtue. Aristotle said that happiness is 'an activity of the soul in accordance with virtue.'[18] But there is no mention of virtue or ethics in Seligman's approach or in other such approaches. And this is also where the Buddha's approach is in fundamental disagreement with the 'happiness industry'. For the Buddha, happiness arises in leading an ethical life and purifying the mind.

A moment's reflection on the specifics of PERMA will expose its shortcomings. Jules Evans comments:

> One could have lots of Positive Emotion, and yet be a happy idiot. One could have a lot of engagement (or 'flow') through being addicted to a computer game. One could have a lot of relationships, but with bad people. One could have a deep sense of meaning, through serving an evil cause. One could have a profound sense of achievement from achieving something that most of humanity might say was worthless or even immoral.[19]

Evans adds that by this definition, Osama bin Laden probably had a life that was objectively very high in PERMA, and comments that if the model of a good life is met by Osama bin Laden, then there's something very wrong with it. I agree with Evans when he concludes that a vision of a life of well-being without an ethical framework for discriminating between good and bad PERMA is simply bankrupt.

How does all this relate to Bhutan, the Buddhist state that was seen as an international leader in happiness measures – at least until July 2013, when the government promoting gross national happiness (GNH) was voted out of office? From 1972, Bhutan recognized GNH to be more important than GNP and carried out much development work to construct an index of GNH. The Bhutan GNH index expanded the concept of happiness to include not just subjective measures of psychological well-being but also various collective, and in some cases more objective, measures, covered in nine domains: psychological well-being; time use (work-life balance); community vitality; community diversity; ecological resilience; living standards; health; education; and good governance.[20] In each domain, an aggregated index was constructed using a complicated system of weights given to the variables that make up the domain. At the level of domains, all nine of them were weighted equally, as they were all considered equally valid for happiness. Bhutan believed that GNH measured the quality of a country in a more holistic way than GNP, and it believed that the beneficial development of human society takes place when material and spiritual development occur side by side to complement and reinforce each other.

This all sounds praiseworthy. But the way in which Bhutan measured GNH, and also some of the values behind its measurement, had critics.[21] For example, a third of Bhutan's 'psychological well-being' indicator consist of measurements of a person's spirituality. The spirituality indicator is based on four elements: a person's self-reported spirituality level and the frequency with which they 1) consider karma, 2) engage in reciting prayers, and 3) meditate. The indicator identified 53 per cent of Bhutanese people as adequate in terms of spirituality. Apart from the practical question of whether or not you can accurately measure a person's genuine level of spiritual attainment simply by asking them how spiritual they are, there's another problem. Bhutan's GNH measured people's well-being according to how far they accepted the spiritual tenets and practices of Buddhism. If you didn't accept Buddhism, you were seen as having a poor level of spirituality. As a Buddhist brought up in the West with a belief in the freedom of religious choice, this makes me feel very uneasy.

And there's a deeper, disturbing history that brings into focus the ethical basis for the measurement of GNH in Bhutan. Accounts of the following historical episode are disputed but various international agencies, such as the UNHCR (the United Nations Refugees Agency) and others, including *The Economist* newspaper and Kai Bird, a Pulitzer Prize- winning historian and author, have raised serious questions about the behaviour of the Bhutanese authorities towards the Nepalese minority living in Bhutan.[22] There was a big influx of economic migrants into Bhutan from Nepal in the 1960s and 1970s; and in the late 1980s, government policy began to make life difficult for Nepali immigrants, resulting in protests, arrests, and expulsions. Others fled and, according to UNHCR estimates, 108,000 refugees ended up in camps in Nepal. As *The Economist* put it, 'one group's GNH starts looking like another group's grief.'[23] When I assess the various alternative indicators to GDP, including Bhutan's gross national happiness, I feel sympathy for the motivation behind creating them even if in practice they are unsatisfactory, particularly in relation to ethics. But I also feel uneasy with the idea that governments can seemingly determine what defines happiness and how to measure it. If we are to have alternative indicators to GDP, my own preference is for what has been called the 'dashboard approach', being developed by the Organisation for Economic Co-operation and Development (OECD).

The OECD's Better Life Index allows users to compare the performance of countries according to eleven criteria covering material conditions such as income and wealth; jobs and earnings; and housing and also quality of life indicators such as health; work-life balance; education and skills; social connections; civic engagement and governance; environmental quality; personal security; and subjective well-being.[24] A person accessing the index can make decisions about which of the component indicators are most important to them and make their judgements accordingly. Assessing which indicators are more important than others becomes a matter for individual choice or for collective discussion.

But the deeper issues of different kinds of happiness and ethics, issues raised by the Buddha, still remain relatively untouched by such statistical indicators.

From a Buddhist perspective, I'm of the view that a much more fruitful way forward on the topic of well-being and happiness is to think in terms of actions rather than indicators or outcomes. The New Economics Foundation has formulated a very useful set of slogans called 'five ways to well-being'.[25] Here they are:

Connect

Connect with the people around you, with family, friends, colleagues, and neighbours at home, work, school, or in your local community. Think of them as the cornerstones of your life and invest time in developing them. Building these connections will support and enrich you every day.

Be active

Go for a walk or run. Step outside. Cycle. Play a game. Garden. Dance. Exercising makes you feel good. Most important, discover a physical activity you enjoy and that suits your level of mobility and fitness.

Take notice

Be curious. Catch sight of the beautiful. Remark on the unusual. Notice the changing seasons. Savour the moment, whether you are walking to work, eating lunch, or talking to friends. Be aware of the world around you and what you are feeling. Reflecting on your experiences will help you to appreciate what matters to you.

Keep learning

Try something new. Rediscover an old interest. Sign up for that course. Take on a different responsibility at work. Fix a bike. Learn to play an instrument or how to cook your favourite food. Set a challenge you will enjoy achieving. Learning new things will make you more confident as well as being fun.

Give

Do something nice for a friend or a stranger. Thank someone. Smile. Volunteer your time. Join a community group. Look out as well as in. Seeing yourself, and your happiness, linked to the wider community can be incredibly rewarding and creates connections with the people around you.

There's a noticeable overlap between these five ways to well-being and positive versions of the five ethical precepts of Buddhism, noted above, of practising loving-kindness; generosity; skilful speech towards others; cultivating stillness, simplicity, and contentment within; and practising mindfulness in all our daily activities.[26]

Combining the two sets would be a good start to finding happiness. But if Buddhists are to offer a fully radical alternative to the typical Western lifestyle, then ideally that whole lifestyle needs to be examined and changed.

Ironically, I believe a pithy vision of what this lifestyle might look like is contained in a piece by Alain de Botton on the Greek philosopher Epicurus.[27]

De Botton tells how Epicurus believes that we make three major mistakes in thinking about happiness. First, we put too much emphasis on romantic relationships and not enough on friendships. Second, we are obsessed by money and careers, instead of seeking meaningful and satisfying work on our own or in small groups, thus obtaining fulfilment through our labour. Third, we dream of luxury but Epicurus believed that what we really want is a life of calm with time to reflect and to be, and to be with a good listener.

Epicurus did not stop with just this analysis. He took practical steps to implement his ideas. First, he decided to live together with friends. He bought a modest plot of land outside Athens where he and his friends could live side by side each with their own living space and with common areas, shared childcare, and everyone eating together. With this, he created the world's first commune. Second, everyone in the commune stopped working for other people, taking a cut in their income so that they could focus on fulfilling work. And, third, Epicurus and his friends spent time every day reflecting and discussing philosophical questions and the workings of their own mind. Epicurean communities arose all round the Mediterranean. They had thousands of participants and thrived for centuries until they were brutally suppressed by the Christian church in the fifth century.

Reading De Botton's account, I was struck by similarities in Epicurus's approach and elements of the lifestyle approach of the Triratna Buddhist Community, of which I am a member. I shall return to the approach of Sangharakshita, who founded the Community, in Chapter 10. Epicurus and the communal living he inspired, together with the Buddha's advice on happiness, offer us a path to happiness alternative to that of the consumer society that dominates today.

9

Inequality

Since 2011 the Occupy Movement has significantly raised awareness of inequality with its slogan 'We are the 99 percent.' Two academic publications have also had a major impact on the awareness and discussion of inequality: Wilkinson and Pickett's *The Spirit Level*[1] and Thomas Piketty's *Capital in the Twenty-first Century*.[2]

In 2009, professors Richard Wilkinson and Kate Pickett published their book *The Spirit Level: Why More Equal Societies Almost Always Do Better*. Taking data from the United Nations, the book focuses on income differentials in rich, developed market democracies. Wilkinson and Pickett measure how much richer the top 20 per cent are than the bottom 20 per cent in each country. In countries such as Japan, Finland, Norway, and Sweden, the top 20 per cent are about three-and-a-half to four times richer than the bottom 20 per cent. But in countries such as the UK, Portugal, the US, and Singapore, the differences are twice as great. Then within each country, they compare the extent of inequality in incomes with key social indicators such as life expectancy, children's maths and literacy scores, infant mortality rates, homicide rates, the proportion of the population in prison, teenage birth rates, levels of trust, obesity, mental illness, and social mobility – all calculated using internationally comparable data.

Although they use different indicators, Wilkinson and Pickett broadly follow an approach similar to the OECD Better Life Index's 'dashboard' approach, outlined in Chapter 8, to measuring well-being. Their indicators give a much more specific and accurate picture of the level of well-being in a society than does any single measure of 'happiness'. They find that the countries with greater differences in income between the top 20 per cent and the bottom 20 per cent are doing worse on all social indicators.

To test the relationship further, they then analyzed the same data for the fifty states of the US. The result was again that the evidence shows the more unequal states to do worse on the social indicators, with less trust, higher rates of mental illness, more homicides, more people in prison, less social mobility, and so on. Wilkinson and Pickett conclude that although for poorer countries the level of national income and economic growth matter very much for the average well-being of society, the well-being of society in the rich, developed world depends very much upon the degree of equality of income in that society. The bottom-line conclusions could not be more compelling. The more equal the distribution of income in a country is, the greater is the extent its well-being. The more unequal the distribution of income is, the lower is the degree of well-being.

In a more recent update for the *New York Times*, Wilkinson and Pickett are more radical in their analysis. They describe how 'inequality hollows out the soul'.[3] Using recent research findings, they write that inequality is divisive and socially corrosive of community life and trust and also damages the individual psyche. Because of our evolutionary inheritance, humans know instinctively how to cooperate and build social ties, but we also inherit both a tendency to compete for status and feelings of superiority and inferiority. We use cooperative and competitive strategies many times in our lives, but inequality shifts the balance of behaviour and feelings towards competition for status and contributes to driving consumerism. This competition helps to create the conditions for psychiatric disorders such as narcissism and mania as well as anxiety and depression.

Greater inequality in a country increases competition for status; it damages our mental health and distorts our personality. A recent study looking at the fifty American states, Wilkinson and Pickett write, found that after taking account of age, income, and educational differences, depression is more common in states with greater income inequality. Another study, looking at data from twenty-six countries, found that schizophrenia is about three times more prevalent in more unequal societies than it is in more equal societies. Moreover, a separate piece of research, on 34,000 people in thirty-one countries, discovered that in countries with bigger income differentials, status anxiety is more common, and not just at lower levels of the social hierarchy but at all levels. The richer in a society do not escape the suffering caused by inequality.

The authors of *The Spirit Level* also point out that countries such as Sweden and Japan that have a low level of inequality of incomes and consequently much greater well-being achieve their low level of inequality by different means.[4] Sweden has very big differences in earnings but it closes the gap between rich and poor by redistributive taxation and by providing a general welfare state with generous benefits. Japan has much smaller differences in earnings before tax, lower taxes, and a smaller welfare state. This suggests that attacking the culture of excessive pay packages for top managers or redistributing income through taxation and benefits are both legitimate and effective means of narrowing income differentials and achieving a higher level of well-being in society.

But in view of the recent runaway pay increases for chief executive officers (CEOs) of major companies in the US, encouraging a culture of more restrained payments for top bosses, at least in that country, may be difficult. For example, in 1978 American CEOs earned 26.5 times more than the average worker. By 2011, they earned 209 times more than the average worker, a dramatic rise in inequality.[5] This trend is one of the key features that Thomas Piketty draws attention to in his book *Capital in the Twenty-first Century*, one of the fastest- selling books on economics ever. (I shall have more to say about it later in this chapter.) One of the causes of the recent growth of inequality in the US and Europe, he argues, is that a new cadre of 'supermanagers' (CEOs) has managed to appropriate more of society's income.

One of the prime reasons for this dramatic shift in the distribution of income can be traced to the rise from the 1970s of free market economics and particularly the ideas of Milton Friedman. In a famous *New York Times* article in 1970, Friedman argues that the sole purpose of a firm is to make money for its shareholders. A corporation should focus totally on making money and forget about any concerns for employees, customers, or society.[6] This idea was adopted six years later in one of the most widely cited academic business articles ever, written by Professor Michael Jensen and Dean William Meckling of the Simon School of Business at the University of Rochester.[7] The article proposes that in order to ensure the exclusive focus is on making money for shareholders, firms should turn the executives running companies into major shareholders by offering them generous annual compensation in the form of shares in the company. Many companies and organizations have since enthusiastically taken on the ideas of professors Friedman, Jensen, and Meckling.

We can measure the result of this embrace of shareholder capitalism by measuring the movement in CEO compensation per dollar of net income earned for the 365 largest publicly traded American companies. Between 1960 and 1980, before shareholder capitalism took hold, CEO compensation per dollar of net income earned for the 365 biggest publicly traded American companies fell by 33 per cent. CEOs earned more for their shareholders for steadily less and less relative compensation. But in the decade from 1980 to 1990, when shareholder capitalism was taking off, CEO compensation per dollar of net earnings produced for the biggest American companies doubled. And from 1990 to 2000, it quadrupled. CEOs earned less for their shareholders for more and more relative compensation.[8] Giving CEOs generous share allocations is the main reason why in 2012, for the first time ever, the ten highest-paid CEOs in the US each received more than $100 million in annual compensation.[9]

But let's return to the effects of unequal distribution of income and wealth, specifically to an exploration of two negative consequences – concerning trust and empathy. Writing in the *New York Times* in December 2013, Joseph Stiglitz, an American economist and a Nobel Prize winner, analyzes the links between inequality and the loss of trust.[10] He argues that trust is becoming yet another casualty of the 'staggering' inequality in the US. As inequality widens the gap between citizens, so the bonds that hold society together become more fragile. As the top 1 per cent become ever richer, people lose faith in the economic system, perceiving that the odds are inexorably stacked against them. Something vital in our way of life is eroded. Stiglitz points out that the undervaluing of trust has its roots in the appropriation of the ideas of Adam Smith. According to the theory of the 'invisible hand', if everyone looks out for just themselves, then we would reach an outcome in which the economy is fully efficient for the benefit of everyone. As I have noted previously, Stiglitz comments, 'To the morally uninspired, it's an appealing idea: selfishness as the ultimate form of selflessness.'

Stiglitz warns that events over the past thirty years have shown not only that we cannot rely on narrow self-interest but also that no economy can function well without trust – and that unmitigated selfishness inevitably diminishes trust. He asks us to examine banking, the industry at the centre of the recent economic crisis. Banking had long been based on trust. At their best, banks were 'stalwart community institutions that made judicious loans to promising small businesses and prospective homeowners'. On a personal level, I can remember visiting my local bank manager in the UK in the early 1970s to ask for a mortgage to buy my first flat. I knew the bank manager personally and he made it his business to know lots about me and the stability of my job and income before he approved a loan, carefully limited to two-and-a-half times my annual salary.

Stiglitz tells us how things have changed:

> In the years leading up to the crisis, though, our
> traditional bankers changed drastically, aggressively
> branching out into other activities, including those
> historically associated with investment banking.
> *Trust went out the window.* Commercial lenders hard-
> sold mortgages to families who couldn't afford
> them, using false assurances. They could comfort
> themselves with the idea that no matter how much they
> exploited their customers and how much risk they had
> undertaken, new 'insurance' products – derivatives
> and other chicanery – insulated their banks from the

consequences. If any of them thought about the social implications of their activities, whether it was predatory lending, abusive credit card practices, or market manipulation, they might have taken comfort that, in accordance with Adam Smith's dictum, their swelling bank accounts implied that they must be boosting social welfare.[11] (my italics)

Let me give you two examples of 'predatory lending'. In one case in Bakersfield, California, a strawberry picker with an annual income of $14,000 was lent $724,000 to buy a house![12] In a second case, a baby (maternity) nurse and her sister ended up owning six townhouses in Queens, New York. When asked how that happened, she said that after she and her sister had bought their first house and its value had risen, the lenders suggested they refinance and borrow $250,000 to buy another townhouse. Then the price of that house rose too and they repeated the trick. Eventually they owned an extra five houses; but when the market fell, they couldn't make any of the repayments.[13]

The mirage created by bankers cost millions their home during and after the crisis. Once the financial crisis started, the destruction of trust was unrelenting. And one of the main reasons why the bubble's bursting in 2007–8 led to such an enormous crisis was that no bank could trust another.

Stiglitz observes, 'Each bank knew the shenanigans it had been engaged in – the movement of liabilities off its balance sheets, the predatory and reckless lending – and so knew that it could not trust any other bank. Interbank lending froze and the financial system came to the verge of collapse, saved only by the resolute action of the public, whose trust had been the most abused of all.'[14]

The Buddha on Wall Street

And what of the effect of inequality of incomes and wealth on empathy? The psychologist Daniel Goleman, author of the best-seller *Emotional Intelligence*, has written about social status and empathy.[15] Reviewing recent research studies, Goleman reports that the richer and more powerful a person is, the less empathy he or she is likely to have for people who are lower in status. For example, in five-minute get-acquainted sessions with strangers, more powerful persons have been observed to show fewer signals of paying attention, such as nodding or laughing. They are more likely to check mobile phones and to express disregard through facial expression and are more likely to take over the conversation and interrupt or to look past the other speaker.

In a 2008 study, social psychologists from the University of Amsterdam and the University of California, Berkeley arranged for pairs of strangers to tell one another about difficulties they had been through, such as a divorce or the death of a loved one. The researchers found that the more powerful were less compassionate towards the hardships described by the less powerful. In another study, Michael Kraus of the University of California found that wealthy people are less adept at reading others' emotions compared to uneducated and poor people. Kraus concluded that poorer people often have to rely on others, whereas wealthy people don't ask for help often. Kraus argues that wealthy people may be ''less concerned and less perceptive of other people's needs and wishes. They show a deficit in empathetic accuracy.'[16] The study's co-author, Dacher Keltner of the University of California, says, 'We are living in a period of historically high inequality [and] people in positions of power are not going to see [the inequality]. They are going to be blind to it and that has enormous implications for how we educate leaders, why they may not see what's obvious and why they may not even understand the suffering of the people below them.'[17]

As Daniel Goleman comments, this has potential repercussions in politics. He argues that the insistence by some Republicans in the United States House of Representatives on cutting financing for food stamps and impeding the implementation of Obamacare (which would allow patients, including those with pre-existing health conditions, to obtain and pay for insurance coverage) may stem in part from the empathy gap. With increasing numbers of 'safe' districts, elected representatives don't even have to encounter many voters from the rival party, much less to empathize with them. Goleman fears that besides the economic gap caused by inequality, a potentially worse gap is caused by 'the inability to see oneself in a less advantaged person's shoes'.[18] If we add to this the concentration of power that comes with increasing inequality of income and wealth by businesses lobbying and financing the political process, the potential for an empathy gap grows even worse. Adam Smith, who wrote so evocatively of empathy, would be dismayed at what is happening in his name (see p.18).

Unfortunately, if the evidence and argument marshalled by Thomas Piketty in *Capital in the Twenty-first Century* is correct, then the recent rise in inequality is not an exception but a consistent feature of capitalism throughout its history.[19] The period in which I was born and grew up, the mid-twentieth century, was a period of *reducing* inequality, a blip in the history of capitalism. This reduction came about because of the circumstances of war, the power of organized labour, and the need for higher taxation and because of other temporary factors.

Basically Piketty argues that the owners of capital, if left unhindered, will always take to themselves a higher percentage rate of return on their capital investment than the average rate of growth and thus that they will appropriate to themselves more and more of the wealth created by economic activity. The implications are bleak. High levels of inequality and low levels of social mobility will become the norm. The neoliberals are taking us back towards 'Dickensian' levels of inequality. Inherited wealth will dominate any wealth accumulated through a lifetime of work. Wealth will therefore concentrate to levels incompatible with democracy. Piketty's recommendations for dealing with this problem are not just to impose higher rates of taxation on higher levels of income but to impose what are essentially confiscatory rates of taxation on wealth.

What might we learn from Buddhism about inequality? In his time, the Buddha saw that governments had a major responsibility for establishing a fairer society. Two stories from the early collections of the Buddha's teachings illustrate this point. In the *Kūṭadanta Sutta*,[20] the story is told of a king, King Wide-Realm, whose land is wracked with discontent and crime to the extent that people are afraid to walk in the streets for fear of violence. The king goes to a wise man for advice. But the advice the king receives is not what he expects. The wise man tells the king that punishment is not the right path. On the contrary, it would increase the problem because the root causes would remain untouched, in this instance economic injustice and poverty. King Wide-Realm is advised to give food and seed corn to farmers, capital to traders, and food to those in government service. He is advised to redistribute income and wealth in the nation.

Earlier, in Chapter 3 on Community, I told the story from the *Cakkavatti Sīhanāda Sutta* of the wheel-turning monarch (see p. 51). Because of the king's neglect of the poor, there was a disastrous decline into lawlessness and violence. The Buddha identified the failure of the state to look after the needs of the poor as the cause of the decline. In my view, a Buddhist perspective would conclude that governments must ensure a more even distribution of income and wealth. It's also worth noting that in the two stories from the Kūṭadanta and Cakkavatti Sīhanāda discourses, kings turn to wise men for advice. These wise men bring a different perspective, one informed by wisdom and compassion. In the absence of fundamental political change, it's difficult to see how such empathetic voices can today reach through to the increasingly closed-off world of the rich and powerful.

What stance should Buddhists take on the issue of inequality? In my view, they have to accept that helping to reduce inequality must involve taking a political stance, one based on Buddhist values. This is because the rise in inequality over the past thirty years has come about through political actions associated with neoliberal capitalist ideology and not through impersonal economic forces.

In the Triratna Buddhist Community, an important principle is 'from each according to their ability to each according to their needs'. This means that in the businesses run by Triratna and in its retreat and urban centres, all those receiving financial support are treated equally according to this principle, whatever their position in the organization. Such a radical stance is unlikely to find widespread acceptance outside the Buddhist community, although its value as a living symbol of what might be achievable should not be underestimated. The view of Triratna's founder Sangharakshita is that in society as a whole, there is no doubt that 'property is inequitably distributed, in the sense of not being distributed in accordance with the genuine needs of people.' This means that in a democratic country, a more equitable distribution of property or wealth must be achieved through legislation, as well as by 'the encouragement of a deeper understanding and a more effective practice, on the grandest possible scale, of the principle of Generosity, or Sharing'.[21]

There are, I believe, two main elements in this Buddhist stance on legislation. First, in keeping with the Buddhist attitude of truthful communication and in the spirit of openness, all companies should publish every year figures showing the ratio of total compensation of their CEO to the median compensation of their employees (a measure of an average worker's pay).[22] Even such a simple measure as this would be a radical step forward. In the United States, the financial reforms of the Dodd-Frank Act contains just such a provision, but strong criticism and resistance from the business sector has already succeeded in delaying the implementation of this measure by four years. More recently, to howls of anguish from the business community, the European Commission in Brussels has proposed that 10,000 of the European Union's companies listed on stock exchanges should reveal their pay ratios and let shareholders vote on whether or not they are acceptable.[23]

Beyond the publication of pay ratios in companies is also the possibility of establishing national restrictions on allowable pay ratios. Recently voters in Switzerland rejected a referendum proposal that would have restricted the pay gap to a ratio of twelve to one (compared to an actual ratio in Switzerland of about 148 to 1).[24] Although it was rejected, it is noteworthy that 35 per cent of those voting were in favour of the proposition. Inevitably discussion about this gets bogged down in arguments about exactly what a realistic ratio would be, but it's noteworthy that in the 1970s the American management guru Peter Drucker recommended a maximum ratio of twenty to one. For me, that would be a reasonable starting point.

A second element in keeping with the approach of a Buddhist 'wheel-turning monarch' (for whose definition see p.51) and with the spirit of generosity and sharing would be to support the redistribution of income and wealth through a progressive system of taxation combined with supportive benefits for the less well off. Combining elements one and two would help to move countries with higher levels of inequality towards those such as Sweden and Japan with lower levels of inequality and much better levels of well-being. From a Buddhist perspective, this policy for reducing inequality would also significantly help to reduce consumerism. Wilkinson and Pickett write that consumerism stands as a marker of the dysfunctional power of status competition in social relations. Reducing inequality, they argue, is the key to reducing consumerism. Because of the pressures of consumerism, people in more unequal societies work longer hours, get more into debt, and are more likely to go bankrupt. Reducing inequality helps to reduce the pressure to consume and encourages more interest in leisure than in material consumption.[25]

Thomas Piketty's recommendations on a wealth tax also need to be considered. And as a former trade unionist, I do believe that Buddhists need to make themselves more aware of the role of trade unions and organized labour in ensuring a fairer distribution of income and wealth.

One final point needs to be made. Notwithstanding the Buddha's advice on looking after the needs of the poor, people sometimes have a serious wrong impression about Buddhism's position on poverty – that poverty is in some way noble or 'spiritual'. The opposite is actually the case: Buddhism sees poverty as a hindrance on the spiritual path. The Buddha firmly took the position that a lack of life's necessities in terms of food and shelter must be rectified in order for the necessary material foundation for spiritual progress to be in place. The Buddhist path is a middle way between asceticism and hedonism, emphasizing that basic material needs must be met before spiritual needs can begin to be fulfilled. It is recounted in the scriptures that the Buddha once made everyone wait for a teaching until a newly arrived poor man had been fed. This story is said to be the basis for the Buddha's phrase 'Hunger is the worst disease.'[26] And as we shall see in Chapter 11, one of the reasons that moved Dr Ambedkar, the leader of the Dalits in India, to convert to Buddhism was because it did not ennoble poverty.

10

The corporation

At the heart of the massive growth of capitalism over the past 300 years is the corporation. From beginnings in the eighteenth century, corporations have grown dramatically; and by 2012, eight of the top fifty economic entities in the world were not countries but corporations such as Royal Dutch Shell, Exxon Mobil, and Wal-Mart Stores. Altogether in 2012, almost two-thirds of the 175 largest economic entities in the world, as measured by GDP or revenue, were corporations.[1] To explain how this situation has arisen, I shall present a brief history of the corporation, its significance and its character, relying on Joel Bakan's book *The Corporation: The Pathological Pursuit of Profit and Power*.[2]

In Bakan's view, we have constructed over the past 300 years an incredibly efficient wealth-creating machine that is now out of control. The genius of the corporation as a form of business is its ability to tap into the financial power of huge numbers of people, originating with the formation of what were known first as joint-stock companies. They were banned in the UK in the seventeenth century because of business frauds, but the Industrial Revolution in the early nineteenth century and its demand for financial investment in large-scale enterprises such as railways and mining led to a change in the law to allow their establishment.

Before the mid-nineteenth century, broader public participation in stock markets was impeded. This was because until then, no matter how much or how little a person had invested in a company, he or she was personally liable, without limit, for the company's debts should it go bankrupt. If a company failed, investors could lose their home, savings, and all their property to the company's creditors. In 1856, this problem was removed in the UK with the introduction of limited liability into law, so that individual investors would be liable only to the extent of their investment in the company's stocks or shares. This is when joint-stock companies in effect became what we know as corporations.

A similar liberalization of this restriction spread across the US in the latter half of the nineteenth century. And at the turn of the century, new laws removed constraints on mergers and acquisitions. In the seven years between 1898 and 1904, a total of 1,800 corporations of all sizes shrank to 157 large corporations. In this way, Bakan writes, 'the US economy had been transformed from one in which individually owned enterprises competed freely among themselves into one dominated by a relatively few huge corporations, each owned by many shareholders. The era of corporate capitalism had begun.'[3]

Two other changes in the legal status of the corporation were significant in determining their future growth and behaviour. The first was the granting by the United States Supreme Court of a legal personality to the corporation in 1886, turning it into a 'person' separate from the real people who are its owners and managers. Corporations were thus empowered to conduct business in their own name, to obtain assets, hire workers, and pay taxes, and to go to court to assert their rights and defend their interests. A second important change occurred in 1916, when Henry Ford cancelled paying a shareholders' dividend in order to divert money to customers. When one of his shareholders objected, the court ruled in favour of the shareholder, commenting that Ford had no right to give shareholders' money away, however good his intentions. Corporations were from that point on legally required to act in the best interests of the profits of shareholders, not for the general good. For the Buddhist activist David Loy, these two changes pose a fundamental problem. Corporations are not people. Corporations cannot feel responsibilities that people feel. Loy writes:

> A corporation cannot laugh or cry. It cannot enjoy the world or suffer with it. It is unable to feel sorry for what it has done (it may occasionally apologise, but that is public relations). Most important, a corporation cannot love. Love is realizing our interconnectedness with others and living our concern for their well-being. Love is not an emotion but an engagement with others that includes responsibility for them, a responsibility that transcends our individual self-interest. Corporations cannot experience such love or act according to it. Any CEOs who try to subordinate their company's profitability to their love for the world will lose their position, for they are not fulfilling their primary – that is, financial – responsibility to its owners, the shareholders.[4]

Later in the twentieth century, corporations moved increasingly from a national to the international stage with the emergence of multinational or transnational corporations, helped by new international trade agreements that facilitated the activities of corporations across national borders. Originally dependent on special permission from national governments for their foundation and continued existence, corporations were now truly independent global economic actors.

More recently, the powers of corporations have been further increased in the US with the Supreme Court's Citizens United decision in 2010 to give corporations the right to spend unlimited sums of money on supporting election candidates. All major companies now have offices in Washington DC. On the international stage, negotiations between the European Union and the United States over a proposed transatlantic trade and investment partnership reveal how the powers of corporations are being further extended.[5] Within the proposed agreement is a mechanism called investor-state dispute settlement (ISDS). This provision allows companies to take governments to international arbitration panels, bypassing national courts, in order to seek compensation if they feel that their investment has been harmed by government action. These agreements already exist in other trade treaties.

Lately ISDS has been used by Vattenfall, a Swedish energy company, to sue the German government for €3.7 billion over the latter's decision to phase out nuclear power in the wake of the Fukushima nuclear disaster. Canada was forced to revoke its ban on the toxic fuel additive MMT under challenge from the US company Ethyl. The US tobacco giant Philip Morris is suing the Australian government for billions of dollars over its public health policy requiring that all cigarettes must now be sold in plain packaging.

Even before these recent developments, Joel Bakan concluded that 'The corporation's legally defined mandate is to pursue, relentlessly, and without exception, its own self-interest, regardless of the often harmful consequences it might cause to others.'[6] As mentioned previously in this chapter, David Loy tells us that a corporation cannot love. Bakan takes this further when he comments, 'The corporation is a pathological institution, a dangerous possessor of the great power it wields over people and societies.'[7] He warns that 'In a world where anything or anyone can be owned, manipulated, and exploited for profit, everything and everyone will eventually be.'[8]

In Chapter 6, on waste, I referred to Jacques Peretti's BBC television series on *The Men Who Made Us Spend*. In the first episode of three, Peretti explains how companies introduced enforced obsolescence into products to increase sales. In the second episode, he reveals how corporations use fear to manipulate people into buying more; and in the third one, he exposes how corporations use advertising targeted at children to increase sales. As using fear and targeting children to increase sales are examples of the pathological behaviour Bakan was alluding to, I shall summarize some of Peretti's reporting.[9]

In this episode, a psychologist says that people are motivated more by fear of losing something than by the prospect of gaining something. Advertising therefore can be designed precisely to create anxiety. An example of the success of this approach was the sales push for SUVs. Their design owes everything to arousing primal fears of harm to the family and to appearing to offer a more secure vehicle. Potential customers are led by emotion, not by reason, to believe that SUVs are safer even though the evidence is that they are less safe, because of their tendency to roll over.

Peretti illustrates too how fear of serious medical conditions is exaggerated in order to promote the sale of pharmaceutical products. Heightened fear increases pressure both on regulatory medical bodies to allow and on doctors to give increased prescriptions even when they are unwarranted. He mentions the sales of statins to deal with high levels of cholesterol as an example of over-diagnosis and over-drugging. The approach of corporations to selling and advertising is aptly summed up in the first episode of the television series *Mad Men* when the character Don Draper says, 'Advertising is based on one thing: happiness. And do you know what happiness is? . . . It's freedom from fear.'[10]

In the third episode Peretti reminds us that in the 1960s, very few products were directly advertised to children; parents were the target. But with the advent of colour television and with the promotion of films such as *Star Wars* and television programmes linked to the toy industry, corporations were able to get past adults and teachers and directly contact children. The selling of sugar-based products was helped in this way also, thus contributing to the obesity problem in children, to which I referred in Chapter 6. In effect, many children's television programmes became advertisements for products. In some cases, such as *Transformers*, the idea for the product was created first and then the story was written to fit in with the product. In this way, Peretti argues, children's programmes became less about imagination and creativity and more about advertising and selling. The attitude of the corporations was that children are consumers just as adults are consumers. Peretti argues further that advertisers set out to get adult consumers to behave more like children, inducing them to channel their inner child with the promotion of games with addictive and compulsive elements designed to give pleasure through dopamine hits in the brain.

Experience in these areas led to another development designed to increase sales. Corporations see the problem with adults to be that they hesitate and think too much at the point of sale. So adults need to be more like children; they must be made to give in to the urge for instant gratification. It was realized from brain studies that adults felt discomfort, equivalent to pain, when handing over cash to pay for something. The result is that when people pay with cash, they think more carefully about what they are buying. Credit cards remove, or at least defer, that discomfort. Other developments, such as 'one-click shopping', disconnect the customer's purchase even further from their discomfort. In 2013, PayPal launched a one-click shopping promotional campaign with the slogan 'Want it, Get it', designed for instant gratification.[11] (Unfortunately, I can attest to the effectiveness of the one-click shopping approach, as evidenced by the number of impulsive e-book purchases I make!) The success of these sales techniques leads Peretti to conclude that Britain is no longer a 'nation of shopkeepers' but a 'nation of shoppers', with manipulated desires that can never be satisfied.

In Chapter 1 of this book, I said Charles Darwin argued in *The Descent of Man* that the human species has succeeded because of characteristics such as sharing and compassion. 'Those communities', he wrote, 'which included the greatest number of the most sympathetic members would flourish best, and rear the greatest number of offspring.' Economics seems stuck, however, in the belief that narrow self-interest is all that matters. Meanwhile scientists working in the field of evolution are developing Darwin's insight with what they call 'multilevel selection theory' and are thinking about its implications for economics. David Sloan Wilson, a specialist in the field, explains it thus:

> The traits that maximise the advantage of an individual, relative to the members of its group, are typically different from the traits required for the group to function as a co-ordinated unit to achieve shared goals. What's good for me is not necessarily good for my family. What's good for my family is not necessarily good for my clan. What's good for my clan is not

necessarily good for my nation. What's good for my nation is not necessarily good for the global environment or economy. . .. *At every rung of this multi-tier hierarchy, self-serving behaviours threaten to undermine the performance of the higher-level unit. This potential for conflict, which I call 'The Iron Law of Multilevel Selection', lies at the heart of all theories of social evolution, and it poses a difficult problem for the 'invisible hand'. If special conditions are required for higher-level functional organisation to evolve, how can one seriously maintain the notion that unregulated self-interest inevitably contributes to the common good?*[12] (my italics)

The modern multinational corporation is a classic example of how unrestrained self-serving behaviour may undermine the potential for the evolution of higher-level organization. What's good for the corporation is not necessarily good for us, our families, our communities, our nations, and our global environment and economy.

From a Buddhist perspective, the corporation can similarly be seen as an example of stifled evolution. The Buddha teaches us that our view of the self as fixed, unchanging, and separate is false. By activating and cultivating our inherited tendencies for generosity and kindness, we can go beyond our equally inherited tendencies for selfishness. We can change or evolve into individuals who realize that they, like all phenomena, are empty of fixed self-nature and are interconnected with all things. The Buddha, the Enlightened human being, stands as a symbol of the potential of human evolution. He embodies all the qualities of a human being who has evolved beyond selfishness. But with the creation of the corporation, we have deliberately designed an 'individual' incapable of evolving beyond selfishness to loving-kindness. If we are to overcome the dangers of allowing such an 'individual' to continue to act in a purely selfish way, then we need to seek different models of governance for corporations and much more vigorous regulation of corporations at both national and international levels in order to control their behaviour.

11

Buddhist voices

During the twenty years of my involvement in Buddhism, I have been inspired by many people, especially those active in 'socially engaged Buddhism'.[1] But in this chapter I want to pick out four individuals, each of whom has given me something specific to consider about our socio-economic world. The first, Sangharakshita,[2] has been a practitioner and teacher of Buddhism since the Second World War. He is also the founder of the Triratna Buddhist Order, of which I am a member, and of the Triratna Buddhist Community. The second, Dr Bhimrao Ramji Ambedkar, was a member of the first government of independent India; and in the 1950s, he instigated a mass conversion movement of Dalits to Buddhism that continues today. The third, David Loy, is a Buddhist scholar and practitioner in the Zen tradition. The fourth, Bhikkhu Bodhi, is one of the best-known translators of the Pali canon of the Buddha's teachings.

Sangharakshita

In early summer 1994, I had just discovered meditation and Buddhism. I was spending lots of time travelling the motorways of England, to get to fire stations where I would interview firefighters as part of a research project for the Fire Brigades

Union. Often, when I arrived at my destination, I would sit in the car park reluctant to get out of the car. This wasn't because of the research, which I enjoyed, but because I was listening to cassette tapes of talks by Sangharakshita.

Among the many fine talks I listened to, what really caught my attention were those on what Sangharakshita called 'the new society' and, separately, on evolution. For the previous twenty-five years, I had read extensively about the history of rebellions and their associated visions of how the world might be made better. As I was fascinated too by the idea of communal living, which was very alive in the west in the 1960s and early 1970s, it's not surprising that Sangharakshita's 'new society' caught my attention. My interest in his talks on evolution derived from one of my favourite pastimes, reading collections of Stephen Jay Gould's wonderful essays on evolution for *Natural History* magazine. Although it wasn't obvious to me then, my interest in evolution, and what was stimulated by Stephen Jay Gould and Sangharakshita, would much later lead to an exploration of an evolutionary perspective on the problem of the corporation in modern capitalism, about which I wrote in the previous chapter. Now I wish to focus on Sangharakshita's 'new society'.

Partly inspired by Dr Ambedkar, one of Sangharakshita's distinctive contributions to modern Buddhism is to see the revolutionary potential of Buddhism in bringing about a 'new society'. Sangharakshita had direct contact in India with Ambedkar and with his followers after his death. This contact opened his eyes to the social and economic potential of Buddhism. Most Dalits lived in extreme poverty, deprived of economic opportunity by their caste status. From their experience, Sangharakshita understood that it was not possible to transform individual lives without a corresponding transformation of the collective life of society. Indeed, what he saw in India was not just a revival of Buddhism but a tremendous positive upheaval brought about in a society by spiritual means. This led him to conclude that a sufficiently alert and inspired group of dedicated Buddhist practitioners working together could exert a substantial influence on whole societies, especially when those societies were in a state of flux and looking for some kind of vision or blueprint for the future. This was the origin of the idea of the 'new society', the practical application of which Sangharakshita sought to encourage in the Triratna Buddhist Community in the UK and in other places around the world. He argued that the nucleus of a new society is the creation of situations in which people live and work together on the basis of Buddhism. From this nucleus, Buddhist community members can go out and transform the larger society around them.

The three principal functions of these 'new societies in miniature', these nuclei, are to support those who are already committed to Buddhism, to exemplify what wider society could become, and to provide points of contact for those who are exploring the Buddhist life.

First, mutual support for those who are already committed to Buddhism is necessary because the work of creating a new society requires a great deal of energy and strength. Few have that strength on their own. They need to live with, to be in regular contact with, or even to work with people who share the same aspiration and who are struggling to realize the same ideals in their life. They also need the support of instruction and guidance from others in order to learn how to apply Buddhism to the concrete realities of daily life. The task of social transformation requires as well as a vast amount of energy a wide range of talents, skills, and experience. It can be carried out on a significant scale only when people cooperate together, pooling their efforts and their abilities through creative teamwork. Such a collective basis is also an important support for those individual Buddhists who wish to become more directly involved in political issues. Without immersion in the nucleus of a new society, political activity is likely to take people over; and as has happened to so many who started out with genuine social and political aspirations, ideals can easily be submerged in the struggle for power. The foundation of active involvement in a spiritual community is indispensable if people are to work effectively to transform society while maintaining their high intention.

Second, the nucleus of a new society can provide an example of what the whole of society could be. Many people have been struck by their experience of visiting an urban Buddhist centre or retreat centre, feeling something different and special in the atmosphere, in the way that people relate with one another, and in the welcome they receive. Such exemplification can have a more subtle dimension. Something is asserted, something is kept alive that affects everyone, however unconsciously. Because such nuclei exist, values are kept alive; and when the circumstances are ripe, they can have a far wider and more effective influence.

A third function of the nucleus of the 'new society' is to provide a point of contact for those who are exploring the Buddhist life. It offers opportunities for contact to those who cannot or do not want to live or to work full-time with Buddhist brothers and sisters. Through Buddhist classes, retreats, festivals, and other events and activities, people can get the support, guidance, and inspiration that will help them to maintain their values. They can stay for a while in a spiritual oasis where they can refresh themselves. And whenever they are ready, they can move closer to the heart of that 'new society' if they want to.

From my own experience, I know that in the Triratna Community much has been tried and done to create the basis of a 'new society'. This includes residential communities, where people can live together in the Dharma and in some working situations and businesses, which give remarkable opportunities for sharing a Buddhist life. There is, for instance, a team-based right livelihood business at Windhorse:Evolution, briefly outlined in Chapter 4. This Buddhist company has people working in it from all over the world and it has a radically different approach to financial remuneration. Its employees receive financial support dependent upon their needs, not upon a hierarchical payment system. These work and remuneration principles apply also at urban centres and retreat centres. In the retreat centre where I lived and worked for six years, there were up to eighteen of us in the community, each performing his own role and having varying levels of practical and spiritual responsibility but all receiving the same level of financial support.

Fulfilling the ideal of the 'new society' has not always been easy. For example, it has been more difficult since the 1990s for the Triratna Buddhist Community to sustain a consistent level of interest in participating in right livelihood businesses and in communities. The reasons for this are not clear, but it's possible that the rising pressures of a consumerist society in the 1990s and 2000s have had an effect on the Buddhist community. Getting the balance right between the ties of affinity and the rules of necessity in intentional communities is not easy. (See chapter 3 for an explanation of affinity and necessity). Perhaps there has been an underestimation of the influence on Buddhist practitioners of the pervasive social and economic environment and a tendency to neglect the need to engage outwardly with society. Sangharakshita himself warned of the danger of ignoring the social dimension:

Inasmuch as the world acts upon you, it is in your interest that it does so in a helpful rather than in a harmful way. That means you have an interest in the particular way in which 'worldly' affairs are organized or run. If you are living in an 'unideal' community or state, it is going to have an unfortunate effect on you. You therefore have an interest in the creation of an ideal state or community.[3]

Notwithstanding these difficulties, Sangharakshita's vision of a 'new society' has, in my view, provided much in the way of practical examples of Buddhist alternatives, and it may yet, with further experimentation, provide more.

To conclude this discussion of Sangharakshita, I would like to touch briefly on the issue of individuality and individualism.[4] He sees this distinction as crucial when considering the sangha, the spiritual community. For Sangharakshita, individuality can be seen as the process by which individuals commit themselves to grow and change. Individualism occurs when a person is absorbed by self-concern. Individuality naturally turns a person in the direction of meaningful connection with others, to help foster each other's creative growth and development, as can happen in the best sangha. Just as Rilke (early twentieth-century poet) declared that the highest task of a bond between two people is that each should stand guard over the solitude of the other,[5] so Sangharakshita identifies as one of the characteristics of individuals that they encourage others to be individual in their own way. Buddhists can thereby encourage each other to become true individuals. Individualism, rooted in selfishness, leads to the materialistic atomization of consumer society, as we see in the modern neoliberal capitalist world. To cultivate sangha, to cultivate the nucleus of a 'new society' is to help cultivate individuality and to counter individualism. To foster spiritual community is to foster freedom of thought and the freedom to grow.

Dr Bhimrao Ramji Ambedkar

In 1956, the great Indian statesman and Buddhist leader Dr Bhimrao Ramji Ambedkar,[6] began a social revolution in India affecting the lives of millions of people known as Dalits. ('Dalit' is a designation for a group of people traditionally regarded in India as untouchable.) In Ambedkar's time, Dalits experienced discrimination and prejudice through the Hindu caste system, and this persists in India today. After becoming a Buddhist himself, he led hundreds of thousands of his followers to convert to Buddhism. Although he died very soon after the initial conversions, the process continues today with new conversions to Buddhism. When the Dalits converted to Buddhism, they gained a new self-confidence and began to assert themselves in society. The effects of this can be seen in Indian census statistics. These show the much greater improvement in social and economic status of those who became Buddhists compared to similar castes in which very few conversions took place.

Dr Ambedkar saw Buddhism as the best way to bring about something like an ideal society. That society could be defined in terms of liberty, equality, and fraternity, which for him were deep spiritual principles, derived not from the French Revolution but from the Buddha. Liberty means that people are free to live the kind of life they consider best – as long as they do not harm or infringe the liberty of others. Equality means that everybody has broadly the same opportunities to make the most of their life. Fraternity means an attitude of respect and reverence of each citizen for every other. This attitude he equates with democracy itself. For Ambedkar, democracy is not merely a means of choosing a government. It is a state of mind, a fraternal attitude that is ultimately one of *mettā*, loving-kindness, which expresses itself in moral action, morality being *mettā* in action. He taught that society should be founded on ethical principles, which themselves are the expression of respect, reverence, and even loving-kindness.

Ambedkar struggled for many years to overcome the terrible historical injustice of untouchability, to which he himself had been subjected simply by his birth. Although born into a caste then considered untouchable, he was fortunate, through the philanthropy of two reformist maharajas, to get an excellent education in the west, and he returned to a senior post in the government of one of those princes. He devoted himself selflessly to freeing his people from the oppressions of caste by every means at his disposal: journalism, social agitation, union and labour organizing, legal action, political activism, and later his position in government – first in the Viceroy's Council and then in the first cabinet of independent India, in which he served as law minister. He was asked by Pandit Nehru, the first Indian prime minister, to chair the committee that oversaw the drawing up of the Constitution of the Republic of India. It is reported that he did the lion's share of the work himself.

Ambedkar's approach can be summed up in his political and social slogan: 'Educate, Agitate, Organize'. Tackle ignorance by getting an education for yourselves and your children. Agitate, in the sense of struggle actively for a better life through economic, social, political, and legal action. And organize yourselves so that you are united and can work together to get what you need and what you deserve as human beings.

Even with all his personal success, he knew that not enough had been done: caste discrimination persisted throughout India, much as it always had, and hundreds of millions of people suffered economically and socially under its oppressions. Frustrated by resistance in Parliament and by a lack of government support for his attempts to bring full equality to women by reforming Hindu family law, he finally became disillusioned with the political process as the sole means of eradicating social injustice. He realized that the problem lay much deeper than laws and constitutions could reach.

Dr Ambedkar came to understand that the roots of caste lay in the mind itself: 'Caste is a notion, a state of mind.' That notion was embedded in the whole Hindu mindset, entwined with its powerful and superstitious beliefs in a social destiny ordained by the gods. But, he realized, this insight also suggested the solution: 'What mind creates, mind can undo.' As early as 1936, he had decided that he would leave Hinduism and search for another religion, both for himself and for his people. He had definite criteria for his search: a new religion must enshrine the principles of liberty, equality, and fraternity and utterly reject caste in all its forms. It must also be compatible with reason and science, not enjoining blind belief in supernatural agencies that control human fate. And it should not justify poverty. Ambedkar was drawn to the Buddha and to his teaching for its spiritual power and emphasis on social morality; and after a lengthy exploration of other major world religions, he concluded that this ancient Indian religion was the best one for his people, indeed for all humanity. On 14 October 1956, he committed himself to the central ideals of Buddhism – in traditional terms he 'went for refuge' to the Buddha, the Dharma, and Sangha – and then, in the same ceremony, he inducted some 400,000 of his followers into Buddhism.

For Ambedkar, real reform comes about only from a change in attitude and outlook on the part of many people. It is the Dharma that offers the firmest basis for that change of heart – a change that would express itself in a transformed society that is truly equal, just, and free and underlain by a powerful sense of shared citizenship, even by respect and love among all citizens. He considered this to be true not just for the oppressed castes from which he himself came or even for all Indians. The Dharma was the surest basis for a truly just economy and society everywhere.

I mentioned earlier that contact with Dr Ambedkar had been one of the inspirations behind Sangharakshita's idea of the 'new society'. This contact continues today with the Triratna Buddhist Community's activities in India, particularly in its economic, social, and cultural work with the Dalits and others under the auspices of the Triratna Bauddha Mahasangha (TBM). More than 600 Indians are members of the Triratna Buddhist Order (about a third of the worldwide total).

With money mainly raised by Triratna Buddhist Community members in the UK, the Karuna Trust is able to fund between 40 and 50 projects across 12 states in India, benefiting more than 50,000 people each year. These projects are run by local community groups, with the dual aims of helping some of South Asia's poorest people to lead more meaningful and dignified lives, and of helping to break down the caste and religious barriers that impede social justice and economic development.

Nagaloka, the Nagarjuna Training Institute, is the TBM's flagship educational project, the largest of its centres. The institute has a fifteen-acre campus on the outskirts of Nagpur, where it offers a ten-month leadership training programme in basic Buddhism and social action for young Dalits. More than 500 young people from many Indian states have graduated from the programme. Most of these students have gone back to their caste-based villages, where life is still marked by discrimination and violence, to offer Dharma teachings and to work for campaigns against social and economic oppression.

Hozan Alan Senauke of the Berkeley Zen Center, author of *The Bodhisattva's Embrace: Dispatches From Engaged Buddhism's Front Lines*, describes his visit to Nagaloka:

> I was inspired by the students at Nagaloka. Meeting them over several days, their stories touched me. Their way-seeking minds glow with the spirit of inquiry. Despite having been involved with engaged Buddhism for twenty years, nowhere else have I met young people with their kind of intuitive grasp of Buddhist practice and social action arising together. Nowhere else have I had deeper discussion that never slipped into abstraction, but focused on the conditions of oppression these students know only too well. Nowhere else have I encountered anything like their determination to remake the world in peace. My heart is with them.[7]

David Loy

My first contact with David Loy was in 2003 when I read *A Buddhist History of the West*, a book that examines how greed, hatred, and delusion have conditioned our history.[8] I was excited by its scale and perspective. Central to the book is the notion of 'lack'.

Buddhism teaches that there is no fixed, separate self and that our sense of self is a construct, an ever-changing process. The self does not exist in its own right. Without a separate reality of its own and any fixed, permanent, or stable ground, the self is haunted by a 'sense of lack', 'lack' for short. Because of our inability to recognize and accept that the self is empty of a separate, fixed existence, we close up and experience a deep-rooted unease or unsatisfactoriness, called *dukkha* or suffering, that we can never quite resolve. One of the ways by which we try to cover up this reality manifests in a consumerism that promises but can never deliver fulfilment. We try to build a sense of identity by consuming. If instead we were to explore this lack of a separate, fixed existence, and even to embrace it, we would discover a tremendous source of creativity and positivity.

Later, I read more of David Loy's books. Loy is also a social activist. He participates in the Buddhist Peace Fellowship and the International Network of Engaged Buddhists and writes blogs and newspaper articles. He regularly appears on Facebook, raising issues and urging responses. His book *Money, Sex, War, Karma: Notes for a Buddhist Revolution* brings together some of his most important thinking on socio-economic topics. One of its distinctive contributions is his focus on the institutionalization of the three poisons of greed, hatred, and delusion in our modern economy,[9] specifically his analysis of greed and the role of the corporation. Buddhism sees greed, hatred, and delusion as root poisons, inherent in the individual human being, but poisons that can be overcome by a path of practice laid down by the Buddha that leads to Enlightenment. On this path, greed is transformed into its opposite generosity, hatred into its opposite loving-kindness, and delusion into wisdom. In Loy's view, the three poisons also operate collectively: our economic system institutionalizes greed, militarism institutionalizes hatred, and our corporate media institutionalize delusion.

The institutionalization of greed has two axioms: corporations are never profitable enough and people never consume enough. The drive for profits means that people must be conditioned into finding meaning in life through more and more buying and consuming. Considering the stock market, Loy points out that investors demand increased earnings through dividends and higher share prices. Executives of companies therefore respond by a constant search for higher profits and growth; their emphasis is on the short run. With the globalization of corporate capitalism, the drive for immediate profitability, higher share prices, and growth is increasingly the engine of the world economy. Everything else, including the environment and quality of life, is subordinate to this anonymous demand for profits and growth. This demand is anonymous because the economic system has attained a life of its own, and we all participate in it as workers, employers, consumers, investors, and pensioners, with a very diffuse sense of moral responsibility. Thus is greed thoroughly institutionalized.

When reflecting on Occupy Wall Street,[10] Loy remarks that Wall Street is the most concentrated and visible part of a much larger nightmare: the collective delusion that there is no alternative to our present economic system. This delusion is reinforced by the ever-increasing closeness of the economic and political spheres in the US. It has been made worse, as described in Chapter 10, by the Supreme Court's Citizens United decision in 2010 to remove limits on corporate spending to influence elections. Loy describes how the elites of the economic and political spheres now move easily from CEO of a corporation to cabinet position and vice versa, managing this comfortably because they share the same belief in unrestrained economic growth. From a Buddhist perspective, this integrated system is incompatible with Buddhist teaching because it encourages greed and delusion, the root causes of our *dukkha*. At the heart of this system is the corporation. To counter the power of corporations, Loy supports groups such as the

Network of Spiritual Progressives, who call for an environmental and social responsibility amendment to the US Constitution that would compulsorily require corporate charters to be rewritten and include social and ecological responsibility.

But by itself, Loy argues, this won't be enough. In Buddhist terms the problem isn't only greed, it's also delusion. He argues that 'realising the nature of these three institutionalised poisons is just as important as any personal realisation we might have as a result of spiritual practice.'[11] Loy also points out that Buddhists have much to learn from Occupy Wall Street. It's not enough for Buddhists to focus just on waking from their own individual dream. They need to join with others and awaken from a collective nightmare. He rhetorically asks, 'Is it time to bring our spiritual practice out into the streets?'[12]

Bhikkhu Bodhi[13]

For many years, I have admired Bhikkhu Bodhi for his tireless dedication to the rigorous translation and elucidation of the meaning of the works of the Pali canon. I have become aware more recently that he has another side. As a student in the 1960s, he was a political activist. But after becoming more interested in working on himself, he became a Buddhist and a monk: he believed this was a better way to help the world in the long run. Apart from five years back in the US, Bhikkhu Bodhi spent the years from 1972 to 2002 in Sri Lanka as a monk. He became one of the top translators of the Pali canon and a respected Dharma teacher. In 1984, he became the editor of the Buddhist Publication Society and in 1988, he became its president.

After a long separation from the outside world, and with the encouragement of his teacher in Sri Lanka, he was gradually drawn back into thinking and writing about world events. As he puts it, 'The social progressive that had gone into deep hibernation decades earlier . . . was starting to re-awaken.' But it was his return to the US in 2002 that led him to fully re-engage with global events from a progressive perspective, and he was also able to closely observe how Buddhism was being assimilated there.

He was troubled by what he saw as complacent and self-absorbed attitudes among many American Buddhists, attitudes that were disconnected from the deepening economic, social, and ecological crises in the world. It seemed to him that many middle class American Buddhists understood suffering mostly in terms of their own individual problems – 'the ennui of material prosperity, the stress of unfulfilling relationships, discontent with their personal foibles'. Outside the group of Engaged Buddhists, many Buddhists seemed barely aware of the misery that overwhelmed some ninety per cent of the world's population because of poverty, tyrannical regimes, social oppression, militarism, and economic globalization. He was critical of the way that Buddhist practice was narrowly understood in terms of one's personal meditation, which appeared to serve a largely therapeutic function. Buddhism, he thought, was being taken up as a path to personal fulfilment rather than as a means of tackling the deepest roots of suffering both for oneself and for others.

These concerns led Bhikkhu Bodhi, with the help of some of his students and Buddhist friends, to found Buddhist Global Relief, whose primary mission is to combat chronic hunger and malnutrition. It has more than fifty hunger-relief projects in countries such as Cambodia, Vietnam, Sri Lanka, India, Kenya, Niger, South Africa, Haiti, and the United States.

His experience has also led Bhikkhu Bodhi to question some aspects of his understanding of Buddhism. In his view, Buddhism, like many traditional forms of contemplative spirituality, is based on the perception of a split between involvement in the world and an exalted sphere of reality transcendent to the world. The spiritual quest aims to ascend from a life normally dominated by contingency, impermanence, illusion, distress and anxiety, and sin or defilement to a spiritual realm in which all these imperfections have finally been overcome. This is a state of Enlightenment, which can be described as 'unconditioned, stable, pure, blissful and serene, a state from which we can never fall back into the swamp of unenlightened living'. He now believes that this perspective on the human condition and its spiritual potential is necessary but incomplete. It is necessary because it sharply illuminates the divide between the deluded condition of our everyday lives and the state of ultimate perfection (Enlightenment) that is ever available to us. It is incomplete because it drives a wedge between the spiritual and mundane spheres. As a result, we may feel compelled either to choose one above the other or 'to settle for an uneasy tension between the ideal and actual'.

Bhikkhu Bodhi now identifies three major domains of human life. One he calls the transcendent domain, 'which is the sphere of aspiration for classical contemplative spirituality'. The second he calls the social domain, which 'includes our interpersonal relations as well as our political, social, and economic institutions'. And the third he calls the natural domain, which includes our physical bodies, other sentient beings, and the natural environment. He concludes that a spirituality that values the transcendent domain over the social and natural domains or sees the two latter as at best stepping stones to realization, is not enough in our current situation; and it may even contribute to putting our future at risk. The pursuits of contemplative spirituality are undertaken by 'spiritual virtuosos', the contemplatives, mystics, and yogis who aspire to transcend the world and express their compassion simply by guiding others to the heights they themselves have reached. At the same time, humanity's future is left solely in the hands of politicians, CEOs of corporations, and technical experts, who are often driven by greed and a narrow belief in the value of technology. This division, he believes, also opens the doors of our communal institutions to religious dogmatists and fundamentalists.

Instead of this division of the three domains of human life, Bhikkhu Bodhi imagines a future that requires the creation of an integral type of spirituality that can bridge them. Until now, he says, the spiritual quest has primarily moved along an ascending track 'from the conditioned to the unconditioned' and 'from mortality to the deathless'. What is required today is 'to complement the ascending spiritual movement with a descending movement, a gesture of love and grace flowing down from the heights of realization into the valleys of our ordinary lives'.

Although both the ascending and descending movements are necessary, Bhikkhu Bodhi's view is that the scale of problems facing humanity now forces us to give special attention to the descending movement. Under the influence of love, this requires that in the social domain we must strive for government that embodies justice, equity, and compassion. (Interestingly Sangharakshita writes about a similar use of what he describes as the 'power mode' subordinated to the 'love mode' in order for government to redistribute income.[14]) Social and economic policies must be grounded in the conviction that all human beings are entitled to live in peace, with sufficient access to food, water, medical care, and housing and with opportunities to fulfil their potential. In the natural domain, Bhikkhu Bodhi urges us to look at the universe with wonder, awe, and reverence, to treat all other living beings with care and kindness, and to ensure that nature's capacity for self-regeneration is preserved. He believes that there is much in the teachings of the Buddha – on ethics, communal harmony, and the duties of governments and kings – that can assist in this project. As he says, the Buddha taught the Dharma on the basis of a far-reaching vision that pierced the depths of suffering in both its personal *and* collective dimensions.

Although Bhikkhu Bodhi warns that we can expect stiff resistance from those who profit by preserving and extending the status quo, he does believe that Buddhists can make a difference. To do so, he urges the creation of Buddhist communities, both locally and globally, that express wisdom, care, and compassion.

When I reflect on what I have learned from these four individuals, what stands out most is how they all base their approach to changing the world upon a deep study and appreciation of the teachings of the Buddha. Sangharakshita reminds me that it's very difficult to transform individual lives without a transformation of the collective life of society and also that the sangha, the Buddhist community, has a key role to play in bringing about this transformation. Dr Ambedkar's life is a model of vigorous political activity in the pursuit of a differently defined liberty, equality, and fraternity. This is combined with a realization that a change in people's consciousness is necessary for fundamental social and economic change to take root. David Loy is an example of taking traditional Buddhist concepts and creatively applying them to modern socio-economic problems and also of unstintingly giving himself to a life of campaigning in support of the Dharma and fundamental economic change. Bhikkhu Bodhi shows that it is never too late for those Buddhists who, like me, became adults in the 1960s to rediscover their radical roots and rethink their approach to Buddhism and social change.

12

Concluding thoughts

Writing in 1904, Winston Churchill predicted the emergence of a new moral ethos in which 'nothing is esteemed except money, nothing accounted except a bank account' and 'quality, education, civic distinction, public virtue are valued less and less'. In future, rich men would greet their day with the prayer 'Give us cash in our time, O Lord.'[1] Churchill could have been describing neoliberal capitalism.

In 1930, the great economist John Maynard Keynes looked ahead 100 years to a life beyond capitalism. In an essay entitled 'Economic Possibilities for our Grandchildren', he concluded that by 2030, the struggle to provide all human beings with decent shelter and the other necessities of life would be over. He predicted:

> When the accumulation of wealth is no longer of high
> social importance, there will be great changes in the code
> of morals. We shall be able to rid ourselves of many of
> the pseudo-moral principles which have hag-ridden
> us for two hundred years, by which we have exalted
> some of the most distasteful of human qualities into the
> position of the highest virtues. We shall be able to afford
> to dare to assess the money motive at its true value.

The love of money . . . will be recognized for what it is;
a somewhat disgusting morbidity, one of those semi-
criminal, semi-pathological propensities which one hands
over with a shudder to the specialists in mental disease.

He went on: 'All kinds of social customs and economic practices,
affecting the distribution of wealth and of economic rewards
and penalties, which we now maintain at all costs, however
distasteful and unjust they may be in themselves, because they are
tremendously useful in promoting the accumulation of capital,
we shall then be free, at last, to discard.'[2]

Keynes believed a time would come when the 'pseudo-moral
principles' of capitalism and the unjust inequalities of income
and wealth that consequently arise could be got rid of. He looked
forward to the day when 'we shall honour those who can teach us
how to pluck the hour and the day virtuously and well.'[3] However,
I believe there to be a flaw in Keynes' thinking. He rightly saw
the provision for everybody in the world of the basic needs for
a nourishing life – clean water, food, clothing, and shelter – as
the key economic problem. But once this economic problem was
solved, he thought, the economy would simply wither away as
the dominant force in our lives.

For Keynes, social attitudes and moral values reflect the
needs and requirements of the economic base. As the economist
Stephen Marglin of Harvard University puts it, Keynes thought
that 'as long as the base is geared toward the accumulation
of capital, the cultural superstructure conforms.'[4] He therefore
believed that once the need for capital accumulation was
removed, cultural values would naturally change. He assumed
that once basic needs are met, greed will disappear and envy
will give way to emulation. On this Keynes was wrong. Marglin

identifies the problem: 'Instead of trying to keep up with the Joneses in the consumption of BMWs and Jacuzzis, we will perhaps try to match Mr. Jones in meditation and Mrs. Jones in awareness of the beauty of the world around us. How the requisite psychological transformation and, dare I say it, spiritual transformation might take place is not even raised as a question, much less answered.'[5]

Change will not happen by itself. From Marglin's perspective, Keynes did not take sufficient account of the 'culture of modernity'. Just as a Buddhist sees consuming more and more things as a vain attempt to construct and reinforce a sense of the self, so Marglin sees individualism and the purchase of goods and services in the market as a misconceived means of solving existential problems. And just as a Buddhist does not believe selfishness to be a fixed and unchangeable part of our evolutionary inheritance, so Marglin does not believe that unlimited wants are 'deeply embedded in human nature, valid for all people at all times'.[6] But these negative values and attitudes are becoming more and more deeply ingrained in our cultural upbringing. It's not the case, as Keynes seemed to suggest, that we must wait until the job of capitalism is done, until we have 'enough', before these values can change. If we do that, then they will never change. As Marglin puts it, *'Rather, we shall have enough when we rethink the premises of modernity* (my italics).'[7] This requires us to start now in promoting different values. Culture needs to push back against the market. Many different voices, both Buddhist and non-Buddhist, are already speaking out on this – I have given examples in this book. I would add to them an observation by one of my favourite poets, Dana Gioia (whose poem on shopping is at the end of this chapter). He says:

The marketplace does only one thing – it puts a price on everything. The role of culture, however, must go beyond economics. It is not focused on the price of things, but on their value. And, above all, culture should tell us what is beyond price, including what does not belong in the marketplace. A culture should also provide some cogent view of the good life beyond mass accumulation. In this respect, our culture is failing us.[8]

What might a Buddhist view of the good life beyond mass accumulation look like? When I try to envisage the kind of economic organization of society I would like to see, my mind turns first to Dr Ambedkar and his three principles of liberty, equality, and fraternity. In the Chapter 11, on Buddhist voices, this is what I wrote about them:

> *Liberty* means that people are free to live the kind of life they consider best – so long as they do not harm or infringe the liberty of others. *Equality* means that everybody has broadly the same opportunities to make the most of their life. *Fraternity* means an attitude of respect and reverence of each citizen for every other. This attitude he equates with democracy itself. For Ambedkar democracy is not merely a means of choosing a government, but is a state of mind, a fraternal attitude that is ultimately one of *mettā* or loving-kindness that expresses itself in moral action – morality being *mettā* in action. Ambedkar taught that society should be founded on ethical principles, which themselves are the expression of respect, reverence, and even of *mettā*, of love.

Concluding thoughts

Having explored the behaviour and the effects of neoliberal capitalism in different aspects of our lives, I hope you agree that our current economic system does not match up to Ambedkar's criteria. If you think I am too harsh in my judgement, listen to these words of Mark Carney, Governor of the Bank of England, speaking in May 2014:

> Just as any revolution eats its children, unchecked market fundamentalism can devour the social capital essential for the long-term dynamism of capitalism itself . . . All ideologies are prone to extremes. Capitalism loses its sense of moderation when the belief in the power of the market enters the realm of faith. In the decades prior to the crisis [of 2008] such radicalism came to dominate economic ideas and became a pattern of social behaviour.[9]

By 'social capital' Carney means the shared values and beliefs in a society that encourage individuals to take responsibility for themselves and their family and to trust each other and work together to offer mutual support. This is what market fundamentalism is destroying. More than that, Carney points to evidence that equality of opportunity is also falling, particularly in the US, 'undercutting the sense of fairness at the heart of American society'. Assessing the effects of inequality of income and opportunity and echoing Thomas Piketty's thoughts on inequality of wealth and opportunity, he concludes, 'Now is the time to be famous or fortunate.'[10]

But if our current form of neoliberal capitalism fails the test of Ambedkar's three principles, so does its opposite extreme, communism, with its oppressive, anti-democratic nature and its stifling of dynamism and creativity. If our economic system is to evolve, it needs to find a middle ground between the two extremes of market fundamentalism and state totalitarianism. It needs to find a middle way between unfettered competition and over-regulation.

Help in finding this middle way may come from evolutionary science. Recently the Evolution Institute launched a long-term research project on rethinking economics, designed to help create a new set of navigational tools for steering an intelligent middle course between market fundamentalism and state totalitarianism. I hope that the study of genetic, psychological, and cultural evolution will help in the exploration of that middle ground for economics.[11] I am not an evolutionary specialist, but this much already seems clear to me. In Chapter 2, I described how leading neoliberal figures in economics have been influenced by Ayn Rand. She believed that altruism is some kind of evolutionary throwback to the past and that the pursuit of self-interest to the exclusion of concern for others is what matters for our economic future. In Chapter 10, on the corporation, I reported on how evolutionary science is showing that, on the contrary, unrestrained self-serving behaviour undermines the potential for the evolution of higher-level organization and the full flowering of human capabilities. As Charles Darwin pointed out in *The Descent of Man*, the human species has succeeded because of characteristics such as sharing and compassion. It is market fundamentalists who are the evolutionary throwbacks, not altruists.

I am not sure whether mainstream economics will be flexible enough to engage with new perspectives such as that being explored by the Evolution Institute, but I am sure Buddhist values will be essential in finding a middle ground for economics. How Buddhists can make their voices heard and affect this process I shall return to shortly. But a foundation for helping to develop that middle ground already exists in economic life in the form of cooperatives and 'the commons'. 'The commons' refers to the cultural and natural resources accessible to all members of a society, including natural materials such as air, water, and a habitable earth. (See below on Elinor Ostrom, 'defender of the commons'.)

There are different forms of business ownership, including single-owner companies and family-owned businesses, partnerships, corporations owned by their shareholders and cooperatives owned by their members. Cooperative members can be customers or employees or both. They own and govern their businesses collectively, sharing benefits between them instead of, in the corporate model, all the profits going to shareholders. Cooperatives are often value-based, with an emphasis on solidarity and responsibility to their members and the local community. Although, like all businesses, they are subject to economic and organizational difficulties, they have withstood well the worst of the recession since 2008. For example, Mondragon in Spain, the world's oldest cooperative, helped to keep the rate of unemployment in the province of Guipuzcoa, where it is based, at half the level for Spain as a whole.[12] Cooperatives exist in many countries and in many sectors of the world economy, among them agriculture and forestry, banking and credit unions, retail, insurance, industrial and craft production, housing, and others.

The scale of cooperatives' economic activity and worldwide membership is impressive. The cooperative sector employs more people than all the mutinationals and their subsidiaries combined.[13] Compared to 328 million private shareholders in the world, there are 1 billion members of cooperatives.[14] Cooperatives touch the lives of many more people than does share ownership. In the heartland of capitalism, the US, some 130 million Americans are members of cooperatives and credit unions. Examples of economic self-determination exist in cities such as Cleveland, where in the struggling Glenville neighbourhood a complex of worker-owned cooperatives sell goods and services to local hospitals, providing local jobs.[15]

Elinor Ostrom, who died in 2012, is the only woman ever to be awarded the Nobel prize for economics. Her obituary in *The Economist* ran under the headline 'Elinor Ostrom, defender of the commons'.[16] What she brought to the world of economics was common sense about common resources. She thought that if left to themselves, people would work out ways of surviving and getting along. She firmly believed that although the world's arable land, forests, and fresh water are finite resources, it is possible to share them without depleting them. She had studied forests in Nepal, irrigation systems in Spain, mountain villages in Switzerland and Japan, and fisheries in Maine and Indonesia. She concluded that women and men tend to make sensible rules for sharing and stewarding common resources provided that they are able to develop a system of caring for the commons from the bottom up and in accord with their cultural norms and that they do not have to put up with solutions imposed from above. In this way, people and communities can often manage common resources as well as or better than markets, companies, or the state.

Ostrom's work reflects the spirit of E.F. Schumacher's *Small is Beautiful* (Chapter 4) and Frederique Apffel-Marglin's emphasis on ritual caring for the land in the native villages of the Peruvian Andes (Chapter 5). It also captures something of the spirit of the initiatives undertaken in Dalit communities of India following in the footsteps of their leader Dr Ambedkar (Chapter 11). This spirit is also alive in the Buddhist Sarvodaya Shramadana movement in Sri Lanka. It works in 15,000 villages bringing a middle way approach to development initiatives, and the emphasis is on Sri Lankans meeting their needs, not their greeds. (For those of you who would like to read more about Sarvodaya Shramadana, I recommend Sallie B. King's book *Socially Engaged Buddhism*.[17])

Self-organized commons offer an alternative to a market-based approach and can be seen in a myriad of emerging initiatives around the world, including seed-sharing cooperatives in India, open-source software programming, open-access journals, Slow Food, permaculture, Transition Towns, the sharing of document, video, and music files under Creative Commons licences, Wikipedia, and also alternative local currencies, time banks, and other collective enterprises.[18]

I am emphasizing cooperatives and the commons because both illustrate the creating of an alternative way of doing economics from the bottom up. It's about engaging people's minds at a local level through activity intended to help themselves and each other. I believe any alternative to the current, neoliberal form of capitalism has to evolve from the bottom up using and trusting in the natural creativity of people.

Buddhists' most important contribution to the evolution of an alternative system is a set of values based on loving-kindness, generosity, simplicity and contentment, truthfulness, and mindfulness. These values can combine with self-interest and ambition, and with a sense of community, to create the conditions from which new ideas and new forms of organization can emerge. So I am not going to offer a blueprint for a new economic system, although I do believe that in the chapters of this book I have given some suggestions for the direction in which changes need to be made. These changes are necessary if we are to stop more damage being done by the current system and if we are to prevent those opposed to change from stifling the evolution of something better.

If you were to persist and ask me whether there would be markets in a future economic system, I would say probably yes. Would there be a variety of business organizations, both profit-based and not-for-profit? Again, I would say probably yes. But in that plurality of organizations there would be a greater emphasis on local production, without the disparity in size of organization that exists now. Would there be a balance of publicly and privately owned enterprises? Yet again, probably yes, but with a shift in public ownership towards the local or community level. But these are personal preferences and speculations. And, to emphasize the point again, I think the key to encouraging a new kind of economic organization to emerge lies in creating the right conditions, ones in which self-interest and personal ambition can work in combination with other human values of generosity, compassion, solidarity, and a sense of community.

In addition to promoting and exemplifying a set of values, Buddhists can take concrete measures to help the move towards a new economic system. Here are some suggestions about what might be done – five steps by individual Buddhists and five steps by the Buddhist community. I put them forward with respect for Buddhist traditions but also in the hope that they will prompt a parallel spirit of exploration and experimentation.

First, as individuals. This may be obvious to Buddhists but it needs to be emphasized: *we must work to transform ourselves*. For Buddhists, a whole-life practice of the path of ethics, meditation, and wisdom is the foundation. Emphasis on transforming the collective is futile unless it is based on transformation of the self. Everyone is subject daily to a barrage of conditioning designed to encourage a desire to consume more and more. Like everyone else, Buddhists are not immune to this conditioning, which penetrates deeply into the psyche. A rigorous approach to self-transformation, in the company of others in the Buddhist community, is necessary if Buddhists are to exemplify and persuade others of the value of generosity and compassion.

Second, *we need to educate ourselves in economics*. If we wish to reduce suffering in the world as aspiring Bodhisattvas, as concerned citizens even, we can't ignore the debate about our economic system and its effects. The future of the world depends on the outcome of this debate. We talk about accountability, about holding politicians or business leaders to account. There was a time when accounting was seen as revolutionary, in that it enabled ordinary people to see for the first time how their rulers acquired and spent their money. The English word 'accountability' comes from accounting. It first came into use in English when the French revolutionary constitution of 1793 was translated into English.[19] There's a clear and close relationship between democracy and accounting. At the moment, we have lost sight of the importance of accounting, especially as it is reflected in the economic behaviour of governments and businesses. We need to reclaim that knowledge, to become literate in economics.

If you want to make a start on this, there are many good books on economics written for a lay reader, but to begin I would recommend five books. The first is E.F. Schumacher's book *Small is Beautiful*.[20] First published in 1973, it's still an inspiring alternative to mainstream economics. It even has a chapter entitled 'Buddhist Economics'. The second and third books are by Dr Ha-Joon Chang, an economist at Cambridge University. They are *23 Things They Don't Tell You about Capitalism*[21] and *Economics: The User's Guide*.[22] Some of you may remember Chairman Mao's 'Little Red

Book' from the 1960s. Slipped inside my copy of *Economics: The User's Guide* was Ha-Joon Chang's 'Little Blue Book', which says:

Five things they don't tell you about economics:
1. 95% of economics is common sense.
2. Economics is not a science.
3. Economics is politics.
4. Never trust an economist.
5. Economics is too important to be left to the experts.

The fourth book is by Michael Sandel and is called *What Money Can't Buy: The Moral Limits of Markets*.[23] It is about the clash of values caused by the encroachment of the market economy into more and more areas of social life. The fifth book is *Prosperity Without Growth: Economics for a Finite Planet* by Tim Jackson.[24] He paints a picture of how human society could flourish within the ecological limits of the planet.

Third, *get involved.* This means that some of us must overcome our reluctance to get involved as individuals in campaigning on issues related to the economy. These might be the closure of a local hospital, a local strike, a protest by the Occupy Movement, an international issue such as the environment, or whatever issue seems to be important. Unless Buddhists are engaged in issues that people care about, and unless we are in dialogue with concerned activists, we are going to be limited in our ability to communicate the Buddhist values that are necessary for a fundamental transformation of the way the world works. And unless we have our ear to the ground, we are going to lose touch with progressive ideas and movements. Rather than a 'scatter gun' involvement with many campaigns, a deeper commitment is required, possibly only to a few campaigns or even to just one. This would allow more opportunity for meaningful, face-to-face communication.

But how might one choose where to get involved, how to find that 'personal calling'? Bhikkhu Bodhi suggests practising what he calls 'conscientious compassion'.[25] This 'conscientious compassion' is different from pity. Compassion calls for a greater commitment to do something, to get involved; pity does not. Pity tends to involve looking down on the object of concern; compassion involves a sense of equality.

Meditate on compassion, perhaps for twenty or thirty minutes. Then focus your attention on the problems that face humanity such as futile and self-destructive wars, global warming, poverty and global hunger, the mistreatment of animals, abuse of the environment, more local issues, or other concerns that come to mind. Reflect briefly on these problems one by one, aware of how you respond to them. You can repeat this procedure for several days, even daily for a week. At some point, Bhikkhu Bodhi advises, you will start to recognize that one of these problems, more than the others, tugs at the strings of your heart. These inner pangs suggest that this is the issue to which you should dedicate your time and energy. But, he cautions, don't rush to a conclusion. Continue instead to explore the issue cautiously and carefully, asking yourself, 'Does this issue break my heart open and cause an outpouring of compassion? Does this urge gnaw at my vital organs? Does it point the finger to the door and tell me to do something?' If your answer to these questions is yes, *that* is your vocation, *that* is your sacred calling, *that* is where you should put conscientious compassion into action. This doesn't mean that you neglect other issues. You remain open and responsive to other concerns but you focus on the issue that tugs at your heart and bids you to act.

Fourth, ***exemplification***. This may be stating the obvious again but we need to consider whether in our individual behaviour we always exemplify the values we espouse. This is not as easy as it sounds – it can be challenging, as I'm sure you know from personal experience. For instance, you may believe that the working methods employed in the mass production computer factories of China are inhumane and must be changed; and as a Buddhist, you make a public argument to that effect. But then how can you reconcile that with your desire to keep up with the latest computer models that your Buddhist friends are proudly showing off? Unlike coffee or tea, there are, as far as I am aware, no 'fair trade' computers.

What can we do to help change the situation? It's easy to dismiss ethical consumerism as a meaningless gesture. But even with a capitalism that maximizes profit, change can happen if we signal a change in what we want loud enough, be it fair trade bananas, recycled paper, clothes made in safe workplaces with free collective bargaining (as publicized by the Clean Clothes Campaign), or computers manufactured in decent factories with independent union organization.[26] I'm sure you can think of your own examples, and maybe sometimes there are no easy answers. But at least we can make these issues in awareness.

The fifth way in which we can be radical is to *become vegetarian or vegan*. Every time we don't eat meat, every time we don't eat or drink dairy products, we act out of empathy for other living beings. We increase our compassion footprint. And at the same time, we reduce our carbon footprint and encourage others to do the same.

Now I want to turn to what Buddhists can do as a spiritual community, as a sangha. First of all, a community needs to *embody dāna, or generosity*, as many do already through their urban centres, retreat centres, or residential communities. The practice of generosity challenges selfishness and is the ethos at the heart of spiritual community. It encourages a culture of sharing.

Buddhist communities can enact the dāna economy, whose basic principle is 'give what you can, take what you need'. Those who come to urban Buddhist centres and retreat centres should be encouraged to give what they can afford, to help the spread of the Dharma. By allowing people to pay what they can afford, Buddhism is open to anyone regardless of individual financial circumstances. The principle of 'give what you can, take what you need' can also apply to levels of financial support given to those who work full-time in Buddhist communities. The dāna economy is one important way in which Buddhism can offer a radical alternative to modern capitalism.

The second way in which Buddhist communities can offer a radical alternative is in *the practice of friendship and community*. Practising friendship and community, perhaps by living in a residential community with other practitioners, goes against the trend of individualism in our society, reduces pressure on economic and natural resources, and encourages sharing.

The third way in which Buddhist communities can offer a radical alternative is in *exploring alternative approaches to work and business* based on the principle of right livelihood. This is where work is not just a means to an end but instead offers people a chance to improve themselves by working together with others, to exercise their creativity, and to contribute to the spreading of Buddhism.

In Chapter 5, on the environment and nature, I talked about the role of rituals and how Buddhists can learn from native societies. Rituals are sidelined or ridiculed today as a hangover from a primitive past and Buddhism is seen as an obstacle to its 'relevant' bits for a modern audience. So *preserving and developing opportunities for participation in meaningful rituals* is a fourth way in which Buddhists can make a distinctive contribution.

The fifth way in which Buddhist sanghas can offer a radical alternative is *to provide space for calm reflection*. People can come together on the basis of shared values and meditate and reflect on their own lives and the lives of others, to change themselves and the world.

The basic instincts for individual survival, greed and hatred, once served us well in a primitive, competitive world. But now, in our interdependent world, where our actions threaten our very survival, the progressive evolutionary impulses of giving, caring, and compassion need to flourish. The Buddha showed us that evolution can lead to a life free of suffering and full of liberation and creativity. But if they continue to get their way, the proponents of free market economics and neoliberal capitalism will suffocate the process of evolution. Which is it to be: a life of Enlightenment or a life of shopping?

Shopping
Dana Gioia

I enter the temple of my people but do not pray.
I pass the altars of the gods but do not kneel
Or offer sacrifices proper to the season.

Strolling the hushed aisles of the department store,
I see visions shining under glass,
Divinities of leather, gold, and porcelain,
Shrines of cut crystal, stainless steel, and silicon.

But I wander the arcades of abundance,
Empty of desire, no credit to my people,
Envying the acolytes their passionate faith.
Blessed are the acquisitive,
For theirs is the kingdom of commerce.

Redeem me, gods of the mall and marketplace.
Mercury, protector of cell phones and fax machines,
Venus, patroness of bath and bedroom chains,
Tantalus, guardian of the food court.

Beguile me with the aromas of coffee, musk, and cinnamon.
Surround me with delicately colored soaps and moisturizing creams.
Comfort me with posters of children with perfect smiles
And pouting teenage models clad in lingerie.
I am not made of stone.

Show me satins, linen, crepe de chine, and silk,
Heaped like cumuli in the morning sky,
As if all caravans and argosies ended in this parking lot
To fill these stockrooms and loading docks.

The Buddha on Wall Street

Sing me the hymns of no cash down and the installment plan,
Of custom fit, remote control, and priced to move.
Whisper the blessing of Egyptian cotton, polyester, and cashmere.
Tell me in what department my desire shall be found.

Because I would buy happiness if I could find it,
Spend all that I possessed or could borrow.
But what can I bring you from these sad emporia?
Where in this splendid clutter
Shall I discover the one true thing?

Nothing to carry, I should stroll easily
Among the crowded countertops and eager cashiers,
Bypassing the sullen lines and footsore customers,
Spending only my time, discounting all I see.

Instead I look for you among the pressing crowds,
But they know nothing of you, turning away,
Carrying their brightly packaged burdens.
There is no angel among the vending stalls and signage.

Where are you, my fugitive? Without you
There is nothing but the getting and the spending
Of things that have a price.
Why else have I stalked the leased arcades
Searching the kiosks and the cash machines?

Where are you, my errant soul and innermost companion?
Are you outside amid the potted palm trees,
Bumming a cigarette or joking with the guards,
Or are you wandering the parking lot
Lost among the rows of Subarus and Audis?

Or is it you I catch a sudden glimpse of
Smiling behind the greasy window of the bus
As it disappears into the evening rush?[27]

Note on classical, neoclassical, and neoliberal economics

Of the many schools of economics, the main focus of this book is on 'neoliberal' or 'free market' economics. With the help of Dr Ha-Joon Chang's book *Economics: The User's Guide*, I shall explain in this note the relationship between classical economics, neoclassical economics, and neoliberal or free market economics.[1]

Adam Smith belonged to the classical school of economics, which has two central assumptions. First, economic actors are motivated by self-interest, but competition in the market guarantees that their actions collectively produce a socially beneficial outcome (the 'invisible hand' argument, see Chapter 1). Second, markets, if left to their own workings, will tend to revert to a stable position. It should be noted that unlike most other classical economists, and unlike many present-day economists, Adam Smith understood that people's behaviour is not just dictated by self-interest but derives from a variety of motives (see Chapter 2).

The neoclassical school takes its basis from classical economics, but puts the emphasis on the economy as an agglomeration of rational and selfish individuals rather than as a collection of distinct classes as the classical school does (and as Marxist economics does too). Moreover, the neoclassical school moves the focus of economics from production to consumption and exchange. Adam Smith was more interested in production and in how changes in the organization of production were transforming the economy (as was Karl Marx). The neoclassical school highlights the role of the individual and the consumer.

The neoclassical school has come under criticism because of its espousal of what's known as the Pareto criterion. For example, if low-wage factory jobs are offered in a poor country, this is a Pareto improvement because without those jobs, there would be no jobs at all. A neoclassical economist might argue that therefore those jobs should not be criticized. As Ha-Joon Chang points out, however, this is true only if we accept the underlying socio-economic structure as fixed. If instead we are willing to contemplate changes in the structure of society, then other options with much better socio-economic outcomes become possible. New labour laws that strengthen workers rights and land reform that encourages more people to stay in the countryside and thus reduces the supply of new labour to factories, combined with new industrial policies that produce more high-skilled jobs, would give a much greater range of choice with better outcomes for workers. Neoclassical economists tend not to think like this.

During the twentieth century, a split arose in neoclassical economics; and in consequence, one cannot always assume that those who define themselves as free market economists and neoclassical economists are identical. This split arose with the emergence of welfare economics, with the recognition that market prices can fail to reflect social costs and benefits, for example when the prices of a factory's products do not reflect the pollution associated with their production. Between the 1930s and the 1970s, many neoclassical economists were not free market economists. But since the 1970s, the prevailing majority of neoclassical economists have aligned themselves with a free market outlook, with the rise of neoliberalism.

Since the beginning of the 1980s and the coming to power of Margaret Thatcher and Ronald Reagan, neoliberalism has been the dominant economic viewpoint both at universities and in economic institutions around the world. Its influence has spread into countries of the former Soviet Union and even into China with the rapid progress of the liberalization and globalization of the world economy. Notwithstanding the excessive liberalization of the financial markets causing the great crash of 2008, neoliberal and free market economics are still the dominant forces in our economic world. Outside the western world, in developing countries especially, neoliberalism is known as the Washington Consensus, because neoliberal economic policies are strongly promoted by the three most powerful economic institutions in the world: the US Treasury, the International Monetary Fund, and the World Bank.

Endnotes

Introduction

1 Smith, Adam. 1904. Book I, I.3.
2 Pin production numbers from Chang, Ha-Joon. 2014. pp.31–3.
3 Smith, Adam. 1904. Book V, I.178.
4 Zizek, Slavoj. 2001. There is also an excellent article on the implications of Zizek's comments, combined with a discussion of Buddhism's response to capitalism, by Stuart Smithers. See Smithers, Stuart (undated).
5 Chang, Ha-Joon. 2014, pp.33–4.
6 John Lanchester has written a short but thorough description of modern neoliberal economics. See Lanchester, John. 2014. pp.53–61.
7 Darwin, Charles. 1871. p.107.

Chapter 1 – An 'invisible hand'

1 Margin Call. 2011.
2 Friedman, Thomas L. 2011.
3 Smith, Adam. 1904. Book IV, 2.9.
4 Paul, Diane B. 1988.
5 Darwin, Charles. 1871. p.107.
6 Stiglitz, Joseph E. 2013.
7 Gethin, Rupert. 2008. pp.116–28.
8 Handy, Charles. 2002. p.36.
9 Jackson, Tim. 2010.

Chapter 2 – The gift relationship

1 Titmuss, Richard M. 1971.
2 Smith, Adam. 1904. Book IV, 2.9.
3 Smith, Adam. 1976. Quoted in Krznaric, Roman. 2013. pp.55-6.
4 Ibid.
5 Śāntideva. 1995. p.80.
6 Seth-Smith, Nikki. 2013.
7 Geoghan, Tom. 2012
8 Johnson, Eric Michael. 2012.
9 Ibid.
10 Geoghegan, Tom. 2012.
11 Isaacs, Jacqueline. 2011.
12 Ñāṇamoli, Bhikkhu. 1992. p.52.
13 Arrow, Kenneth J. 1972. Quoted in Sandel, Michael J. 2013. pp.125–6. The argument I develop in this chapter relating to Richard Titmuss's *The Gift Relationship* draws on Michael Sandel's discussion in *What Money Can't Buy*.
14 Nasser, Alan. 2012.
15 Sandel, Michael. 2013. p.126.
16 Arrow, Kenneth J. 1972. Quoted in Sandel, Michael. 2013. p.127.

17 Robertson, Sir Dennis H. 1954. Quoted in Michael Sandel, 2013. pp.127–8.
18 Summers, Lawrence H. 2003. Quoted in Michael Sandel, 2013. p.130.
19 Sandel, Michael. 2013. p.130.
20 Marglin, Stephen A. 2008. p.18.
21 Sandel, Michael. 2013. pp.61–4.
22 Ibid. p.64.
23 Ibid. pp.132–6.
24 Schultz, Ellen E. and Francis, Theo. 2002.
25 Meserve, Myles. 2012.
26 *Wall Street*. 1987.
27 Watt, Nicholas. 2013.
28 Wang, Long. Malhotra, Deepak. Murnighan, J. Keith. 2011.
29 Weissmann, Jordan. 2012.
30 Amaravati Sangha. 2004.
31 Ṭhānissaro, Bhikkhu. 1997(b).
32 Sangharakshita. 2009. pp.573–4.
33 Andre, Clair and Velasquez, Manuel. 1992.
34 Unno, Taitetsu. 2003.

Chapter 3 – The decline of community

1 The term 'Sangha' has several meanings in Buddhism. It can refer to the community of Buddhist monks and nuns. More strictly, as the third of Buddhism's Three Jewels, 'Sangha' applies only to those who have reached a high level of spiritual attainment. In more modern times, 'Sangha' has come to connote in the west any community of Buddhists, whether monastic or lay or a combination of the two. In this chapter, I refer to the Buddhist spiritual community according to the latter meaning.
2 Marglin, Stephen A. 2008. The discussion in this chapter of the enclosure movement and its significance, and of the Amish community, draws on Marglin's book.
3 Marglin, Stephen A. 2008. p.20.
4 Calder, Angus. 2008. p.251. The background story to the Beveridge Report and the formation of the NHS is also taken from this book.
5 Calder, Angus. 2008. p.540.
6 Marglin, Stephen A. 2008. pp.21–7.
7 Appleby, Joyce Oldham. 1978. Quoted in Apffel-Marglin,
Frederique. 2011. p.36.
8 Ibid. p.36.
9 Ibid. p.39.
10 *Witness*. 1985.
11 Marglin, Stephen A. 2008. pp.1–2.
12 Details drawn from Sandel, Michael. 2013. pp.155–60.
13 Connolly, Kate. 2012.
14 Marglin, Stephen A. 2008. p.27.
15 Ibid. p.20.
16 Heller, Nathan. 2012.
17 An argument developed in Klinenberg, Eric. 2012.
18 Putnam, Robert D. 2000. Quoted in Heller, 2012.
19 Heller, Nathan. 2012.
20 Bodhi, Bhikkhu. 2000. p.1524.
21 Ñāṇamoli, Bhikkhu and Bodhi, Bhikkhu. 2001. pp.301–6.
22 Walshe, Maurice. 1995. pp.461–9.
23 Bodhi, Bhikkhu. 2005. p.110.
24 Ṭhānissaro, Bhikkhu. 1997(c).
25 Ñāṇamoli, Bhikkhu. 1992. pp.109–19.
26 Walshe, Maurice. 1995. pp.395–405.
27 Vajragupta. 2010.

Chapter 4 – Work

1 Wikipedia. Unemployment in the United Kingdom. Undated.
2 Haraszti, Miklós. 1977.
3 Ibid. p.142.
4 Crabtree, Steve. 2013. Figures are for 2011–12.
5 International Labour Organization. 2014.
6 Wikipedia. Marie Jahoda. Undated.
7 Zajonc, Arthur. 1997.
8 Wikipedia. The Protestant Ethic and the Spirit of Capitalism. Undated.
9 Zajonc, Arthur. 1997.
10 Ibid.
11 Chamberlain, Gethin. 2011.
12 Schumacher, E.F. 1993. p.39.
13 Walshe, Maurice. 1995. p.336.
14 Bodhi, Bhikkhu. *The Noble Eightfold Path*. No date.
15 Bodhi, Bhikkhu. 2005. pp.107–14.
16 Ñāṇamoli, Bhikkhu. 1992. p.120.
17 Wikipedia. Baizhang Huaihai. Undated.
18 Work As Practice. Undated.
19 Sangharakshita. 1995(a). p.12.
20 Ibid. pp.38–46.
21 Ibid. pp.39–40.
22 Ibid. p.40.
23 Ibid. p.40.
24 Zajonc, Arthur. 1997.
25 Jackson, Tim. 2012.
26 Adams, Richard. 2014.
27 Jackson, Tim. 2012.
28 Feinberg, Cara. 2013.
29 Ashley, Jackie. 2014.
30 Jackson, Tim. 2012.
31 Ibid.
32 Schumacher, E.F. 1993. p.41.
33 Big Rock Candy Mountain. Undated.
34 Gutting, Gary. 2013.
35 Sangharakshita. 1995(b). pp.106–8.
36 See Windhorse:Evolution. Undated. Sadly, after the completion of this manuscript, early in January 2015, it was announced that Windhorse:Evolution would be closing.

Chapter 5 – Nature and the environment

1 Kenneth Boulding. Quote from Attenborough, David. 2011.
2 Source of figures on energy use from Geoffrey West. Quoted in Krulwich, Robert. 2012.
3 Mooney, Chris. 2014.
4 Wikipedia. *E. J. Mishan.* Undated.
5 Orrell, David. 2010. p.106.
6 Robert Solow. Quoted in Orrell, David. p.203.
7 Ibid. p.203.
8 Vulture figures taken from Juniper, Tony. 2013. pp.131–5.
9 E. O. Wilson. Quoted in Orrell, David. 2010. p.199.
10 Hamilton, Clive. 2003.
11 Marx, Karl. Undated. Vol. 1. Ch. 24. Section 3.
12 Jackson, Tim. 2011.
13 Vishvapani. 2012.
14 Ibid.
15 Ibid.
16 Ibid.
17 Olendzki, Andrew. 2013.
18 de Silva, Lily. 2005.
19 Olendzki, Andrew. Mettā Sutta. Undated.
20 Walshe, Maurice. 1995. p.466.
21 Abrams, Lindsay. 2013.
22 Ibid.
23 Quoted in Krulwich, Robert. 2011.
24 Olendzki, Andrew. Undated.
25 Appfel-Marglin, Frederique. 2011. pp.3–4.
26 Ibid. p.6.
27 Ibid. p.75.

28 Appfel-Marglin, Frederique. 2011.
   p.88.
29 Ibid. p.88.
30 Harding, John. 2013.
31 Whitely, Peter. 2013.
32 Bodhi, Bhikkhu. 2000. Part II.
   p.552.
33 Orrell, David. 2006. pp.205–6.
34 Cline, Eric H. 2014.
35 Frank, Adam. 2014.
36 Ibid.
37 Ibid.
38 Buddhafield. Undated.

39 Eco Dharma. Undated.
40 Schumacher, E. F. 1993. p.42.
41 Hamilton, Clive. 2010.
42 Jianguo Liu figures. Quoted in
   Morrison, Ewan. 2012.
43 Carus, Felicity. 2010.
44 Bekhechi, Mimi. 2013.
45 Lancaster University. 2012.
46 Figures taken from Lancaster
   University. 2012.
47 Bekhechi, Mimi. 2013.
48 Leonard, Annie. 2013.

Chapter 6 – The waste economy

1 Handy, Charles. 2008. pp.122–3.
2 Monbiot, George. 2012.
3 Handy, Charles. 1994. p.32.
4 Wikipedia. E.J. Mishan.
5 Handy, Charles. 2008. pp.122–3.
6 Jackson, Tim. 2010.
7 Handy, Charles. 2008. pp.122–3.
8 Anālayo, Bhikkhu. 2012. p.194.
9 Bodhi, Bhikkhu. 2005. p.127.
10 Wijayaratna, Mohan. 1990. pp.56–75.
11 Ibid. p.68.
12 Ibid. p.73.
13 Hayes, Shannon. 2012.
14 Ball, Philip. 2013.
15 Ibid.
16 Peretti, Jacques. 2014.
17 Hamzelou, Jessica. 2012.
18 Ibid.

19 Smithers, Rebecca. 2013.
20 Ibid.
21 Moss, Michael. 2013.
22 Ibid.
23 Ibid.
24 Su, Christine. 2012.
25 Berreby, David. 2013.
26 Ibid.
27 Ibid.
28 Ibid.
29 Ibid.
30 Ibid.
31 Berreby, David. 2012.
32 Electronics Take Back Coalition.
   Undated.
33 IFIXIT. Undated.
34 Lavars, Nick. 2014.
35 See Lama's Pyjamas. Undated.

Chapter 7 – The attention economy

1 Sangharakshita. 1993.
2 Crary, Jonathan. 2013. Location 871
   of 1577.
3 Ratnaguna. 2010. p.14.
4 Ñāṇamoli, Bhikkhu and Bodhi,
   Bhikkhu. 2001. pp.207–10.
5 W.H. Auden. Quoted in
   Konnikova, Maria. 2013. Location
   33 of 4687.

6 Olendzki, Andrew. 2009.
7 Auden, W.H. Undated.
8 KPCB. 2013.
9 Leo Burnett. Quote from Loy,
   David R. 2009. p.28.
10 Carr, Nicholas. 2007.
11 City of Ten Thousand Buddhas.
   Undated.
12 Burak, Jacob. 2014.

13 Konnikova, Maria. 2014.
14 Loy, David. 2009. p.28.
15 Crary, Jonathan. 2013. Location 22–30 of 1577.
16 Crary, Jonathan. 2013. Location 128 of 1577.
17 Campbell, Denis. 2012.
18 Crary, Jonathan. 2013. Location 136 of 1577.
19 Shakespeare and Edison. Quotations from Foster, Russell. 2013.
20 Ibid.
21 Ibid.
22 Tan, Declan. 2012.
23 Huffington, Arianna. 2013.
24 Ibid.
25 Ibid.
26 Ibid.
27 Hutton, Will. 2013.
28 Carr, Nicholas. 2007.
29 Ibid.
30 NPR Books. 2010. Includes extract from Carr, Nicholas. 2010.
31 Carr, Nicholas. 2007.
32 Carr, Nicholas. 2013.
33 See Gelles, David. 2012 and Rathbone, John Paul. 2013.
34 Heuman, Linda. 2014.
35 Gelles, David. 2012.
36 Rathbone, John Paul. 2013.
37 Manjusura. 2003.
38 *The Third Man*. 1949.
39 Vishvapani. 2014.
40 Ream, Amanda. 2014.
41 Rathbone, John Paul. 2013.
42 Shachtman, Noah. 2013.
43 Kreider, Tim. 2012.
44 Sangharakshita. 2013. pp.93–4.
45 Eliot, T.S. Undated.

Chapter 8 – The happiness industry

1 Huxley quoted in Evans, Jules. 8 February 2012.
2 Brittan, Sam. 2012.
3 Ñāṇamoli, Bhikkhu and Bodhi, Bhikkhu. 2001. pp.188–9.
4 Olendzki, Andrew. 2005.
5 Anālayo. 2012. p.157.
6 Ṭhānissaro, Bhikkhu. 1997(a).
7 Sangharakshita. 2001. p.13.
8 Anālayo, Bhikkhu. 2012. p.161.
9 Summarized in Stoll, Laura and Michaelson, Juliet. 2013.
10 O'Connor, Sarah. 2014.
11 Pilling, David. 2014.
12 Gleeson-White, Jane. 2012.
13 Layard, Richard. 2012.
14 English, Cynthia. 2010.
15 Baggini, Julian. 2011.
16 Evans, Jules. 2 March 2011.
17 Ibid.
18 Evans, Jules. 8 July 2011.
19 Ibid.
20 Kelly, Annie. 2012.
21 Evans, Jules. 17 April 2012.
22 See Bird, Kai. 2012, and *The Economist*. 2010.
23 *The Economist*. 2010.
24 OECD. 2011.
25 NEF. Undated.
26 The formulation of the positive versions of the five precepts is that used in the Triratna Buddhist Community.
27 de Botton, Alain. 2014.

Chapter 9 – Inequality

1 Wilkinson, Richard and Pickett, Kate. 2010.
2 Piketty, Thomas. 2014.
3 Wilkinson, Richard and Pickett, Kate. 2 February 2014.
4 Wilkinson, Richard. 2011.

5 Kavoussi, Bonnie. 2012.
6 Denning, Steve. 2013.
7 Ibid.
8 Ibid.
9 Rushe, Dominic. 2013.
10 Stiglitz, Joseph E. 2013.
11 Ibid.
12 Lewis, Michael. 2011. pp.97–8.
13 Ibid. pp.97–8.
14 Stiglitz, Joseph E. 2013.
15 Goleman, Daniel. 2013.
16 Williams, Ray. 2012.
17 Ibid.
18 Goleman, Daniel. 2013.
19 Piketty's book is more than 900 pages long. I cannot claim to have read it all. However, I have read several lengthy summaries and articles that contain the gist of his statistics and argument. My description here of the book is based on Mason, Paul. 2014.
20 Walshe, Maurice. 1995. pp.133–41.
21 Sangharakshita. 1989. pp.69–70.
22 Measuring 'average' pay can sometimes be confusing. Most often when we read about 'average pay', we are reading about average pay as measured by the arithmetic mean. This mean value is calculated by adding up all the pay earned by all the employees in a company (from the lowest paid to the highest paid executives) and then dividing the total by the number of employees. The resulting average is pulled upwards if there are a few very high-paid executives, and thus the average figure can overestimate the true pay levels in the company. A usually more representative figure is derived when all employees' pay is plotted in a league table from the lowest to the highest and the median figure is then found. The median figure is found at the half-way point of the league table. It tells you the pay level below which 50 per cent of employees will be found and above which 50 per cent will be found. In most companies the median will be significantly lower than the arithemtic mean.
23 Hargreaves, Deborah. 2014.
24 Garofalo, Pat. 2013.
25 Wilkinson, Richard and Pickett, Kate. July 2014.
26 Sangharakshita. 2001. p.72.

Chapter 10 – The corporation

1 White, D. Steven. 2012.
2 Bakan, Joel. 2005. See also Kemmerer, Lisa. 2008.
3 Bakan, Joel. 2005. Location 301 of 6078.
4 Loy, David R. 2011.
5 Monbiot, George. 2014.
6 Bakan, Joel. 2005 Location 106 of 6078.
7 Bakan, Joel. 2005.Location 106 of 6078.
8 Bakan, Joel. 2005. Location 2479 of 6078.
9 Peretti, Jacques.2014.
10 *The Daily Telegraph*. 2010.
11 See PayPal. Undated.
12 Wilson, David Sloan. 2013.

Chapter 11 – Buddhist voices

1 For those interested in gaining an overview of the world of socially engaged Buddhism and of major figures and movements involved in this contemporary movement, see King, Sallie B. 2009.
2 Much of the material on Sangharakshita is taken from Subhuti, 1994.
3 Subhuti. 1994. p.227.
4 This paragraph is drawn from a summary prepared by Atkinson, Hannah. 2012.
5 Rilke, Rainer Maria. 2002.
6 Much of the information on Dr Ambedkar has been gathered from Subhuti. 2010.
7 Senauke, Hozan Alan. 2011. For more information on the Karuna Trust see http://www.karuna.org/
8 Loy, David R. 2002.
9 Loy, David R. 2008.
10 Loy, David R. 2011.
11 Loy, David R. 2008. p.94.
12 Loy, David R. 2011.
13 This section on Bhikkhu Bodhi draws on Bodhi, Bhikkhu. *Bridging the Spiritual and the Mundane*. No date.
14 Sangharakshita. 1989. p.70.

Chapter 12 – Concluding thoughts

1 Rose, Jonathan. 2014. pp.99–100.
2 Keynes, John Maynard. 1963. Quoted in Marglin. 2008. p.204.
3 Marglin, Stephen A. 2008. p.205.
4 Ibid. p.205.
5 Ibid. p.211.
6 Ibid. p.201.
7 Ibid. p.222.
8 Gioia, Dana. 2007.
9 Monaghan, Angela. 2014.
10 Carney, Mark. 2014.
11 Wilson, David Sloan. 2013.
12 Phillips, Tom. Undated.
13 Ibid.
14 International Cooperative Alliance. 2010.
15 Gast, Scott. 2014.
16 *The Economist*, 2012.
17 King, Sallie B. 2009.
18 Bollier, David. 2014.
19 Derbyshire, Jonathan. 2014.
20 Schumacher, E.F. 1993.
21 Chang Ha-Joon. 2010.
22 Chang, Ha-Joon. 2014.
23 Sandel, Michael. 2013.
24 Jackson, Tim. 2011.
25 Bodhi, Bhikkhu. 2011.
26 Baggini, Julian. 2013.
27 Gioia, Dana. 2012. p.10.

Note

1 Chang, Ha-Joon. 2014. pp.115–27.

References

Abrams, Lindsay. 'When Trees Die, People Die'. *The Atlantic*, 22 January 2013. http://www.theatlantic.com/health/archive/2013/01/when-trees-die-people-die/267322/. Accessed 25 January 2013.

Adams, Richard. 'Teachers spend less than half their working week in the classroom'. *The Guardian*, 25 June 2014. http://www.theguardian.com/education/2014/jun/25/teachers-classroom-working-week-england-survey. Accessed 29 August 2014.

Amaravati Sangha. *Karaniya Metta Sutta: The Buddha's Words on Loving-Kindness.* Access to Insight, 2004. http://www.accesstoinsight.org/tipitaka/kn/snp/snp.1.08.amar.html. Accessed 29 August 2014.

Analāyo, Bhikkhu. *Excursions into the Thought-World of the Pali Discourses.* Onalaska, WA: Pariyatti Press. 2012.

Andre, Clair and Velasquez, Manuel. Giving Blood: The Development of Generosity. Santa Clara University, 1992. http://www.scu.edu/ethics/publications/iie/v5n1/blood.html. Accessed 16 September 2014. http://www.scu.edu/ethics/publications/iie/v5n1/blood.html. Accessed 2 August 2014.

Apffel-Marglin, Frederique. *Subversive Ritualities: How Rituals Enact the World.* Oxford: Oxford University Press. 2011.

Appleby, Joyce Oldham. *Economic Thought and Ideology in Seventeenth-Century England.* Princeton, NJ: Princeton University Press. 1978.

Arrow, Kenneth J. *Gifts and Exchanges.* Philosophy and Public Affairs. vol. 1, no.4. 1972.

Ashley, Jackie. 'I've seen the future of Britain's healthcare – and it works'. *The Guardian*, 6 June 2014. http://www.theguardian.com/commentisfree/2014/jun/06/i-have-seen-future-of-britain-healthcare-and-it-works. Accessed 6 June 2014.

Atkinson, Hannah. A spiritual community is not a group. It is a free association of individuals. Windhorse Publications. 30 October 2012. https://thebuddhistcentre.com/windhorsepublications/%E2%80%9C-spiritual-community-not-group-it-free-association-individuals%E2%80%9D. Accessed 30 August 2014.

Attenborough, David. RSA President's Lecture 2011: People and Planet. RSA, March 2011. http://www.thersa.org/events/audio-and-past-events/2011/rsa-presidents-lecture-2011. Accessed 25 August 2014.

Auden, W.H. *Canzone.* http://www.poemhunter.com/best-poems/wh-auden/canzone-2/. Accessed 9 September 2014.

Baggini, Julian. 'Flourish'. *The Financial Times*, 13 May 2011. http://www.ft.com/cms/s/2/2fac01e0-7ce3-11e0-a7c7-00144feabdc0.html#ixzz1Mm929T5K. Accessed 19 May 2011.

Baggini, Julian. 'Move your money from the high street and help to achieve a fairer society'. *The Guardian*, 31 December 2013. http://www.theguardian.com/commentisfree/2013/dec/31/move-your-money-high-street-fairer-society. Accessed 1 June 2014.

Baizhang Huaihai. http://en.wikipedia.org/wiki/Baizhang_Huaihai. Accessed 25 August 2014.

Bakan, Joel. *The Corporation: The Pathological Pursuit of Profit and Power*. London: Constable. 2005 (Kindle edition).

Ball, Philip. 'Making Good'. *Aeon*, 29 May 2013. http://aeon.co/magazine/culture/philip-ball-art-of-repair/. Accessed 29 May 2013.

Bekhechi, Mimi. 'Eating quinoa may harm Bolivian farmers, but eating meat harms us all'. *The Guardian*, 22 January 2013. http://www.theguardian.com/commentisfree/2013/jan/22/quinoa-bolivian-farmers-meat-eaters-hunger. Accessed 22 January 2013.

Berreby, David. 'Is Capitalism To Blame for Worldwide Obesity?' *Big Think*, 24 March 2012. http://bigthink.com/Mind-Matters/is-capitalism-to-blame-for-worldwide-obesity. Accessed 26 August 2014.

Berreby, David. 'The Obesity Era'. *Aeon*, 19 June 2013. http://www.aeonmagazine.com/being-human/david-berreby-obesity-era/?utm_source=Aeon+newsletter&utm_campaign=769936c921-Aeon_newsletter6_19_2013&utm_medium=email&utm_term=0_411a82e59d-769936c921-49705477. Accessed 19 June 2013.

Big Rock Candy Mountains. www.youtube.com/watch?v=0-ftai12IOM. Accessed 25 August 2014.

Bird, Kai. 'The Enigma of Bhutan'. *The Nation*, 26 March 2012. http://www.thenation.com/article/166667/enigma-bhutan. Accessed 30 March 2012.

Bodhi, Bhikkhu. *The Connected Discourses of the Buddha: A Translation of the Saṃyutta Nikāya*. Boston: Wisdom Publications. 2000.

Bodhi, Bhikkhu. *In the Buddha's Words: An Anthology of Discourses from the Pali Canon*. Boston: Wisdom Publications. 2005.

Bodhi, Bhikkhu. 'The Need of the Hour'. *Tricycle Magazine*, Fall 2011. http://www.tricycle.com/feature/need-hour. Accessed 28 December 2013.

Bodhi, Bhikkhu. 'Bridging the Spiritual and the Mundane: A Personal Odyssey'. *Parabola Magazine*. Undated. http://www.parabola.org/bridging-the-spiritual-and-the-mundane.html. Accessed 28 December 2013.

Bodhi, Bhikkhu. *The Noble Eightfold Path*. Undated. http://www.beyondthenet.net/dhamma/nobleEight.htm. Accessed 3 April 2013.

Bollier, David. 'FabLabs, Time Banks, and Other Hidden Treasures You Didn't Know You Owned'. *Yes! Magazine*, 16 July 2014. http://www.yesmagazine.org/issues/the-power-of-story/these-days-it-s-cool-to-be-a-commoner?utm_source=YTW&utm_medium=Email&utm_campaign=20140718. Accessed 19 July 2014.

Brittan, Sam. 'Diogenes was right to value more than happiness'. *The Financial Times*, 27 January 2012. http://www.samuelbrittan.co.uk/text417_p.html. Accessed 24 April 2013.

Buddhafield. http://www.buddhafield.com/index.php.

Burak, Jacob. 'Escape from the Matrix'. *Aeon*, 28 May 2014. http://aeon.co/magazine/being-human/can-we-break-free-from-the-fear-of-missing-out/?utm_source=Aeon+newsletter&utm_campaign=cb73d0c20b-Daily_Newsletter_28_may_20145_28_2014&utm_medium=email&utm_term=0_411a82e59d-cb73d0c20b-49705477. Accessed 13 July 2014.

Calder, Angus. *The People's War: Britain 1939–1945*. London: Pimlico. 2008.

Campbell, Denis. 'Chronic lack of sleep affects one in three British workers'. *The Observer*, 1 April 2012. http://www.theguardian.com/lifeandstyle/2012/apr/01/chronic-sleep-deprivation-uk-staff . Accessed 26 August 2014.

Carney, Mark. 'Inclusive capitalism: creating a sense of the systemic talk'. Bank of England, 27 May 2014. http://www.bankofengland.co.uk/publications/Documents/speeches/2014/speech731.pdf. Accessed 27 August 2014.

Carr, Nicholas. 'Is Google Making Us Stupid?' *The Atlantic*, July 2007. http://www.theatlantic.com/magazine/archive/2008/07/is-google-making-us-stupid/6868/. Accessed 27 January 2012.

Carr, Nicholas. *The Shallows: What the Internet Is Doing to Our Brains*. New York: W.W. Norton & Co. 2010.

Carr, Nicholas. 'The Patience Deficit'. *Edge*, 2013. http://edge.org/response-detail/23721. Accessed 18 September 2013.

Carus, Felicity. 'UN urges global move to meat and dairy-free diet'. *The Guardian*, 2 June 2010. http://www.guardian.co.uk/environment/2010/jun/02/un-report-meat-free-diet. Accessed 6 July 2013.

Chamberlain, Gethin. 'Apple's Chinese workers treated "inhumanely, like machines"'. *The Observer*, 1 May 2011. http://www.guardian.co.uk/technology/2011/apr/30/apple-chinese-workers-treated-inhumanely. Accessed 4 April 2013.

Chang, Ha-Joon. *23 Things They Don't Tell You About Capitalism*. London: Penguin Books. 2010.

Chang, Ha-Joon. *Economics: The User's Guide*. London: Pelican. 2014.

City of Ten Thousand Buddhas. *The Sutra in Forty-Two Sections Spoken by the Buddha*. Undated. http://

www.cttbusa.org/42s/42sections. asp. Accessed 9 September 2014.

Cline, Eric H. *1177 B.C.: The Year Civilization Collapsed*. Princeton University Press. 2014.

Connolly, Kate. 'Germany exporting old and sick to foreign care homes'. *The Guardian*, 26 December 2012. http://www.theguardian. com/world/2012/dec/26/ german-elderly-foreign-care-homes . Accessed 26 December 2012.

Crabtree, Steve. 'Worldwide, 13% of Employees Are Engaged at Work'. Gallup, 8 October 2013. http://www.gallup.com/poll/ 165269/worldwide-employees-engaged-work.aspx. Accessed 30 June 2014.

Crary, Jonathan. *24/7: Late Capitalism and the Ends of Sleep*. Verso. 2013 (Kindle edition).

The Daily Telegraph. '20 of the most memorable *Mad Men* quotes'. 1 December 2010. http:// www.telegraph.co.uk/culture/ tvandradio/8170937/20-of-the-most-memorable-Mad-Men-quotes.html. Accessed 19 July 2014.

Darwin, Charles. *The Descent of Man*. D. Appleton and Company. 1871.

de Botton, Alain. *The Great Philosophers 3: Epicurus*. The School of Life, 10 July 2014. http://www. theschooloflife.com/blog/2014/ 06/the-great-philosophers-3-epicurus/. Accessed 26 August 2014.

de Silva, Lily. *The Buddhist Attitude Towards Nature*. Access to Insight, 2005. http://www.accesstoinsight. org/lib/authors/desilva/attitude. html. Accessed 26 November 2013.

Denning, Steve. 'The Origin Of "The World's Dumbest Idea": Milton Friedman'. *Forbes*, 26 June 2013. http://www.forbes.com/sites/ stevedenning/2013/06/26/the-origin-of-the-worlds-dumbest-idea-milton-friedman/. Accessed 27 August 2014.

Derbyshire, Jonathan. 'Accounting and Accountability'. *Prospect*, 29 April 2014. http://www. prospectmagazine.co.uk/ derbyshire/accounting-and-accountability-interview-with-jacob-soll/#.U2Xn-vmSzzo. Accessed 4 May 2014.

Eco Dharma. http://www.ecodharma. com/.

The Economist. 'Elinor Ostrom', 30 June 2012. http://www.economist. com/node/21557717. Accessed 20 July 2014.

The Economist. 'Unhappiness exported', 27 December 2010. http://www. economist.com/blogs/banyan/ 2010/12/refugees_bhutan. Accessed 30 January 2012.

Electronics Take Back Coalition. http:/ /www.electronicstakeback.com/ home/.

Eliot, T.S. *Burnt Norton*. No date. http:/ /www.coldbacon.com/poems/ fq.html. Accessed 9 September 2014.

English, Cynthia. 'Global Wellbeing Surveys Find Nations Worlds Apart'. Gallup, 25 March 2010. http://www.gallup.com/poll/ 126977/global-wellbeing-surveys-find-nations-worlds-apart.aspx. Accessed 6 April 2012.

Evans, Jules. 'A technocratic solution to a spiritual question'. Philosophy for Life, 2 March 2011. http://philosophyforlife. org/a-technocratic-solution-to-a-

spiritual-question/. Accessed
2 May 2013.

Evans, Jules. *PoW: Is Osama bin
Laden the model of a flourishing
life?* Philosophy for Life, 8 July
2011. http://philosophyforlife.
org/pow-is-osama-bin-laden-
the-model-of-a-flourishing-life/.
Accessed 27 April 2013.

Evans, Jules. *Aldous Huxley on the
politics of well-being.* Philosophy
for Life, 8 February 2012. http://
philosophyforlife.org/category/
politics/page/2/. Accessed 8
February 2012.

Evans, Jules. *Bhutan's problematic
definition of well-being.* Philosophy
for Life, 17 April 2012. http://
philosophyforlife.org/bhutans-
problematic-definition-of-well-
being/. Accessed 24 April 2013.

Feinberg, Cara. 'The Placebo
Phenomenon'. *Harvard Magazine*,
January–February 2013. http:/
/harvardmagazine.com/2013/
01/the-placebo-phenomenon.
Accessed 12 January 2013.

Foster, Russell. *Why do we sleep?* TED,
June 2013. https://www.ted.com/
talks/russell_foster_why_do_we_
sleep. Accessed 17 September 2013.

Frank, Adam. *Lessons From The Last
Time Civilization Collapsed.* npr. 13.7
cosmos and culture, 19 August
2014. http://www.npr.org/blogs/
13.7/2014/08/19/341573332/
lessons-from-the-last-time-
civilization-collapsed. Accessed 20
August 2014.

Friedman, Thomas L. 'Did You Hear
the One About the Bankers?' *The
New York Times*, 29 October 2011.
http://www.nytimes.com/2011/
10/30/opinion/sunday/friedman-
did-you-hear-the-one-about-the-
bankers.html?_r=0. Accessed 2
August 2014.

Garofalo, Pat. 'What We Can Learn
From Switzerland's CEO Pay Cap
Vote'. *U.S. News*, 25 November,
2013. http://www.usnews.com/
opinion/blogs/pat-garofalo/
2013/11/25/the-importance-of-
switzerlands-112-ceo-pay-cap-
vote. Accessed 1 August 2014.

Gast, Scott. 'Gar Alperovitz on Why
the New Economy Movement
Needs to Think Big'. *Yes! Magazine*,
2 July 2014. http://www.
yesmagazine.org/issues/the-
power-of-story/what-then-must-
we-do?utm_source=YTW&utm_
medium=Email&utm_
campaign=20140703. Accessed 4
July 2014.

Gelles, David. 'The Mind Business'.
The Financial Times, 24 August
2012. http://www.ft.com/cms/
s/2/d9cb7940-ebea-11e1-985a-
00144feab49a.html#axzz2f7tPLrkE.
Accessed 25 August 2014.

Geoghegan, Tom. 'Ayn Rand: Why
is she so popular?' *BBC News
Magazine*, 17 August 2012.
http://www.bbc.com/news/
magazine-19280545. Accessed 3
February 2013.

Gethin, Rupert. *Sayings of the Buddha.*
Oxford: Oxford University Press.
2008.

Gioia, Dana. 'Gioia to graduates: Trade
easy pleasures for more complex
and challenging ones'. *Stanford
Report*, 17 June, 2007. http://news.
stanford.edu/news/2007/june20/
gradtrans-062007.html. Accessed
15 October 2012.

Gioia, Dana. *Pity the Beautiful.*
Minneapolis: Graywolf Press. 2012.

Gleeson-White, Jane. 'Is the reign of GDP as the only measure of wealth coming to an end?' *The Guardian*, 22 October 2012. http://www. theguardian.com/commentisfree/ 2012/oct/22/gdp-only-measure-wealth. Accessed 23 October 2012.

Goleman, Daniel. 'Rich People Just Care Less'. *The New York Times*, 5 October 2013. http://opinionator. blogs.nytimes.com/2013/10/ 05/rich-people-just-care-less/ ?partner=rss&emc=rss&_r=2&. Accessed 25 December 2013.

Gutting, Gary. 'Happiness, Beyond the Data'. *The New York Times*, 10 April 2013. http://opinionator. blogs.nytimes.com/2013/04/ 10/happiness-beyond-the-data/. Accessed 30 June 2014.

Hamilton, Clive. *Growth Fetish*. Allen & Unwin. 2003 (Kindle edition).

Hamilton, Clive. 'Consumerism, self-creation and prospects for a new ecological consciousness'. *Journal of Cleaner Production*, vol. 18 (2010). www.elsevier.com/locate/jclepro. Accessed 25 August 2014.

Hamzelou, Jessica. 'Overeating now bigger global problem than lack of food'. *New Scientist*, 13 December 2012. http://www.newscientist. com/article/mg21628963.600-overeating-now-bigger-global-problem-than-lack-of-food. html#.U_yAGPkbUXE. Accessed 14 December 2012.

Handy, Charles. *Age of Paradox*. Harvard Business School Press. 1994.

Handy, Charles. *The Empty Raincoat*. London: Arrow Books. 2002.

Handy, Charles. *The Elephant And The Flea*. London: Random House. 2008 (Kindle edition).

Haraszti, Miklós. *A Worker In A Worker's State*. Harmondsworth: Penguin. 1977.

Harding, John. 'How shark skin makes aeroplanes go faster'. *Daily Mail*, 17 January 2013. http://www. dailymail.co.uk/home/books/ article-2264009/How-shark-skin-makes-aeroplanes-faster-WHAT-HAS-NATURE-DONE-FOR-US-BY-TONY-JUNIPER. html#ixzz2IsNvBkLN. Accessed 24 January 2013.

Hargreaves, Deborah. 'Can We Close The Pay Gap?' *The New York Times*, 29 March 2014. http://opinionator. blogs.nytimes.com/2014/03/29/ can-we-close-the-pay-gap/#more-152647. Accessed 1 April 2014.

Hayes, Shannon. 'The Endangered Repairman'. *Yes! Magazine*, 23 November 2012. http://www. yesmagazine.org/blogs/shannon-hayes/the-endangered-repairman. Accessed 24 November 2012.

Heller, Nathan. 'The Disconnect: Why are so many Americans living by themselves?' *The New Yorker*, 16 April 2012. http://www. newyorker.com/magazine/2012/ 04/16/the-disconnect. Accessed 16 October 2013.

Heuman, Linda. 'The Science Delusion: An interview with cultural critic Curtis White'. *Tricycle Magazine*, Spring 2014. http://www.tricycle. com/feature/science-delusion. Accessed 4 February 2014.

Huffington, Arianna. 'Hemingway, Thoreau, Jefferson and the Virtues of a Good Long Walk'. *Huffington Post*, 29 August 2013. http:/ /www.huffingtonpost.com/ arianna-huffington/hemingway-thoreau-jeffers_b_3837002. html?ir=World&utm_

campaign=083013&utm_
medium=email&utm_
source=Alert-world&utm_
content=Title. Accessed 14
September 2013.

Hutton, Will. 'Give us back our public
spaces so we can have access to all
areas'. *The Observer*, 16 June 2013.
http://www.guardian.co.uk/
commentisfree/2013/jun/16/
retail-development-public-access-
planning. Accessed 14 September
2013.

IFIXIT. https://www.ifixit.com/.

International Cooperative Alliance.
Global 300 Report 2010.

International Labour Organization.
Global Employment Trends 2014:
Executive Summary.

Isaacs, Jacqueline. 'A Need to Rethink
Altruism'. *Values and Capitalism*,
2011. http://valuesandcapitalism.
com/a-need-to-rethink-altruism/.
Accessed 2 August 2014.

Jackson, Tim. *An economic reality check*.
TED, July 2010. http://www.
ted.com/talks/tim_jackson_s_
economic_reality_check. Accessed
1 December 2012.

Jackson, Tim. *Prosperity Without
Growth: Economics for a Finite
Planet*. London: Earthscan. 2011.

Jackson, Tim. 'Let's Be Less
Productive'. *The New York Times*,
26 May 2012. http://www.
nytimes.com/2012/05/27/
opinion/sunday/lets-be-less-
productive.html?_r=0. Accessed 1
April 2013.

Johnson, Eric Michael. 'Ayn Rand
on Human Nature'. *Scientific
American*, 5 October,2012. http:/
/blogs.scientificamerican.com/
primate-diaries/2012/10/05/ayn-
rand-on-human-nature/. Accessed
2 August 2014.

Johnson, Eric Michael. 'Survival of the
. . . Nicest?' *Yes! Magazine*, 3 May
2013. http://www.yesmagazine.
org/issues/how-cooperatives-
are-driving-the-new-economy/
survival-of-the-nicest-the-other-
theory-of-evolution. Accessed 2
August 2014.

Juniper, Tony. *What Has Nature Ever
Done For Us?* London: Profile
Books. 2013.

Kavoussi, Bonnie. 'CEO Pay Grew
127 Times Faster Than Worker
Pay Over Last 30 Years: Study'.
The Huffington Post, 2 May 2012.
http://www.huffingtonpost.com/
2012/05/02/ceo-pay-worker-
pay_n_1471685.html. Accessed 27
August 2014.

Kelly, Annie. 'Gross national
happiness in Bhutan: the big
idea from a tiny state that could
change the world'. *The Observer*,
1 December 2012. http://www.
theguardian.com/world/2012/
dec/01/bhutan-wealth-happiness-
counts. Accessed 11 February 2013.

Kemmerer, Lisa. 'Review'. *Philosophy
Now*, July 2008. http://
philosophynow.org/issues/
65/The_Corporation_The_
Pathological_Pursuit_of_Profit_
and_Power_by_Joel_Bakan.
Accessed 19 July 2014.

Keynes, John Maynard.
'Economic Possibilities for
our Grandchildren'. In *Essays
in Persuasion*, New York:
W.W.Norton & Co. 1963.

King, Sallie B. *Socially Engaged
Buddhism*. University of Hawai'i
Press. 2009.

Klinenberg, Eric. 'I want to be alone:
the rise and rise of solo living'.
The Guardian, 30 March 2012.
http://www.theguardian.com/

lifeandstyle/2012/mar/30/the-rise-of-solo-living. Accessed 31 March 2012.

Konnikova, Maria. *Mastermind: How to think like Sherlock Holmes.* New York: Penguin, 2013 (Kindle edition).

Konnikova, Maria. 'What's Lost as Handwriting Fades'. *The New York Times*, 2 June 2014. http://www.nytimes.com/2014/06/03/science/whats-lost-as-handwriting-fades.html?WT.mc_ev=click&WT.mc_id=NYT-E-I-NYT-E-AT-0611-L12&nl=el&nlid=33368331&_r=0. Accessed 13 July 2014.

KPCB. A Few More Thoughts On Our Internet Trends Report. 6 June 2013. http://www.kpcb.com/news/a-few-more-thoughts-on-our-internet-trends-report. Accessed 30 August 2014.

Kreider, Tim. 'The "Busy" Trap'. *The New York Times*, 30 June 2012. http://opinionator.blogs.nytimes.com/2012/06/30/the-busy-trap/?_r=0. Accessed 14 September 2013.

Krulwich, Robert. 'The World's Tallest Tree Is Hiding Somewhere In California'. NPR, 8 April 2011. http://www.npr.org/blogs/krulwich/2011/04/08/135206497/the-worlds-tallest-tree-is-hiding-somewhere-in-california. Accessed 25 August 2014.

Krulwich, Robert. *Jonah And His Many, Many Whales.* NPR. 12 April 2012. http://www.npr.org/blogs/krulwich/2012/04/12/150492481/jonah-and-his-many-many-whales. Accessed 13 April 2012.

Krznaric, Roman. *How Should We Live? Great Ideas from the Past for Everyday Life.* New York: BlueBridge. 2013.

Lama's Pyjamas. http://www.lamaspyjamas.com/.

Lancaster University, 'Research reveals the true cost of a burger'. Lancaster University News Archive. 7 February 2012. http://news.lancs.ac.uk/Web/News/Pages/Research-reveals-the-true-cost-of-a-burger.aspx. Accessed 16 July 2014.

Lanchester, John. *How To Speak Money: What the money people say – and what they really mean.* London: Faber & Faber Ltd. 2014.

Lavars, Nick. 'Germany's first waste-free supermarket about to open its doors'. *Gizmag*, 3 June 2014. http://www.gizmag.com/original-unverpackt-germany-waste-free-supermarket/32376/. Accessed 4 June 2014.

Layard, Richard. 'Why measure subjective well-being?' *OECD Observer*. No 290–91, Q1–Q2. 2012. http://www.oecdobserver.org/news/fullstory.php/aid/3767/Why_measure_subjective_well-being_.html. Accessed 1 May 2013.

Leonard, Annie. 'Can We Change the World Just by Changing Our Own Actions?' Alternet, 15 October 2013. http://www.alternet.org/print/environment/can-we-change-world-just-changing-our-own-actions. Accessed 9 July 2014.

Lewis, Michael. *The Big Short: Inside the Doomsday Machine.* Penguin Books Ltd. 2011 (Kindle edition).

Loy, David R. *A Buddhist History of the West.* Albany NY: State University of New York Press. 2002.

Loy, David R. *Money, Sex, War, Karma: Notes For A Buddhist Revolution.* Somerville MA: Wisdom Publications. 2008.

Loy, David R. *Awareness Bound And Unbound.* Albany NY: State University of New York Press. 2009.

Loy, David R. 'Waking Up from the Nightmare: Buddhist Reflections on Occupy Wall Street'. *Tikkun*, 18 October 2011. http://www.tikkun. org/nextgen/buddhist-reflections-on-occupy-wall-street-by-david-loy. Accessed 9 January 2013.

Manjusura. 'The View From Above'. *Tricycle*, Summer 2003. http:// www.tricycle.com/my-view/ view-above. Accessed 26 August 2014.

Margin Call. Film. 2011.

Marglin, Stephen A. *The Dismal Science: How Thinking Like an Economist Undermines Community.* Cambridge, Massachusetts: Harvard University Press. 2008.

Marx, Karl. *Capital, Volume 1: A Critical Analysis of Capitalist Production.* Ch. 24, section 3. https://www. marxists.org/archive/marx/ works/1867-c1/ch24.htm. Accessed 25 August 2014.

Mason, Paul. 'Thomas Piketty's *Capital*: everything you need to know about the surprise bestseller'. *The Guardian*, 28 April 2014. http://www.theguardian.com/ books/2014/apr/28/thomas-piketty-capital-surprise-bestseller. Accessed 29 April 2014.

Meserve, Myles. 'Meet Ivan Boesky, The Infamous Wall Streeter Who Inspired Gordon Gekko'. *Business Insider*, 26 July 2012. http://www. businessinsider.com/meet-ivan-boesky-the-infamous-wall-streeter-who-inspired-gordon-gecko-2012-7?op=1. Accessed 2 August 2014.

Monaghan, Angela. 'Bank of England governor: capitalism doomed if ethics vanish'. *The Guardian*, 28 May 2014. http://www. theguardian.com/business/2014/ may/27/capitalism-critique-bank-of-england-carney. Accessed 21 July 2014.

Monbiot, George. 'The Gift of Death'. *The Guardian*, 10 December 2012. http://www.monbiot.com/ 2012/12/10/the-gift-of-death/. Accessed 11 December 2012.

Monbiot, George. *All Give and No Take.* George Monbiot 10 March 2014. http://www.monbiot.com/2014/ 03/10/all-give-and-no-take/. Accessed 19 July 2014.

Mooney, Chris. 'Finally, Cosmos Takes On Climate Change'. *Huffington Post Green*, 5 May 2014. http:/ /www.huffingtonpost.com/ 2014/05/05/cosmos-climate-change_n_5268839.html. Accessed 25 August 2014.

Morrison, Ewan. 'What I'm thinking about . . . why capitalism wants us to stay single'. *The Guardian*, 11 August 2012. http://www. theguardian.com/books/ booksblog/2012/aug/11/ewan-morrison-capitalism-single. Accessed 12 October 2013.

Moss, Michael. 'The Extraordinary Science of Addictive Junk Food'. *The New York Times*, 20 February 2013. http://www.nytimes. com/2013/02/24/magazine/ the-extraordinary-science-of-junk-food.html?pagewanted=all&_r=0. Accessed 27 February 2013.

Ñāṇamoli, Bhikkhu. *The Life of the Buddha.* Kandy, Sri Lanka: Buddhist Publication Society. 1992.

Ñāṇamoli, Bhikkhu and Bodhi, Bhikkhu. *The Middle Length Discourses of the Buddha: A Translation of the Majjhima Nikāya.*

References

Boston: Wisdom Publications. 2001.

Nasser, Alan. ' Economy of Blood: What the Market Does to Our Souls'. *Counterpunch*, 28 June 2012. *http://www.counterpunch.org/2012/06/28/what-the-market-does-to-our-souls/*. Accessed 27 January 2013.

NEF. *Five ways to well-being*. Undated. http://www.neweconomics.org/projects/entry/five-ways-to-well-being. Accessed 9 September 2014.

NPR Books. 'The Shallows': This Is Your Brain Online. 2 June 2010. Includes extract from Carr, Nicholas. *The Shallows: What the Internet Is Doing to Our Brains*. W.W. Norton & Co. http://www.npr.org/templates/story/story.php?storyId=127370598. Accessed 18 September 2013.

O'Connor, Sarah. 'Drugs and prostitution add £10bn to UK economy'. *The Financial Times*, 29 May. 2014. http://www.ft.com/intl/cms/s/2/65704ba0-e730-11e3-88be-00144feabdc0.html#axzz37QEGvrid. Accessed 16 July 2014.

OECD. Compendium of OECD Well-Being Indicators. OECD. 2011.

Olendzki, Andrew. 'Busy Signal'. *Tricycle*, Winter 2009. vol. 19, no. 2. http://www.tricycle.com/meditation-buddhist-practices/calm-abiding-shamatha/busy-signal. Accessed 9 September 2014.

Olendzki, Andrew (trans.). *Culaka: The Call of the Peacock*. Thag 2. Access to Insight, 2005. http://www.accesstoinsight.org/tipitaka/kn/thag/thag.02.46.olen.html. Accessed 9 September 2014.

Olendzki, Andrew (trans.). *Mahā Kassapa Thera: At Home in the Mountains*. Theragata 18. Access to Insight (Legacy edition). 2 November 2013. http://www.accesstoinsight.org/tipitaka/kn/thag/thag.18.00x.olen.html. Accessed 29 August 2014.

Olendzki, Andrew (trans.). *Mettā Sutta* [Discourse on Lovingkindness] *Sutta Nipāta* 143–52. A Sourcebook. Barre Centre for Buddhist Studies. Undated.

Orrell, David. *Economyths: How the Science of Complex Systems is Transforming Economic Thought*. Icon Books. 2006 (Kindle edition).

Paul, Diane B. 'The Selection of the "Survival of the Fittest"'. *Journal of the History of Biology*, vol. 21, no.3 (Autumn 1988). http://www.dianebpaul.com/uploads/2/3/2/9/23295024/selection_of_survival_of_fittest.pdf. Accessed 29 August 2014.

PayPal. https://www.paypal.co.uk/Blog/Want-It-Get-It-With-PayPal/. Accessed 19 July 2014.

Peretti, Jacques. *The Men Who Made Us Spend*. BBC TV. 2014.

Phillips, Tom. *Defeating the Digital Oligopoly*. iai news, undated. http://iainews.iai.tv/articles/defeating-the-digital-oligopoly-auid-382?utm_source=Institute+of+Art+and+Ideas&utm_campaign=49940fbefb-IAI+Weekly+Newsletter+03%2F07%2F2014&utm_medium=email&utm_term=0_33593fe9fa-49940fbefb-47003645. Accessed 3 July 2014.

Piketty, Thomas. *Capital In The Twenty-First Century*. London: The Belknap Press of Harvard University Press. 2014.

Pilling, David. 'Has GDP outgrown its use?' *Financial Times*, 4 July 2014. http://www.ft.com/

References

intl/cms/s/2/dd2ec158-023d-11e4-ab5b-00144feab7de.html#axzz36PVt3fPS. Accessed 15 July 2014.

Putnam, Robert D. *Bowling Alone: The Collapse and Revival of American Community*. New York: Simon & Schuster. 2000.

Rathbone, John Paul. 'Zen and the Art of Management'. *Financial Times*, 16 September, 2013. http://www.ft.com/intl/cms/s/2/32e0b9b4-1c5f-11e3-8894-00144feab7de.html#axzz3BW6DmYha. Accessed 17 September 2013.

Ratnaguna. *The Art of Reflection*. Cambridge: Windhorse Publications. 2010.

Ream, Amanda. 'Why I Disrupted the Wisdom 2.0 Conference'. *Tricycle Blog*, 19 February 2014. http://www.tricycle.com/blog/why-i-disrupted-wisdom-20-conference. Accessed 4 June 2014.

Rilke, Rainer Maria. *Letters to a Young Poet*. Dover Publications. 2002.

Robertson, Sir Dennis H. *What Does the Economist Economise?* Columbia University. May 1954.

Rose, Jonathan. *The Literary Churchill: Author, Reader, Actor*. Yale University Press. May 2014.

Rushe, Dominic. 'US CEOs break pay record as top 10 earners take home at least $100m each'. *The Guardian*, 22 October 2013. http://www.theguardian.com/business/2013/oct/22/top-earning-ceos-100m-paychecks-record. Accessed 27 August 2014.

Sandel, Michael J. *What Money Can't Buy: The Moral Limits Of Markets*. London: Penguin. 2013.

Sangharakshita. *The Ten Pillars of Buddhism*. Glasgow: Windhorse Publications. 1989.

Sangharakshita. *Fifteen Points for Old and New Order Members*. Freebudhist audio, 1993. http://www.freebuddhistaudio.com/audio/details?num=180. Accessed 26 January 2013.

Sangharakshita. *Peace is a Fire*. 1995(a). http://www.sangharakshita.org/_books/peace-fire.pdf . Accessed 25 August 2014

Sangharakshita. *Vision and Transformation*. Birmingham: Windhorse Publications. 1995(b).

Sangharakshita. *Living Wisely: Further Advice from Nagarjuna's Precious Garland*. Cambridge: Windhorse Publications. 2013.

Sangharakshita. 'Staying with Boredom'. *Tricycle Magazine*, Summer 2013. http://www.tricycle.com/brief-teachings/staying-boredom. Accessed 17 September 2013.

Sangharakshita (trans.). *Dhammapada*. Birmingham: Windhorse Publications. 2001.

Sangharakshita. *The Essential Sangharakshita*. Karen Stout, ed. Boston: Wisdom Publications. 2009.

Śāntideva. *The Bodhicaryāvatāra*. Kate Crosby and Andrew Skilton (trans.). Oxford: Oxford University Press. 1995.

Schultz, Ellen E. and Francis, Theo. 'How Life Insurance Morphed Into a Corporate Finance Tool'. *The Wall Street Journal*, 30 December 2002. http://online.wsj.com/news/articles/SB1041197687392508913. Accessed 2 August 2014.

Schumacher, E.F. *Small Is beautiful: a study of economics as if people mattered*. London: Vintage. 1993.

Senauke, Hozan Alan. 'Ambedkar's Vision'. *Buddhadharma*, 3

February 2011. http://www.thebuddhadharma.com/web-archive/2011/2/3/ambedkars-vision.html. Accessed 27 August 2014.

Seth-Smith, Nikki. 'Partying With Britain's New Randian Ubermensch'. *Vice*. 1 November 2013. http://www.vice.com/en_uk/read/i-crashed-an-ayn-rand-love-in-for-the-super-rich. Accessed 2 August 2014.

Shachtman, Noah. 'In Silicon Valley, Meditation Is No Fad. It Could Make Your Career'. *Wired*, 18 June 2013. http://www.wired.com/2013/06/meditation-mindfulness-silicon-valley/all/. Accessed 25 August 2014.

Smith, Adam. *An Inquiry into the Nature and Causes of the Wealth of Nations*. Edwin Cannan ed. London: Methuen & Co. Ltd. 1904. Library of Economics and Liberty [Online] available from http://www.econlib.org/library/Smith/smWN1.html. Accessed 2 August 2014.

Smith, Adam. *The Theory of Moral Sentiments*. Indianapolis: Liberty Classics. 1976

Smithers, Rebecca. 'Nearly half of the world's food ends up as waste, report finds'. *The Guardian*, 10 January 2013. http://www.theguardian.com/environment/2013/jan/10/half-world-food-waste. Accessed 10 January 2013.

Smithers, Stuart. *Occupy Buddhism: Or Why the Dalai Lama is a Marxist*. Tricycle Wisdom Collection (undated). http://www.tricycle.com/web-exclusive/occupy-buddhism. Accessed 2 April 2014.

Stiglitz, Joseph E. 'In No One We Trust'. *The New York Times*,

21 December 2013. http://opinionator.blogs.nytimes.com/2013/12/21/in-no-one-we-trust/?_r=0#more-151136. Accessed 24 December 2013.

Stoll, Laura and Michaelson, Juliet. 'The truth about money and happiness'. *The NEF Blog*, 9 May 2013. http://www.neweconomics.org/blog/entry/the-truth-about-money-and-happiness. Accessed 16 July 2014.

Su, Christine. *Justifiers of the British Opium Trade: Arguments by Parliament, Traders, and the Times Leading Up to the Opium War*. http://web.stanford.edu/group/journal/cgi-bin/wordpress/wp-content/uploads/2012/09/Su_SocSci_2008.pdf . September 2012. Accessed 24 October 2013.

Subhuti. *Sangharakshita: a new voice in the Buddhist tradition*. Birmingham: Windhorse Publications. 1994.

Subhuti. *The Dharma Revolution and the New Society*. October 2010. Available for download from http://subhuti.info/essays.

Summers, Lawrence H. 'Economics and Moral Questions'. *Harvard Magazine*, November–December 2003.

Tan, Declan. 'The Art of Wandering: The Writer as Walker by Merlin Coverley' (review). *Huffington Post culture*, 8 July 2012. http://www.huffingtonpost.co.uk/declan-tan/the-art-of-wandering-the-_b_1750928.html. Accessed 14 September 2013.

Ṭhānissaro, Bhikkhu. *Anana Sutta: Debtless*. Access to Insight. 1997(a). http://www.accesstoinsight.org/tipitaka/an/an04/an04.062.than.html. Accessed 26 August 2014.

References

Ṭhānissaro, Bhikkhu (trans.). *Dhammapada*. Access to Insight, 1997(b). http://www. accesstoinsight.org/tipitaka/kn/ dhp/dhp.13.than.html#dhp-177. Accessed 2 August 2014.

Ṭhānissaro, Bhikkhu. *Kucchivikara-vatthu: The Monk with Dysentery*. Access to Insight, 1997(c). http:// www.accesstoinsight.org/tipitaka/ vin/mv/mv.08.26.01-08.than.html. Accessed 2 August 2014.

The Third Man. Film. 1949.

Titmuss, Richard M. *The Gift Relationship: From Human Blood to Social Policy*. New York: Pantheon. 1971.

Unno, Taitetsu. 'Three Grapefruits'. *Tricycle Magazine*, Summer 2003. http://www.tricycle.com/ practice/three-grapefruits. Accessed 6 February 2013.

Vajragupta. *The Triratna Story: Behind the Scenes of a New Buddhist Movement*. Cambridge: Windhorse Publications, 2010.

Vishvapani. 'How The Buddha Discovered Nature'. *Wise Attention*, 29 November 2012. http://www. wiseattention.org/blog/2012/11/ 29/how-the-buddha-discovered-nature/. Accessed 18 January 2013.

Vishvapani. 'Mindfulness is Political'. *Wise Attention*, 20 February 2014. http://www.wiseattention.org/ blog/2014/02/20/mindfulness-is-political/. Accessed 13 July 2014.

Walshe, Maurice. *The Long Discourses of the Buddha: A Translation of the Dīgha Nikāya*. Boston: Wisdom Publications. 1995.

Wang, Long. Malhotra, Deepak. Murnighan, J. Keith. 'Economics Education and Greed'. *Academy of Management Learning & Education* 10, no. 4 (December

2011): 643–60. http://www. hbs.edu/faculty/Pages/item. aspx?num=44223. Accessed 2 August 2014.

Watt, Nicholas. 'Boris Johnson invokes Thatcher spirit with greed is good speech'. *The Guardian*, 27 November 2013. http://www. theguardian.com/politics/ 2013/nov/27/boris-johnson-thatcher-greed-good. Accessed 28 November 2013.

Weissmann, Jordan. 'Research Says: Studying Economics Turns You Into a Liar'. *The Atlantic*, 18 December 2012. http://www. theatlantic.com/business/archive/ 2012/12/research-says-studying-economics-turns-you-into-a-liar/ 266423/. Accessed 2 August 2014.

White, D. Steven. *The Top 175 Global Economic Entities 2011*. http:// dstevenwhite.com/2012/08/11/ the-top-175-global-economic-entities-2011/. Accessed 19 July 2014.

Whitely, Peter. 'The fire burns yet'. *Aeon*, 25 November 2013. http:/ /aeon.co/magazine/culture/ native-american-worldviews-and-the-environment/. Accessed 25 August 2014.

Wijayaratna, Mohan. *Buddhist Monastic Life: According to the texts of the Theravada tradition*. Cambridge: Cambridge University Press. 1990.

Wikipedia. *The Protestant Ethic and the Spirit of capitalism*. Undated. http://en.wikipedia.org/wiki/ The_Protestant_Ethic_and_the_ Spirit_of_Capitalism. Accessed 25 August 2014.

Wikipedia. *E. J. Mishan*. Undated. http://en.wikipedia.org/wiki/ E._J._Mishan. Accessed 10 July 2014.

Wikipedia. *Unemployment in the United Kingdom.* Undated. http://en.wikipedia.org/wiki/Unemployment_in_the_United_Kingdom. Accessed 2 July 2014.

Wikipedia. *Marie Jahoda.* Undated. http://en.wikipedia.org/wiki/Marie_Jahoda. Accessed 25 August 2014.

Wilkinson, Richard. *How economic inequality harms societies.* TED, July 2011. https://www.ted.com/talks/richard_wilkinson. Accessed 25 December 2013.

Wilkinson, Richard and Pickett, Kate. *The Spirit Level: Why Equality is Better for Everyone.* London: Penguin. 2010.

Wilkinson, Richard and Pickett, Kate. 'How Inequality Hollows Out The Soul'. *The New York Times*, 2 February, 2014. http://opinionator.blogs.nytimes.com/2014/02/02/how-inequality-hollows-out-the-soul/?_php=true&_type=blogs&_r=0#more-151712. Accessed 17 July 2014.

Wilkinson, Richard and Pickett, Kate. *The importance of the labour movement in reducing inequality.* Class: Centre for Labour and Social Studies, July 2014.

Williams, Ray. 'What Price Will We Pay For Greed?' *Psychology Today*, 29 February 2012. http://www.psychologytoday.com/blog/wired-success/201202/what-price-will-we-pay-greed. Accessed 27 August 2014.

Wilson, David Sloan. 'A good social Darwinism'. *Aeon*, 4 July 2013. http://aeon.co/magazine/living-together/how-evolution-can-reform-economics/. Accessed 14 July 2014.

Windhorse: Evolution. http://windhorse.biz/cat/.

Witness. Film. 1985.

Work As Practice. Undated. http://www.sfzc.org/sp_download/Work%20as%20Practice1.pdf. Accessed 25 August 2014.

Yake, Bill. *Unfurl, Kite, and Veer.* Astoria, Oregon: Radiolarian Press. 2010.

Zajonc, Arthur. *Buddhist Technology: Bringing a New Consciousness to Our Technological Future.* New Economy Coalition. October 1997. http://neweconomy.net/publications/lectures/zajonc/arthur/buddhist-technology. Accessed 25 August 2014.

Zizek, Slavoj. 'From Western Marxism to Western Buddhism'. *Cabinet*, Spring 2001. http://www.cabinetmagazine.org/issues/2/western.php. Accessed 1 September 2013.

Index

Introductory Note

References such as '178–9' indicate (not necessarily continuous) discussion of a topic across a range of pages. Wherever possible in the case of topics with many references, these have either been divided into sub-topics or only the most significant discussions of the topic are listed. Because the entire work is about 'Buddha', the use of this term (and certain others which occur constantly throughout the book) as an entry point has been restricted. Information will be found under the corresponding detailed topics.

Index

Big Rock Candy Mountain 70
bin Laden, Osama 150
biofuels 91
Bird, Kai 152
blamelessness 142–3
  happiness of 142
bliss 63, 65
  land of 71
blood 17, 21–4, 28, 32
  donation 17, 21–3
blood donor system 21–2
blue whales 75
Bodhi, Bhikkhu 48–9, 181, 194–9, 213, 224
Bodhisattvas 49, 191
  aspiring 211
  of Compassion 132
Boesky, Ivan 28–9
bonuses 92, 148
boredom 137–8
boro clothes 106
Boulding, Kenneth 75
Brahmins 13–14, 62–3
brain 68, 111, 125, 127, 137, 176
Brave New World 139
bread 25–6, 58, 92, 98, 102
brewers 10
Bridgewater 131–2
Britain 36–8, 40, 72, 96, 107, 126, 139, 177
Bronze Age, Late 92–3
Buddha, *see* Introductory Note
Buddha-to-be 122
Buddhafield 94
Buddha's followers 46, 62, 85, 122
Buddha's Sangha 85, 103
Buddha's teachings 82, 95, 120, 146, 166, 181
Buddhism, see also Introductory Note
  modern 94, 182
  Western 3–4
Buddhist attitude to work 61, 64
Buddhist centres 33, 53, 98, 116
  urban 73, 184, 215

Buddhist communities 33, 36, 63, 73, 198, 210–11, 215, 224
Buddhist Economics 60, 64–5, 71, 95, 211
Buddhist History of the West, A 191
Buddhist life 183–5
Buddhist path 15, 125, 170
Buddhist Peace Fellowship 192
Buddhist perspective 20, 143, 153, 167, 169, 178, 193
Buddhist practice 72, 191, 195
Buddhist Publication Society 194
Buddhist values 6, 73, 167, 206, 212
Buddhist voices 7–8, 181–204
Buddhists 7, 52–3, 70–3, 130–3, 194–5, 203–4, 209–12, 214–15
  American 195
  individual 71, 184, 210
  Western 4
business leaders 20, 134, 211
business mindfulness 132, 135
business studies 30
businesses 12–13, 33, 73–4, 76–7, 79, 131–2, 162, 207
butchers 10

Cakkavatti Sīhanāda Sutta 51, 82, 166
calculations 70, 145
campaigns 117, 135, 191, 212
  to change behaviour of industry and government 99–100
capacity 66, 130
  imaginative 18
capital 6, 165–6
  accumulation of 202
  owners of 79, 165
capitalism 1–7, 10, 12, 37, 39–41, 58, 201–3, 205

history of 114, 165
  modern 3–4, 10, 13, 182, 215
  neoliberal 6–7, 10–12, 18, 167, 201, 205, 209, 216
  shareholder 161
carbon footprint 97–8, 214
care, economy of 70–1
caring 15, 19, 37, 39, 50, 69, 208, 216
Carney, Mark 205
Carr, Nicholas 124, 129–30
cash 43, 176, 201, 218
  prizes 29
caste 187–91
  system 14, 187
cattle 77–8
CCD (colony collapse disorder) 78
cement-lined channels 88
CEOs (chief executive officers) 36, 160–1, 168, 173, 193
  compensation 161
ceramics 106
cereals 98
channels 88, 176
  cement-lined 88
  earthen 88–9
  irrigation 88–9
chaos 52
charity 68–9
cheese 98
Cheetos 111
chief executive officers, *see* CEOs
Chief Fire Officers 36
children 31, 35, 48, 109, 114–15, 125, 144–5, 175–6
China 6, 60, 63, 92, 214, 221
chindogu 101–3
Chinese 63, 106, 112
choice 16, 22–3, 108, 111, 116, 123, 220
cities 59, 128, 134–5, 208
Citigroup 9, 92
citizens 36, 100, 161, 188, 190, 204, 211
civic engagement 152
civilization 21, 65
clans 177
classical economics 219

Index

Index

Index

Index

Index

Index

Index

253

Index

Index

WINDHORSE PUBLICATIONS

Windhorse Publications is a Buddhist charitable company based in the UK. We place great emphasis on producing books of high quality that are accessible and relevant to those interested in Buddhism at whatever level. We are the main publisher of the works of Sangharakshita, the founder of the Triratna Buddhist Order and Community. Our books draw on the whole range of the Buddhist tradition, including translations of traditional texts, commentaries, books that make links with contemporary culture and ways of life, biographies of Buddhists, and works on meditation.

As a not-for-profit enterprise, we ensure that all surplus income is invested in new books and improved production methods, to better communicate Buddhism in the 21st century. We welcome donations to help us continue our work – to find out more, go to www.windhorsepublications.com.

The Windhorse is a mythical animal that flies over the earth carrying on its back three precious jewels, bringing these invaluable gifts to all humanity: the Buddha (the 'awakened one'), his teaching, and the community of all his followers.

Windhorse Publications
169 Mill Road
Cambridge CB1 3AN
UK
info@windhorsepublications.com

Perseus Distribution
210 American Drive
Jackson TN 38301
USA

Windhorse Books
PO Box 574
Newtown NSW 2042
Australia

THE TRIRATNA BUDDHIST COMMUNITY

Windhorse Publications is a part of the Triratna Buddhist Community, which has more than sixty centres on five continents. Through these centres, members of the Triratna Buddhist Order offer classes in meditation and Buddhism, from an introductory to a deeper level of commitment. Members of the Triratna community run retreat centres around the world, and the Karuna Trust, a UK fundraising charity that supports social welfare projects in the slums and villages of South Asia.

Many Triratna centres have residential spiritual communities and ethical Right Livelihood businesses associated with them. Arts activities and body awareness disciplines are encouraged also, as is the development of strong bonds of friendship between people who share the same ideals. In this way Triratna is developing a unique approach to Buddhism, not simply as a set of techniques, but as a creatively directed way of life for people living in the modern world.

If you would like more information about Triratna please visit www.thebuddhistcentre.com or write to:

London Buddhist Centre
51 Roman Road
London E2 0HU
UK

Aryaloka
14 Heartwood Circle
Newmarket NH 03857
USA

Sydney Buddhist Centre
24 Enmore Road
Sydney NSW 2042
Australia

Buddhism: Tools for Living Your Life

by Vajragupta

In this guide for all those seeking a meaningful spiritual path, Vajragupta provides clear explanations of the main Buddhist teachings, as well as a variety of exercises designed to help readers develop or deepen their practice.

Appealing, readable, and practical, blending accessible teachings, practices, and personal stories . . . as directly relevant to modern life as it is comprehensive and rigorous. – Tricycle: The Buddhist Review, 2007

I'm very pleased that someone has finally written this book! At last, a real 'toolkit' for living a Buddhist life, his practical suggestions are hard to resist! – Saddhanandi, Director of Adhisthana

ISBN 9781 899579 74 7
£11.99 / $18.95 / €17.95
192 pages

Change Your Mind

by Paramananda

An accessible and thorough guide, this best-seller introduces two Buddhist meditations and deals imaginatively with practical difficulties, meeting distraction and doubt with determination and humour.

Inspiring, calming and friendly . . . If you've always thought meditation might be a good idea, but found other step-by-step guides lacking in spirit, this book could finally get you going. — Here's Health

ISBN 9781 899579 75 4
£9.99 / $13.95 / €12.95
208 pages

Not About Being Good: A Practical Guide to Buddhist Ethics

by Subhadramati

While there are numerous books on Buddhist meditation and philosophy, there are few books that are entirely devoted to the practice of Buddhist ethics. Subhadramati communicates clearly both their founding principles and the practical methods to embody them.

Buddhist ethics are not about conforming to a set of conventions, not about 'being good' in order to gain rewards. Instead, living ethically springs from the awareness that other people are no different from yourself. You can actively develop this awareness, through cultivating love, clarity and contentment. Helping you to come into greater harmony with all that lives, this is ultimately your guidebook to a more satisfactory life.

1SBN: 9781 909314 01 6
£10.99 / $16.95 / €13.95
336 pages

Wildmind: A Step-by-Step Guide to Meditation

by Bodhipaksa

From how to build your own stool to how a raisin can help you meditate, this illustrated guide explains everything you need to know to start or strengthen your meditation practice. This best-seller is in a new handy format and features brand new illustrations.

Of great help to people interested in meditation and an inspiring reminder to those on the path. – Joseph Goldstein, cofounder of the Insight Meditation Society and author of *One Dharma: The Emerging Western Buddhism*

Bodhipaksa has written a beautiful and very accessible introduction to meditation. He guides us through all the basics of mindfulness and also loving-kindness meditations with the voice of a wise, kind, and patient friend. – Dr. Lorne Ladner, author of *The Lost Art of Compassion*

ISBN 9781 899579 91 4
£11.99 / $18.95 / €15.95
240 pages